Education Policy and Equal Opportunity in Japan

ASIA-PACIFIC STUDIES: PAST AND PRESENT

Series Editors: J. S. Eades, *Ritsumeikan Asian Pacific University*; and David Askew, *Ritsumeikan Asian Pacific University*

The Asia Pacific is the most economically dynamic region of the world, due to the emergence of China as an economic superpower, and following on from the economic miracles of the Japanese and other Asian dragon economies. It can boast large numbers of new economic and political groupings that extend from the Russian Far East in the north to Australia and New Zealand in the south. The forces of globalization are producing new population, cultural, and information flows throughout the region, movements that are the product of a vast and increasingly cosmopolitan middle class. At the same time, the past continues to cast a long shadow, with unresolved conflicts adding fuel to current tensions among the major regional players over a wide range of issues from the environment to future energy supplies.

This series provides an outlet for cutting-edge academic research on Asia-Pacific studies. The major focus is the politics, histories, societies, and cultures of individual countries, together with overviews of major regional trends and developments.

VOLUME 1
Media and Nation Building: How the Iban Became Malaysian
John Postill

VOLUME 2
The Nanking Atrocity, 1937–38: Complicating the Picture
Edited by Bob Tadashi Wakabayashi

VOLUME 3
The Body in Asia
Edited by Bryan S. Turner and Zheng Yangwen

VOLUME 4
Education Policy and Equal Opportunity in Japan
Akito Okada

EDUCATION POLICY AND EQUAL OPPORTUNITY IN JAPAN

Akito Okada

Berghahn Books

New York • Oxford

Published in 2012 by

Berghahn Books

www.berghahnbooks.com

Library of Congress Cataloging-in-Publication Data

Okada, Akito, 1967–

Education policy and equal opportunity in Japan / Akito Okada.

p. cm. — (Asia-Pacific studies: past and present)

Includes bibliographical references and index.

ISBN 978-0-85745-267-2 (hardcover : alk. paper) — ISBN 978-0-85745-268-9 (ebook)

1. Educational planning—Japan. 2. Educational equalization—Japan.
3. Education and state—Japan. I. Title.

LA1312.O4145 2011

371.2'070952—dc23   2011037470

British Library Cataloguing in Publication Data

A catalogue record for this book is available from the British Library

Printed in the United States on acid-free paper

ISBN 978-0-85745-267-2 (hardback)
ISBN 978-0-85745-268-9 (e-book)

Contents

Figures and Tables		VII
Acknowledgements		IX
Notes on Style		XI
Japanese Terms		XIII
Abbreviations		XV

Introduction   1

1   The Initial Application of Equal Opportunity to the Education System in Japan, 1868–1944   19

2   The Initial Position of the Concept of Equal Opportunity in Education, 1945–1950   31

3   The Development of the New Perspective on Equal Opportunity in Education, 1951–1959   54

4   The Development of the Concept of Equal Opportunity under the High Economic Growth Period, 1960s–1970s   80

5   From Human Capital to Market Values in Education, 1980s–Present Day   108

6   Educational Reform and Equality of Opportunity in Contemporary Japan   139

Conclusion   160

APPENDIX 1. THE JAPANESE SCHOOL SYSTEM IN 1937   181

APPENDIX 2. THE JAPANESE SCHOOL SYSTEM IN THE 1980S   183

APPENDIX 3. THE JAPANESE SCHOOL SYSTEM IN 2008   185

BIBLIOGRAPHY   187

INDEX   195

Figures and Tables

Figures

3.1. Three Main Schemes in ACOR's Recommendations   58

6.1. Fathers' Occupations and Percentages of Students
Who Advance to Higher Education   140

6.2. Details in Total Learning Expenditure of Households
for Children   146

6.3. Gini Co-efficients of Income Concentration in
27 OECD Countries, Most Recent Year   147

A.1. The Japanese School System in 1937   182

A.2. The Japanese School System in the 1980s   184

A.3. The Japanese School System in 2008   186

Tables

I.1. Elements of "Trilemma"   11

I.2. The Combined Husén-Fishkin Model   12

I.3. Three Phases of Historical Shift in the Concept of
Educational Opportunity as Identified by Halsey   14

2.1. RUDIMENTARY CONTENT OF THE EQUALITY OF EDUCATIONAL
OPPORTUNITY IN THE VARIOUS GROUPS   37

4.1. THE QUANTITATIVE EXPANSION OF TECHNICAL EDUCATION IN JAPAN   82

4.2. PERCENTAGES OF BOYS AND GIRLS ENTERING UPPER
SECONDARY SCHOOL   93

5.1. COMPARISON OF THE CHARACTERISTICS OF THE IMPERIAL RESCRIPT,
THE FLE, AND THE ERNC's PROPOSED LEGISLATION   129

5.2. POLITICAL POINTS OF VIEW CONCERNING THE ERNC's
EDUCATION REFORM   131

C.1. THE HISTORICAL SHIFTS OF THE CONCEPT OF EQUALITY
OF EDUCATIONAL OPPORTUNITY IN POST-WAR JAPAN AND
EXPLANATORY MODEL   169

C.2. THE SENSE OF "UNFAIRNESS" AMONG JAPANESE PEOPLE   178

ACKNOWLEDGEMENTS

First, I would like to express my greatest appreciation, thanks and respect to David Phillips and Roger Goodman, for their valuable guidance and for their commitment of considerable time and energy over the years. This book originally developed from a doctoral thesis supervised by them. Through their astute and constructive criticisms, I learned the value of rigorous critical standards and exacting accuracy in research and writing. I wish to also thank Dr. Peter Cave for advising on the entire contents of this study and providing many helpful comments and suggestions. Thanks are due also to Professor Ehara Takekazu and Professor Kariya Takehiko for their suggestions, help, and constructive criticism from the initial stage of this study; and to Professor Horio Teruhisa whose interest in this study provided incentive as well as academic enlightenment. I would also like to thank Professor Maekawa Kyōichi, Professor Inoue Katsuya, Professor Tsudaka Masafumi, Professor Ozawa Shūzō, and Professor Suzuki Shin'ichi who provided invaluable assistance in setting up many of the interviews.

Thanks go to all those friends, colleagues, and students, too numerous to mention, in England and Japan whose support, advice, and encouragement have helped sustain me along the course of study and research that has culminated in this study; in particular, Robert Aspinall, Sato Chizu, Gregory Poole, Yusof Othman, Jilia Bekker, Akiko Vandenberg Sakamoto, Nakajima Kusu, and Terada Ryōta. I would particularly like to thank Jason Edward Collinge for his great efforts in editing the drafts of this book.

I wish also to thank Professor Jeremy Eades and Ann Przyzycki for advice, suggestions, and comments on publishing this study. I also express my appreciation to Taylor & Francis Ltd which permitted me to print revised and updated material from the following articles written by me: "Secondary Education Reform and the Concept of Equality of Opportunity in Japan" in *Compare* 29, no. 2 (1999):

171–89; "Japan as a Prototype of the 'Degreeocracy' Society?" in *Educational Review* 23, no. 3 (2001): 303–12; and "Education of Whom, for Whom, by Whom? Revision of the Fundamental Law of Education in Japan" in *Japan Forum* 14, no. 3 (2002): 425–41.

Finally, this study is dedicated to my family: to my parents Yūzō and Taneko Okada and parents-in-law Ken'ichi and Eiko Nakanishi, who always had great confidence in me and rescued me financially, emotionally, and intellectually on a number of occasions when I needed help; to my sisters Machiko and Harue; to my twin brother Kazuto; to the memory of my grandfather and grandmother; and to my nephew Masaki, who fought against leukemia for a long time and finally went to his eternal rest during my second year in Oxford.

Last, but not least, I wish to express the gratitude I feel to my wife, Naomi, and my daughters, Mariya and Nana, for their support, encouragement, and love during the writing of this study. Without their warm support, this book would not have been completed.

Notes on Style

Japanese names are given in their proper order, with the surname first and personal name second. With names of Westerners of Japanese descent, Western order is preserved. Macrons are used over vowels that are lengthened in Japanese pronunciation, in order to distinguish them from short vowels, for example at the end of *Monbushō*. For the names of Tokyo, Osaka, and some other major cities and place names, however, they are omitted. It should be noted that a long vowel is given in pronunciation approximately twice the length of a short vowel. Japanese political parties and ministries are referred to by the initial letters of their English names. Thus, the Ministry of Education is referred to as the MOE and the Liberal Democratic Party as the LDP. A list of the main abbreviations and Japanese terms used is included for the benefit of readers more familiar with different conventions. Unless stated otherwise, all translations of Japanese texts are my own.

Japanese Terms

Doryoku	Efforts for Studying
Gakubatsu	School cliques
Gakurekishugi	Meritocracy
Furiitā	Youth who do not find employment as full-time permanent employees and work in non-permanent short-term and or part-time jobs after leaving school
Hensachi	T-score
Jiyūka	Liberalization
Juku	Private exam preparatory schools attended by children
Kakusa Shakai	Gap Society
Keizai Shingikai	Economic Deliberation Council
Koseika	Individualization
Kokusaika	Internationalization
Kōkō Sangensoku	Three principles of upper secondary school ("small school district system," "co-education," and "comprehensive system")
Kyōikuken	Right to learning
Nikkyōso	Japan Teachers' Union
Nōryokushugi	Ability-first principle
Rinkyōshin	Ad Hoc Council on Education
Shiken jigoku	Examination hell

Shōshika	Declining birthrate
Sabetsu = Senbetsu Kyōiku	Discrimination = Selection by Ability
Tayōka	Diversification
Yutori	Time for creative and exploratory activity
Zaikai	Industrial circles
Zenjin Kyōiku	Education to create whole people
Zen-nyū	Upper secondary school for all
Zoku	Cliques of politicians with similar interests

ABBREVIATIONS

ACOR   Advisory Committee for Ordinance Revision
        (Seirei Shimon Iinkai)
AHCE   Ad Hoc Council on Education (Rinji Kyōiku Shingikai)
CCE   Central Council on Education (Chūō Kyōiku Shingikai)
CI&E   Civil Information and Education Section (Minkan Jōhō
        Kyōiku Kyoku)
EDC   Economic Deliberation Council (Keizai Shingikai)
ERC   Educational Reform Council (Kyōiku Sa'ssin Iinkai)
ERNC   Education Reform National Conference (Kyōiku Kaikaku
        Kokumin Kaigi)
FLE   Fundamental Law of Education (Kyōiku Kihonhō)
GDCE   Group for Discussion of Culture and Education (Bunka to Kyōiku
        ni Kansuru Kondankai)
GHQ   General Headquarters (Rengōgun Saikō Sireikan Sousireibu)
JAP   Japan Advancement Party (Nihon Shinpotō)
JCP   Japan Communist Party (Nihon Kyōsantō)
JDP   Democratic Party of Japan (Minshutō)
JLP   Japan Liberal Party (Nihon Jiyūtō)
JSP   Japan Socialist Party (Nihon Shakaitō)
JTU   Japan Teachers' Union (Nikkyōso)
KGSGI   Kyoto Group for the Study of Global Issues (Sekai o Kangaeru
        Kyoto Zaikai)

KSHI	Editorial Committee of Postwar Education History (Kyōiku no Sengoshi Henshū Iinkai)
LDP	Liberal Democratic Party (Jiyū Minshutō)
MEXT	Ministry of Education, Culture, Sports, Science, and Technology (Monbu Kagakushō)
MOE	Ministry of Education (Monbushō)
NEET	Not in Education, Employment or Training
NIDP	National Income Doubling Plan (Kokumin Shotoku Baizō Keikaku)
SAT	Scholastic Achievement Test (Zenkoku Gakuryoku Tesuto)
SCAP	Supreme Command for the Allied Powers
SNKSHI	Sengo Nihon Kyōiku Shiryō Shūsei Henshū Iinkai
USEM	United States Education Mission
ZKKS	Zenkoku Kyōiku Kenkyu Shūkai (JTU's annual meeting)

INTRODUCTION

In many societies today, it is virtually impossible to read any document about educational aims or goals without encountering such phrases and terms as "equality," "equal opportunity," "equal access," "equal rights" and so forth. The underlying assumption seems to be that "equality" in some form is an intelligible and sensible educational ideal, yet there are different views about what sort of equality should be pursued. The issue of equality in education has been greatly debated, especially that of equality of opportunity, which served as a justification for much of the post-World War II restructuring of educational systems around the world.

The Purpose of This Study

In the 1960s and 1970s, equality of educational opportunity became an important subject in many industrialized Western countries.[1] A number of definitions of the concept were developed by social scientists. Compared with England and the United States, there was less research about changes in the understanding and use of the concept in Japan. Moreover, previous research dealt particularly with the shift of the concept during the American Occupation period in Japan, and focused on the process of creating the new Constitution and the Fundamental Law of Education (FLE).[2] It is therefore necessary to update the work of previous scholars concerning equality of opportunity and to also ascertain whether the kind of changes the concept underwent in other industrial societies could also be seen in the case of Japan. As the first nation outside the Western cultural context to have achieved a high level of expansion of educational opportunities, Japan represented a critical case for the theory of the shifting equality of educational opportunity—a test of its predictive power. This book will specially address the following four questions:

1) What kinds of equality of educational opportunity did Japan aim to achieve during the last century, especially since World War II?

2) How did decision-makers and interest groups apply equality of opportunity to educational policies?

3) What influenced changes in attitudes towards equal educational opportunity in Japan?

4) What kinds of criteria were used to measure equality of educational opportunity?

There was much English-language research concerning these questions carried out from various perspectives—historical, socio-political, and anthropological. Yet it seemed that there still remained a need for the examination of basic questions, such as what forms of equality of educational opportunity did the Japanese aim to achieve in the post-war period? Despite the proliferation of criticisms and analyses of existing educational policies concerning opportunity in Japan, an understanding of the original formation of the concept of equal opportunity and of its development and transformation up to the present was still required. There was very little detailed research that threw light on the historical transformation of the concept of equality of opportunity as applied to post-World War II educational policies or on the multiplicity and complexity of factors which brought about changes in the meaning of equality of opportunity. Here, indeed, was an issue demanding attention.

Post-war Ideological Shift of the Concept of Equal Opportunity in Japan's Educational Policies

Equality of opportunity was one of the ideals that Japan developed in its educational policies during the last century (see chapter 1). Since the latter half of the nineteenth century, when the Meiji government was able to transform feudal Japan into a fast-growing modern nation state, equality of opportunity as the underpinning rationale for mobilizing the talents of the whole nation was applied to almost all domains of national policy, including education.[3] The need to catch up with Western countries impelled the nation to move towards realizing this ideal by fostering a national elite. Likewise the growth of liberalism, with its call for distributive justice, helped to bring equality of opportunity to the forefront as a national ideal. However, despite the fact that elementary education was already universal by 1886, the principle had rarely—if ever—been applied beyond the post-primary education level until the American Occupation authorities scrapped the pre-war Japanese education system. In fact, opportunities in secondary education and above were dependent in part upon, and generally corresponded with, the contemporary patterns of social stratification, regional disparity, and different treatments of boys and girls. Pre-war secondary education was a complex and hierarchical system comprising middle schools for a (male) elite, and vocational, higher elementary, and youth schools for the majority (see appendix 1).

The post-war education system was introduced by the American Occupation, which aimed at the 'democratization', 'demilitarization', and 'decentralization' of Japanese society (see chapter 2).[4] The new system was the American model: the first nine years were compulsory education—composed of six years of elementary school and three years of lower secondary school—after which came three years of upper secondary school (see appendix 2). All higher educational institutions were integrated into either four-year universities or two-year junior colleges. The new system was thus called the '6-3-3-4' system. This system was simpler than the pre-war system and was aimed at providing greater opportunities to advance to secondary and higher education. The general trend of the post-war Occupation reforms in Japan was originally to interpret the concept of equality of opportunity in an "egalitarian" way, emphasizing self-realization, rather than as a justification for differentiation among children. This ideal of equal opportunity was incorporated into Article 26 of the post-war Constitution and Article III of the Fundamental Law of Education (FLE). As explained in chapter 2 of this book, in the general circumstances of the post-war period, the ideological emphasis was placed upon "equality" rather than "meritocracy" or "efficiency," and the FLE's aims were fundamentally divergent from those supported by the state before the war—allocation of national children into different types of secondary schools in terms of their social function for national prosperity.

The period of the 1950s could be described as essentially one of consolidation, but also a time when the implementation of the FLE began to be challenged (see chapter 3). Towards the end of the 1950s, criticism of the new systems began to emerge, along with pressure to redefine the concept of equality of opportunity declared in the FLE. Once the American Occupation of Japan ended in 1952, the Japanese government began to undertake a revision of various legislative legacies of the Occupation and to modify them according to the domestic conservative ideology of the day. This process became known as the "reverse course."[5] In education, the conservative government, together with the Ministry of Education (MOE) and industrial interest groups, attacked some aspects of the Occupation reforms. Behind these criticisms, the philosophical basis of the concept of equality of opportunity in the Occupation's educational reform began to be eroded by a strong emphasis on "efficiency" and "meritocracy." In this context, conservatives insisted that equality of educational opportunity should mean *equal cultivation of different ability* in order to foster a national elite. The fiercest opponent of these conservative groups was the Japan Teachers' Union (JTU). The JTU had emerged as a major force in defending the 6-3-3-4 system, and in maintaining the system's emphasis on equality of educational opportunity as stipulated in the FLE. Strong obstruction from the JTU prevented any change taking place until the late 1980s when it split into two unions.[6] Thus, from the 1950s to the end of the early 1990s, severe disputes frequently unfolded between conservatives and the JTU over the principle of equality of educational opportunity.

There was no doubt that post-war Japan made enormous strides in providing the nation's children with expanded educational opportunities covering the whole range of pre-school to higher education, particularly since the period of high-speed economic growth in the 1960s (see chapter 4). The widespread popularity of the idea of equality of opportunity resulted from the belief that expansion of education would bring about greater social equality and at the same time a stronger national economy. The "labor force policy" and "human capital policy" provided a theoretical basis for this expansion.[7] Nevertheless, equality of opportunity was conceived in a specifically Japanese way at the beginning of the 1970s. During the long economic boom, Japan experienced rapid changes in its economy and became a leading industrial society. It was confronted with the task of adjusting the nation's industrial structure to emphasize industries on the cutting edge of scientific and technological change. In addition, the Japanese government was once again forced to look at its educational system. Even though it was successful in terms of past performance, it had been designed to emphasize examinations and to create a large number of quality workers for the catch-up phase of Japan's development. With the Japanese economy becoming increasingly dependent on international business, fast-changing science, and technological industries, the government was faced with demands from many quarters, especially industrial circles, calling on it to reform its educational system in order to bring it into line with the growing need for more diversely talented and creative workers. Against this background, the concept of equality of educational opportunity became interpreted as the *same* possibility of access for each pupil to *diversified* schools, curriculum, teaching methods, and treatment corresponding to ability.

Accordingly, the established 6-3-3-4 system began to be seen as failing to foster talent at a national level, and also failing to provide various educational opportunities, "which were suited to each individual's abilities and aptitudes."[8] Twice in the twenty-year period between 1970 and 1990, the Japanese government embarked on major educational reforms. The first was the Central Council on Education's (CCE) comprehensive reform program in 1971, which sought to introduce a greater degree of diversity into the educational system so it would be capable of producing the type of workers required for the next stage in Japan's economic advance (see chapter 4). The second, the Ad-Hoc Council on Education (*Rinji Kyōiku Shingikai* or *Rinkyōshin*), set up in 1984, similarly tried to achieve more flexibility by introducing "market competition" into the educational system in order to restore the high standards of attainment that existed in the pre-war middle schools, effectively select national elites, and triumph in international industrial competition (see chapter 5)[9]. The Ad-Hoc Council on Education also advocated the adoption of the notion of "freedom of choice," which meant more choice for parents, and more emphasis on a child's "individuality" to achieve these goals. The CCE's reform proposal of the late 1990s to diversify the 6-3-3-4 system could be seen as essentially continuous with the aims of both previous initiatives of the government from the 1970s as indicated in the following passage:

> Since World War II Japan has experienced a dramatic spread and development of education based on the principle of equality of opportunity for all and has at the same time succeeded in maintaining its high standards and improving its quality. . . . However, since we have placed too much value not only on formal equality, but also on equality of outcomes in education, it is true that our school system is uniform and inflexible. . . . We have not considered education which is suited to each individual's abilities and aptitudes. . . . As to the present education [6-3-3-4] system, it is extremely important for us to promote diversification, liberalization and flexibilization (flexibility) of the system and to expand more children's and parents' choices in order to provide each child with an education according to their different abilities and aptitudes.[10]

The CCE's series of reports in the 1990s concluded an era of almost four decades of attempts by Conservatives to create an elite track in the present 6-3-3-4 system by introducing the six-year state secondary school system (see appendix 3). As will be discussed later in this book, the gloss on equality insisted on by successive governments of the post-war period—*Nōryokushugi* (diversification based on children's different abilities)—was reappraised as the most important yardstick in evaluating equality in education for the coming new century.[11] In other words, the diversification of the system together with the notion of freedom of choice was demanded and justified in the name of equality of educational opportunity. This represented the existing trend in official educational statements.

Arguing over Equality of Opportunity

In order to trace the evolutionary shifts in interpretation of the concept of equal opportunity and to explore the reasons for changes in policy, this study uses a historical approach. In this perspective, the studies of Passin, Kobayashi, Beauchamp and Vardaman, and Marshall provide useful explanations of the general history of contemporary Japanese schooling in terms of its contribution to modernization and economic development.[12] Also, in selecting historical documents, this study focuses upon public statements, particularly those that use the term "equality" or "equality of opportunity," and that were made mainly by the central administrative (Ministry of Education) and advisory bodies (for example, Central Council for Education). It also traces the major political parties' interpretations of equality of opportunity as reflected in their publications and in parliamentary debates, and compares them with one another.

This study also analyzes the policy formulation process. This follows the practice of several important studies. For example, Schoppa provided detailed analysis of the educational policy-making process by using the models of the many "actors" (i.e., major political parties, bureaucracy, and industrial groups) during the Ad-Hoc Council's education reform of the 1980s.[13] Schoppa described how the Japanese policy-making process in education could become paralyzed when there was disagreement between conservatives (the LDP, industrial groups and the conservative bureaucrats) and progressives (the JTU and Japan Socialist Party) and argued that this "immobilism" could become an element that would delay the progress of educational arguments at the national level. Duke, Thurston, and Aspinall analyzed the history of the Japan Teacher Union within the contemporary Japanese political system and introduced the various theoretical models which accounted for the roles of the JTU in the wider context of Japanese unionism and party politics.[14]

In addition, of the various lenses used to view equality of educational opportunity in Japan, this study is particularly concerned with the following two paradigms: "meritocracy" and "egalitarianism." Indeed, throughout this book, we will see an interplay between meritocracy and egalitarianism, which eventually caused a transformation in the concept of equality of opportunity over the period. It might also be said that the Japanese educational policies formulated to promote equality of opportunity reflected the attitudes of two distinct groups toward education—the conservatives and the progressives, as categorized by Schoppa. The concept's shifting meaning was always inseparably connected with the ethos, philosophy, and aims of the two groups. The conservatives had a tradition of encouraging the idea of meritocracy and insisting on allocating the nation's children according to their different abilities within a diversified school system.[15] On the other hand, the progressives, particularly the JTU, demanded a common secondary schooling for all children regardless of family background and children's different abilities (see chapter 4). Their demand was generally characterized as idealistic and impractical by conservatives. Also, their ideological emphasis upon the egalitarianism of educational opportunity and their suggested policies were fundamentally divergent from those of conservatives over the period. Thus, in using these two significant paradigms of Japanese education, this study examines the shifting meaning of the concept of equal opportunity, declared overtly in, or reflected implicitly by, educational policies over the period.

This study also analyzes criticisms of inequalities in educational opportunity. The findings of social scientific research provided a growing volume of evidence that the expansion of the formal and legal meaning of equal opportunity in Japanese education had a limited effect in bringing about equality for children in their adult lives in terms of social mobility and income.[16] It was also suggested that equality in education should be defined not only in terms of equal access, but in terms of equal achievement among children.[17] These arguments and findings have far-reaching implications for the efficacy of educational policies. Recently, there were even concerns that equality of educational opportunity was lost and that this was leading to the stratification of Japanese society through the widening of income differentials in the "gap society" (*kakusa shakai*). In the gap society, secure full-time jobs were becoming increasingly limited to those who graduated from prestigious universities, and entry to those institutions was becoming connected more clearly with family income and investments. Therefore, as will be discussed in chapter 6, the CCE's education reforms since the 1990s, which were executed to give students more free time to explore their own interests (so-called *yutori kyōiku*), in reality possibly led to the creation of children who could no longer see the point of working hard in school, and who then ended up unemployed or in casual work because educational success was so visibly related to family background, dropping out of the system altogether, or becoming disruptive within it.[18]

Social Class Issues in the Debate over Equal Opportunity in Education

A key element of the debate over equality of opportunity concerned the inequality between different social groups in education. Terms such as "class inequality" or "social group bias" were widely used in industrial Western countries. In those countries, there was also a growing volume of evidence that the quantitative expansion of educational opportunity did not bring qualitative equality to children from the lower social groups, and social and educational reforms were introduced to tackle this problem.

However, in Japan the social background issue did not attract much attention in the official debates on education, although some educational sociologists revealed the existence of social bias in both children's academic achievement and in the proportion of graduates entering higher education.[19] The Japanese government maintained a policy based on the meritocratic principle. Indeed, the issue of inequality between social groups faded from the educational debate, and instead concern increased about other issues such as "examination hell" or "ijime" (bullying). Thus, although social inequality in educational opportunity existed in Japan as well as in Western countries, governments took different roads to reform the structure of their national education systems especially in the period between the 1950s and 1970s. Here another important question arose: Why had the class issue not attracted attention from the general population of Japanese people in the official educational debate? As will be discussed in more detail in chapter 6, Kariya attributed this phenomenon to people's sense of egalitarianism, which was probably the most significant variable that distinguished Japan from Western nations in the post-war period.[20] Kariya argued that Japanese teachers tended to treat all school children equally regardless of socioeconomic differences that might exist prior to schooling. In such a society, it was taboo to treat them differently, and in that sense Japanese egalitarianism was the antithesis of the underlying compensatory education in England or so-called "head-start" programs in the United States.

Theoretical Perspective

Husén's Models of the Concepts of Equality of Educational Opportunity

It is necessary first to examine theoretical insights into the concept of equality of opportunity. In the 1960s and 1970s, equality of educational opportunity became an important subject in many industrialized countries.[21] A number of definitions of the concept were developed by social scientists. One of the most important participants in this debate was the Swedish scholar Torsten Husén.[22] Kang Hee-Chun summarized Husén's concepts and created four major theoretical models of the concept of equal opportunity in British education.[23] This study uses the four major explanatory models, which took the work of Husén as their starting point and were further developed by Kang.

(1) The Conservative Concept of Equality of Educational Opportunity

The conservative perspective, which was prevalent in most industrial countries until World War I, defined equality of opportunity on the basic assumption that God had bestowed different amounts of capacity upon each human being and it was up to the individual to make the best possible use of whatever he or she had been given. Hyper-conservative variants of this philosophy maintained that God had given each pupil the aptitudes that corresponded to the caste or social class into which he or she had been born. The tacit assumption of the conservative interpretation, then, was that pupils had not only to make optimal use of their capacity, but also to be content with it, because they had been given what they deserved at birth.

(2) The Liberal Concept of Equality of Educational Opportunity

The liberal concept of equal opportunity sought to go beyond the conservative one by considering what barriers might actually restrict access to schooling. The liberal concept was that "all pupils should be given the same opportunity to start their life career and not necessarily that it should ultimately bring about greater equality in terms of social and/or economic status."[24] In this view, as well as in the legal or formal meaning of equal access to education, there was a practical meaning; that is to say, active steps needed to be taken to eliminate economic or regional handicaps, which prevented talented, but socio-economically disadvantaged children from developing their innate ability by means of a good education. Yet, the liberal view held that once external barriers were removed, success or failure in school primarily depended upon each individual child: Thus this concept supported the idea of the meritocratic nature of educational selection, by which allocation of children into diversified tracks was assumed to be desirable. This perspective received its justification both from a presumed relation to national efficiency and from a desire to ensure distributive justice according to the criterion of deserts. Since the liberal interpretation tended to allow for a diversified education system, it consequently involved a risk of reproducing the social stratification in a society.

(3) The Egalitarian Concept of Equality of Educational Opportunity

Since James Coleman's landmark study of equal opportunity,[25] a third interpretation gained currency; according to this view, opportunities are equal only when results are equal. While the liberal concept of equal opportunity focused on the possibility of the same *access* to schooling, the egalitarian concept focused on the same educational *achievement* in school. The egalitarian view assumed from the start that the elimination of early selection of those judged to have academic ability alone would not be sufficient to ensure equality of educational opportunity. This was because a person's intelligence was a product not only of genetic make-up, but also of social background, and therefore the child from a socio-economically disadvantaged background would fail to develop academically because of a lack of adequate support at home. Based on this view, the egalitarian interpretation tended to place a greater emphasis on a unified educational system, such as the comprehensive school in England and the United States. However, in this concept equal opportunity was not defined by the identity of schooling, teaching method, or curricula provided to all children, but rather by optimal opportunity to fully develop children's personal abilities, if necessary by providing special treatment such as compensatory educational programs. From the egalitarian position, the principle of individuality was much more important than a consideration of national efficiency or the needs of the economy. It differed significantly from the liberal position in its view of the relationship between education and the wider social and economic structures.

(4) The Neo-Marxist Concept of Equality of Educational Opportunity

In addition to the above three models, which Husén provided, the Neo-Marxist view of equal opportunity was adopted by Kang as one more explanatory model.[26]

A particularly influential version of this perspective was concerned with theories of cultural reproduction that were well represented in the works of Bowles and Gintis, Bourdieu and Passeron, Bernstein, and Collins.[27] They shared the view that educational attainment was largely influenced by various resources from the family background, and education in turn played the role of reproducing social inequality and class structure from one generation to the next. Central to this perspective was the view that there was a high degree of correspondence between school and work, as its proponents argued that the education system helped to integrate pupils into the economic system. In particular, in this concept, schools socialized pupils into the disciplines of work and into the main social habits that were demanded by the working world. Thus the Neo-Marxist theorists accused schools of not acting as the prime equalizer, but on the contrary of being geared to reproduce the prevailing class inequalities in the name of a "technocratic-meritocratic" ideology suitable only for a capitalist society.

Fishkin's "Trilemma" Model

Each of these four different concepts of equality of educational opportunity had many intrinsic attractions, but their transformation into practical policies was characterized by much confusion. The crucial question was whether to evaluate the concepts in terms of equality or of liberty. When we look carefully at the relationship of these four different concepts, the conflicts among them were, in fact, both dramatic and inescapable in regard to the relative priorities given to equality and liberty or, to put it in another way, to egalitarianism and meritocracy. As we will see later, although there was widespread agreement that equality of opportunity was a requirement of a just society in Japan, there was also widespread disagreement about just what this requirement amounted to and how it was to be balanced against other requirements such as maintaining a meritocracy. Was equality of educational opportunity consistent with liberty? If egalitarianism and meritocracy conflict, how did one decide which was to be given precedence? In fact, no society or individual ever fully resolved the conflict between equality and liberty. Fishkin investigated the apparent tension between liberty and equality and proposed the concept of the 'trilemma' which focused on three positions that could be distinguished in terms of their different accounts of liberty and equality.[28] The trilemma consisted of a forced choice among three principles, namely: merit, equality of life chances, and the autonomy of the family.[29]

Fishkin argued that no society could consistently embody all three principles. Each of these positions sacrificed some degree of either liberty or equality in order to achieve a higher degree of the other. Given background conditions of inequality, according to Fishkin, "it is a trilemma because realization of any two of these principles can realistically be expected to preclude the third."[30] For example, he explained that:

Table I.1. Elements of "Trilemma"

Elements of "Trilemma"	Contents
1. Merit	There should be procedural fairness in the evaluation of qualifications for positions.
2. Equality of Life Chances	Children's prospects for eventual positions in society should not vary in any systematic and significant manner according to their arbitrary native characteristics.
3. The Autonomy of the Family	Consensual relations within a given family governing the development of its children should not be coercively interfered with, except to ensure for the children the essential prerequisites for adult participation in society.

implementing the first [merit] and third [family autonomy] undermines the second [equal life chances]. The autonomy of the family protects the process whereby advantaged families differentially contribute to the development of their children. Given background conditions of inequality, children from the higher strata will have been systematically subjected to developmental opportunities which can reliably be expected to give them an advantage in the process of meritocratic competition. Under these conditions, the principle of merit—applied to talents as they have developed under such unequal conditions—becomes a mechanism for generating unequal life chances.[31]

In the same manner, Fishkin argued that realization of another pair of these principles (merit and equal life chances) could be expected to preclude family autonomy. Likewise, adoption of equal life chances and family autonomy could reasonably be expected to preclude merit. Thus Fishkin contended that the concept of equality of opportunity was contradictory in the sense that attempts to achieve it involved society in this trilemma.

Combined Husén-Fishkin Model

This study combines Husén's and Fishkin's theses to create a new research model—the combined Husén-Fishkin Model—that we can then use for the analysis of the historical transformation of the concept of equality of educational opportunity in Japan and for an examination of the relationships and conflicts amid the four different concepts detailed above. In the following section, the conflict among the four concepts of equality of educational opportunity in Husén's explanatory model (conservative, liberal, egalitarian, and Neo-Marxist) will be explained by focusing on the three positions of Fishkin's trilemma, each of which can be considered in terms of its corresponding account of liberty and equality. Table I.2 illustrates the relationship of these concepts:

Table I.2. The Combined Husén-Fishkin Model

	Conservative	Liberal	Egalitarian	Neo-Marxist
Merit	−	+	−	+
Equal life chances	−	−	+	+
Family autonomy	+	+	+	−

Note: A minus sign denotes de-emphasis; a plus sign denotes emphasis.

Thus, if one chose one of the above four models, one had to give up some of the attractions afforded by the other different interpretations. Each interpretation involved different consequences for educational policy. Some saw the most important task of education as achieving the egalitarian concept of equal opportunity to realize equal life opportunities for children and so required what some called "reverse discrimination" for socially disadvantaged children. Others, although acknowledging the desirability of excluding "irrelevant" factors such as class, income, religion, race, or early handicaps, stressed the liberal concept of the necessity of maintaining meritocracy. Yet another factor, the needs of society, was included by the Neo-Marxists who asserted that it was dangerous to attempt to consider equality of opportunity in isolation from its connection with a larger occupational structure.

What could equality of educational opportunity mean in this situation where competing priorities and diversity of educational aims existed? As will be examined later, these different priorities in equality of opportunity were at the core of the conflict between the two main groups—conservatives and progressives. Such conflict forms the basis of an attempt to explain the historical shift of equality of educational opportunity—particularly meritocracy and the demands of counter-egalitarianism. In fact, the meaning that was given to the concept of equality of educational opportunity underwent considerable change, and clarification is needed as to how the different interpretations and their resultant consequences developed.

Studies of the Historical Transformation of the Concept of Equality of Educational Opportunity

The study of equality of educational opportunity in a particular society cannot address the question of whether the process of historical transformation of the concept is typical or anomalous. However, through comparative analysis, it becomes possible to identify what is similar and dissimilar in the patterns and processes of the historical transformation of the concept. Therefore, this study attempts to use explanatory models developed in Western societies to analyze the concept changes in Japan.

There is much sociological and educational research in industrial Western countries that can contribute to our understanding of trends in the historical transformation of the concept of equality of opportunity during the last century in Japan, particularly after World War II. As we shall see later in this study, some of this research had direct implications for educational policy and reform. Major empirical studies by Coleman, Jencks, and Bowles and Gintis in the United States and by Halsey, Floud, and Anderson in the England have examined the historical trend of the concept and also documented persistent inequalities of educational outcome despite dozens of major policy reforms instituted in the name of "equality of educational opportunity" in these countries.[32] Generally speaking, however, the issue of equality arose in the United States initially with regard to race (mainly black and white) and in the England in relation to the lower socioeconomic classes.

Halsey's Model

Since the issues of race and ethnicity were not taken up in debates on educational opportunity in Japan during the period researched, this study uses Halsey's thesis of equal opportunity in preference to U.S. models to evaluate the historical shift of the concept of equality of educational opportunity. Halsey identified three historical phases of the concept in the England since World War II, each characterized by different thinking about how education could be used to produce equality:[33]

1. From the turn of the century to the late 1950s, the definition of equality was predominantly a liberal one, concerned with the idea of equality of opportunity. Combined with a concern for efficiency, the logical outcome of this view was in terms of equality of *access* for all children to the more advanced stages of education regardless of their sex, social class, religion, ethnic group, or region of origin. This meritocratic view of equal opportunity was consistently demonstrated to be failing. The class composition of grammar school and student proportions were not changing markedly, for example, despite expansion in both sectors.

2. The second phase occurred throughout the 1960s when the meaning of equality of opportunity changed to become equality of *achievement*. On this basis, equality of educational opportunity came about if the proportion of pupils from different social, economic, or ethnic groups at all levels of education was more or less the same as the proportion of these pupils in the population. If this did not occur then injustice could be said to have

taken place. In the early 1960s, sociological research indicated that particular groups were at a disadvantage in terms of educational achievement. As a consequence, positive discrimination in the form of compensatory education was suggested. This problem was tackled in the USA through the Project Headstart Programme and in England by implementing some of the recommendations of the Plowden Committee. One important implication of this shift was to emphasize the need to work upon those social conditions in the home and the community which helped to produce unequal educational outcomes.

3. In the third phase, in the 1970s, the debate was taken well beyond the concept of equality of opportunity, to attempts to reappraise the function of education in contemporary societies.

Halsey's theory of equality of opportunity, similarly to the others, was based on three assumptions: (1) since the industrializing nations were subject to a common set of technological imperatives, educational opportunities were expanded quantitatively in an attempt to find national talent; (2) however, the quantitative expansion of educational opportunities brought about little equality for children from lower social groups in terms of social mobility and income; and (3) in this situation, the notion of equality of educational opportunity tended to shift from equality of *access* to equality of *outcome*. In short, a characteristic common to these studies was that the principle of equal opportunity could not guarantee equal outcome in education, though it did preserve rights of free choice where reform policies that demanded equal results did not. Although there were appropriate reasons for desiring a more equal range of educational outcomes, it was not within the power of the liberal concept to ensure this goal, in theory or in practice. Of particular interest here was Halsey's claim that cross-national similarities in the process and in patterns of shifts in the concept would emerge in industrial countries. Since Japan and England experienced continuous expansions of educational opportunity after the war, Halsey's thesis predicted a historical shift in

Table I.3. Three Phases of Historical Shift in the Concept of Educational Opportunity as Identified by Halsey

	Phase of the debate on equality of opportunity		
	Up to the late 1950s	The 1960s	The 1970s and after
Type of equality of opportunity	Equality of access (Liberal concept)	Equality of outcome (Egalitarian concept)	Various definitions (Emergence of Neo-Marxist views)

the concept of equality of opportunity and a corresponding increase in universalism in the process of the shift in these countries.

Educational Models: Borrowing from the West

Japan shares important historical and socio-economic affinities with England and the United States in the field of education. The major education reforms in Japan, including those of Meiji, the Occupation, and even the present day, have relied heavily on Western models, particularly from Germany, England, and the United States. Indeed in the immediate post-war period after World War II, the first priority of the government was to remove all traces of the pre-war period and adopt instead an American education model aimed primarily at the democratization of society, while in the debates of the 1980s priority was given to the Western notion of individuality, which was aimed at encouraging creativity by introducing more freedom and choice into the education system. The recent agenda on education is regarded by many as having similarities to that of the Thatcher government in England and the Reagan government in the United States in the late 1980s.

On the other hand, there are also great differences among Japan, the United States, and England. They have vastly different historical and cultural backgrounds. The Western education system and its educational ideology is generally influenced by ancient Greek and Roman thought and practice; while Japan is primarily influenced by Eastern philosophical thinkers, particularly those in the Confucian tradition. If these different cultural ideologies are reflected in thinking about equality of educational opportunity, the conceptual shift that has taken place in England, the United States, and Japan over the period may be somewhat different. For the sake of clarity, it is therefore important to identify the way in which the debates have been pursued in these different countries. Thus, this study has used the English and the American cases of equality of opportunity as an explanatory model, where possible drawing comparisons and contrasts with Japan.

Structure of the Book

This study concentrates in particular on secondary education, a field in which major changes, events, and decisions took place during the period covered. Little attention has been given to the other tiers of the system (pre-school, elementary, further education, and higher education). Similarly, no examination is made of religious, ethnic, gender, or minority issues in the debate on equality of educational opportunity—debates which lie for the most part outside the scope of this study. Furthermore, in selecting historical documents, the focus has been on public statements, especially those which contain the terms "equality," "equality of opportunity," and "social background" and which were made mainly by the central administrative and advisory bodies. I mainly consult evidence available in the MOE and the CCE in Japan. I also trace interpretations of equality of educational opportunity by the major political parties, industrial organizations, academic scholars, and teachers' unions as reflected in their publications and in parliamentary debates.

The main body of this book focuses on two essential notions of equality of opportunity—egalitarianism and meritocracy—and examines how equality of educational opportunity was realized when applied to educational policy in these two paradigms.

Chapter 1 looks back to the evolution of modern secondary education systems in Japan, traces the origins of the concept of equality of educational opportunity, and classifies the major interpretations up to the post-war educational reform.

Chapters 2 and 3, covering phase one from 1945 to 1959, trace the initial application of equality of opportunity to post-war educational reforms and examine the notion of equality of opportunity that the central government, the MOE, the CCE, and others subscribed to for the first stage of the observation period. They also examine how, in the process, initial interpretations of equality of opportunity were gradually eroded by new interpretations. They focus closely on conflict over equality of educational opportunity between two major groups—conservatives and progressives. Chapter 2 (1945–1950) analyzes the debate on the process of formulation of educational clauses of the New Constitution and the FLE and examines how the pre-war educational policies differed from the New Constitution and the FLE in relation to equality of opportunity. Chapter 3 (1951–1959) describes how the egalitarian concept of equality supported by the FLE began to be attacked by the series of "reverse course" policies under the conservative governments after the Occupation period.

Chapter 4 looks at phase two, covering roughly the 1960s and the 1970s, in order to examine the notions of equality of educational opportunity that the CCE, the Economic Deliberation Council (EDC), and the Teachers' Union held when the unprecedented enthusiasm for expansion of education began to appear. This chapter focuses particularly on the conflict between conservatives and the Teachers' Union over the interpretation of equality of opportunity and examines how the Japanese conservatives partly succeeded in implementing the principle of *Nōryokushugi* ("ability first") in educational policy.

Chapter 5 discusses phase three, covering roughly the 1980s and 1990s onward. It analyzes the series of educational reform proposals and policies based on the "market principle" measures introduced by the Nakasone's Ad-Hoc Council and the CCE. These reforms fall under the slogan of "individuality" and are purportedly aimed at encouraging creativity by introducing more freedom and choice into education. This chapter also describes the debates over revising the Fundamental Law of Education under the Koizimi cabinet.

Chapter 6 analyzes how, in Japan during the period under investigation, the meaning of equality of educational opportunity shifted in the educational policies of the different first phases, whether there was a universal trend behind the historical shift of the concept or not, and if not, what factors led to the uniqueness of it. This chapter also re-examines popular conceptions of *gakurekishugi* ("degreeocracy") in Japan and throws light on the issue of social class inequality of educational opportunity. This chapter also expands upon the existing literature on educational reform in the twenty-first century by examining how the decline in the birth rate affects equality of educational opportunity among children from different family backgrounds.

The conclusion returns to the substantive themes underlying this study that were spelled out in this introduction and also attempts to bring together the major findings in the preceding chapters in order to arrive at some general conclusions about the historical transformation of the concept of equality of educational opportunity in Japan.

Notes

1. For instance, Coleman et al., *Equality of Educational Opportunity*; Halsey, *Educational Priority* (The Halsey Report); Husén, *Social Background and Educational Career*; and Musgrove, *School and the Social Order*.
2. See Suzuki, *Kyōiku Gyōsei*; Duke, *Japan's Militant Teachers*; Horio and Yamazumi, *Kyōiku Rinen*; Sato, H., *Beikoku Tai'Nichi Kyōiku Shisetsudan ni Kansuru Sōgtōteki Kenkyu*; Kubo, *Tai'nichi Senryō Seisaku to Sengo Kyōiku Kaikaku*; and Tsuchimochi, *Education Reform in Post-War Japan*.
3. See Passin, *Society and Education in Japan*; Hunter, *The Emergence of Modern Japan*; Linicome, *Principles, Praxis, and the Politics of Educational Reform in Meiji Japan*; and Marshall, *Learning to be Modern*.
4. For further details of tasks undertaken by the American Occupation, see Duke, *Japan's Militant Teachers*; Sato, H., *Beikoku Tai'Nichi Kyōiku Shisetsudan ni Kansuru Sōgtōteki Kenkyu*; Kubo, *Tai'nichi Senryō Seisaku to Sengo Kyōiku Kaikaku*; and Tsuchimochi, *Education Reform in Post-War Japan*.
5. Schoppa, *Education Reform in Japan*, 38–52.
6. For further details about the JTU, see Duke, *Japan's Militant Teachers*; and Thurston, *Teachers and Politics in Japan*. For a recent analysis of the schism in the JTU that occurred in 1989, see Aspinall and Cave, "Lowering the Flag."
7. Keizai Shingikai (EDC), *Jinteki Nōryoku Seisaku ni Kansuru Tōshin* (Task and Countermeasure for Development of Human Abilities and in Pursuits of Economic Expansion), January 13. Useful information on the report is given by Inui, *Nihon no Kyōiku to Kigyō Shakai*, 38–76.
8. Fundamental Law of Education, Article III.
9. For further details of Nakasone's educational reform during the 1980s, see Schoppa, *Education Reform in Japan*, 211–50; Goodman, *Who's Looking at Whom?*; Hood, *Japanese Education Reform*; and Okano and Tuchiya, *Education in Contemporary Japan*.
10. Chūō Kyōiku Shingikai (The Central Council on Education), 57–68.
11. See Okada, "Secondary Education Reform and the Concept of Equality of Opportunity in Japan."

12. Passin, *Society and Education in Japan*; Kobayshi, *Society, Schools and Progress in Japan*; Beauchamp and Vardaman, *Japanese Education since 1945*; and Marshall, *Learning to be Modern*.

13. Schoppa, *Education Reform in Japan*.

14. Duke, *Japan's Militant Teachers*; Thurston, *Teachers and Politics in Japan*; and Aspinall, *Unions and the Politics of Education in Japan*.

15. Horio, *Gendai Shakai to Kyōiku*; Okano and Tsuchiya, *Education in Contemporary Japan*.

16. On this subject, see Ishida, *Social Mobility in Contemporary Japan*; Tachibanaki, *Nihon no Keizai Kakusa*; Yoneyama, "Japanese 'Education Reform'"; Cave, "Educational Reform in Japan in the 1990s"; and Miura, *Karyū-Shakai*.

17. Fujita, *Kyōiku Kaikaku*; and Kurosaki et al., *Kyōiku Shi-zō no Saikouchiku*.

18. See Genda and Kyokunuma, *NEET*.

19. Ehara, *Gendai Kōtō Kyōiku no Kōzō*; and Kariya, *Kaisōka Nihon to Kyōiku Kiki*.

20. Kariya, *Taishū Kyōiku Shakai no Yukue*.

21. For instance, Coleman et al., *Equality of Educational Opportunity*; Halsey, *Educational Priority* (The Halsey Report); Husén, *Social Background and Educational Career*; and Musgrove, *School and the Social Order*.

22. Husén, *Social Background and Educational Career*, 27–39.

23. Kang, *Educational Policy and the Concept of Equal Opportunity in England*, xi–xii.

24. Husén, *Social Background and Educational Career*, 32.

25. Coleman et al., *Equality of Educational Opportunity*.

26. See Kang, *Educational Policy and the Concept of Equal Opportunity in England*.

27. Bowles and Gintis, *Schooling in Capitalist America*; Bourdieu and Passeron, *Reproduction in Education, Society, and Culture*; Bernstein, *Class Codes and Control*, vol. 3; and Collins, *The Credential Society*.

28. Fishkin, "Liberty versus Equal Opportunity," 32–48.

29. Ibid., 38–39.

30. Ibid., 39.

31. Ibid., 39.

32. Coleman et al., *Equality of Educational Opportunity*; Jencks et al., *Inequality*; Bowles and Gintis, *Schooling in Capitalist America*; and Halsey, Floud and Anderson, *Education, Economy and Society*.

33. Halsey, *Educational Priority* (The Halsey Report), 6–11.

I

The Initial Application of Equal Opportunity to the Education System in Japan, 1868–1944

The concept of "equality of opportunity" emerged along with the establishment of a modern school system. The transition from a pre-industrial society where formal education was a prerogative of birth, wealth, and connection and was designed for upper-class positions, to a modern society in which access to and promotion within the education system depended upon academic ability, was regarded as a tremendous step forward by means of which justice and efficiency alike were expected to be achieved.[1] In attempting to perfect equality of educational opportunity, objectively-assessed academic ability seemed to be the self-evident selection criterion to replace social class, economic background, and personal connections. It is thus that in modern industrial times it has been regarded, not only in Japan but also in other industrial societies, as desirable and even an obligation of the state to organize such a flow of ability and talent through the national education system. This has been done partly out of the individual Japanese sense of self-interest and partly out of a concern for national wealth. In comparing the historical movement of the concept of equality of opportunity in other industrial nations with Japan's in the modern industrial period, a number of parallels can be found.

Towards a State System: The Establishment of Compulsory Education Education in the Pre-Industrial Period

The birth of the modern school system of Japan originated in 1872. However, almost twenty years earlier the Tokugawa shōgunate had settled on an education system that was considered able to meet the foreign challenge. The long, continuous development of the Edo period (1600–1867) generated a distinctively Japanese style of life and thought, which was destined to have a significant influence on the development of modern educational institutions.[2] One distinctive feature of the feudal society of the Tokugawa shōgunate was the traditional stratification of classes into *samurai* (warriors), *nōmin* (farmers), *kōin* (artisans), and *shōnin* (merchants), with an especially strict distinction made between the samurai and the remaining strata. Tokugawa education already offered a wide range of schooling for each stratum—*hankō* or *hangaku* (the fief schools) for the samurai and the *terakoya* (parish school) for others. Under the rigid class divisions of the feudal system, schools, where they existed, were operated and sponsored by the respective classes for the benefit of their members. The fief schools were set up primarily to inculcate in the samurai moral values rooted in the study of Confucianism (Chinese classics) in order to stabilize their position; and the *terakoya* was a purely secular institution for the common people that mainly offered the so-called "three Rs": reading, writing, and arithmetic. Except for the *terakoya*, all of these institutions were only for boys. Besides these schools, private institutions (*shijuku*) were also opened to the samurai class. Thus the education that children received was designed to equip them with the knowledge and skills that they would require in performing the tasks of their respective classes when they reached adulthood.

Meiji Restoration and Education Reform

The Meiji Restoration in 1868 marked a turning point in transforming feudal Japan into a modern nation state by directing all of the nation's energies toward the goal of catching up with the Western countries. The urgent task of the newly established government was to create a centralized imperial state. The four most important changes in Japanese society were accomplished simultaneously between 1871 and 1875:

1. To set up a national land tax (*chiso kaisei*)

2. To abolish the social class system (*shimin byōdō*)

3. To establish a rich nation and a strong military (*fukoku kyōhei*)

4. To abrogate the traditional domain system and create prefectures (*haihan chiken*)

Although these four significant changes could not be accomplished independently, perhaps the most fundamental change that facilitated the establishment of a new state education system was the abolition of the four-class social system, because it broke down inherited social class distinctions within the Tokugawa education system. The abolition of the social class system was tied with the increase in production and the foundation of industries (*shokusan kōgyō*) and became a driving force both to prepare the nation's youth for their future careers and to certify meritorious achievement. These political movements paved the way for the establishment of a central authority for national education, the Monbushō (Ministry of Education), in 1871, and its subsequent development.

The Demand for Equal Opportunity

Equality of educational opportunity in the early Meiji period meant equal access to universal elementary school. As an illustrative case, one can cite the *Gakusei* (Education Law) in 1872. The Meiji reformers—themselves lower ranking samurai—were deeply conscious of the prime importance of mass education and advanced knowledge in meeting the challenge of the West and in mobilizing the talents of the whole nation regardless of social class. Accordingly, the government promulgated the *Gakusei* which ordered the provision of compulsory elementary education for all children. The preamble of the *Gaisei*, which indirectly denied Confucian ideology as the foundation for Japanese education, stipulated a liberal view of equal opportunity as explained in the introduction of this study:

> Henceforth, in the future, there shall be no community among the people as a whole—whether they be noble, samurai, farmer, artisan, merchant, or woman—where there is neither an uneducated household nor a family with an uneducated person. . . . Parents and guardians should be held at fault if they fail to have a child—whether boy or girl—attend primary school.[3]

This was the first time in Japanese history that an official statement declared that educational opportunity should be open to all citizens irrespective of social class or sex. Throughout the preamble, two principles were emphasized: (1) the removal of feudalistic barriers and the securing of equal opportunities of schooling according to one's abilities; and (2) the consideration of the individual's success in life and enlightenment concerning the goals of study and education. What is noteworthy here is that the *Gakusei* changed the role of education, which ceased to be the promulgation of a self-perpetuating social unit or a training ground. This functional definition of education as the best means for an individual's success in life, and national efficiency was already being advocated by some new intellects such as Fukuzawa Yukichi, Nakamura Masanao, Nishi Amane, and Mitsukuri Rinshō, who had preached the benefits of "Civilization and Enlightenment" (*bunmei kaika*). They believed that there was a necessary and close link between society, the state school system and national efficiency, and that, of all the factors impairing efficiency, the lack of a suitable education system was most grievous.[4]

It was in this context that such intellects counted education as having crucial importance and saw it in essentially utilitarian terms. Underpinning national efficiency, a natural corollary was to let able children continue their studies up to higher education through state scholarships. This view was widely supported by the Meiji government and reflected in the *Gakusei*. Indeed, seeking knowledge of an essentially practical kind, unrelated to appropriate socioeconomic roles and political loyalty, became the hallmark of the Meiji Restoration. However, although these new intellects contributed to the abandonment of Tokugawa feudalism, some of them did not totally deny the different roles of social class in the new education system. It should be noted that in their demands for a national system of post-elementary education in the early Meiji period, they did not advocate it as a universal system.[5] Their primary concern was the development of a limited number of post-elementary education institutions on one hand and the establishment of private higher education for able and wealthy middle-class children on the other. They insisted on "voluntary efforts" for creating a higher education, rather than a state provision, and on the principle of leaving education costs to individuals. One of the leading figures, Fukuzawa Yukichi, for instance, stated his educational philosophies in his various publications. In his book *Public Education*, he stated:

> State education should be a most basic, low-budget allocation, and stick to the lowest level in the whole education system. Secondary education above the state elementary education should not be a public concern. . . . It is a task for sages that university education should be entrusted to privatize, elaborate its curriculum, demand high fees, and open doors wholly to children of wealthy families.[6]

Fukuzawa's educational interest was mainly concerned with private school systems and producing a class-biased secondary education system, which may be characterized by a small number of middle-class people who had a high educational background ruling the remaining majority of uneducated people. In other words, the principle of equality of educational opportunity was not yet fully infused into an elitist concept of society. Thus, under a narrow sense of equal rights before the law, some new intellects did not repudiate the conservative perspective of equality of educational opportunity which admits privilege to birth and wealth in the education system.

In short, the *Gakusei* made several regulations which constituted a prophetic blueprint for the move to end the existing class-biased system of education. The *Gakusei* laid down the foundations for a national system of eight years of compulsory elementary education for all children aged six to thirteen, and parents were placed under an obligation to make their children attend school. Secondly, it characterized the nature of elementary school as a sequential process towards post-elementary education. This birth process of elementary school is different from those in Europe. Thirdly, it separated education and religion, and it required the teaching of the "three Rs" or "secular knowledge" (e.g., mainly technology and medicine, etc.) in the school. Fourthly, the law adopted a school district system, modeled on the French system, in order to create a unified school system. It prescribed that the country would be divided into 8 university districts, each with one university, and these districts were to be divided into 32 middle school districts, and again each of these into 210 primary school districts. In every grand school district, a board of school inspection was provided to administer under the supervision of Monbushō. Finally, it imposed the duties for parents to pay the fees of the school for their children and placed the entire burden of the expense to establish and maintain the school onto people and boards in local areas. Thus, the *Gakusei* is remarkable for the move it represents by the state away from the reliance on the initiative of respective classes towards the provision of a complete national system of education according to central instruction established by law.

The Development Process of Secondary Education

Towards a National System of Secondary Education

The establishment of a state elementary system was soon accompanied by the development of secondary education.[7] Compared to the elementary schools, however, after a decade of the 1872 *Gakusei*, the Meiji government was not active enough to provide secondary education for all the nation's children. Under the policy of "non-interference by state but private-management" (*minni hounin*) it was wholly left in the hands of voluntary initiatives made by the local boards or people concerned with managing old fief schools.[8] In 1875, the total number of secondary schools was estimated at about 116, with 11 in the state sector and 105 private. The total number of students was 5,437 (1,052 state and 4,385 private). Due to the lack of initiative on the part of the government in secondary education, the existing regional disparity in opportunity of secondary education was also enormous. Thus, the first priorities of the educational reform in the early Meiji period were placed on setting up compulsory elementary education and normal schools, and therefore, the establishment of the secondary schools took a back seat to the provision of those schools.

A New Education Ordinance, enacted in 1879 by Monbushō, stated that "secondary education gives a higher level of general education." Yet this ordinance, and other relevant regulations enacted by the mid 1880s, had left undefined what type of secondary education system was the most desirable and who was eligible for it. The 1886 Middle School Ordinance, laid down by the first Minister of Education Mori Arinori, specified the characteristics of secondary education and led to the expansion of the secondary school system along the lines of strictly determined priorities given the limited resources available. Three elements of secondary education were clarified in this ordinance:[9] First, the ordinance defined the nature of secondary education by stipulating that "secondary schools provide essential education for students who want to work for the business world (*jitsugyō*) or to advance to higher institutions." At the time "business world" did not have the same usage as that in the present day: It included as meanings not only "industry" but also "bureaucracy." Secondly, the secondary education was organized as two stages: One is a five-year lower secondary school which was under the jurisdiction of the prefectures, and the other is a two-year higher secondary school which was set up and administrated directly by the minister of education. Thirdly, the ordinance strictly restricted the number of secondary schools; there is one in each prefecture. The assumption underlying policies implemented under such ministers of education as Mori and Inoue Kowashi, who accepted a large part of Mori's plans, was to create a dual system comprising a compulsory sector of elementary schools confined to the 3Rs and heavily indoctrinated in the spirit of morality and nationalism, and an Imperial university sector for a male elite, with high fees charged, which enjoyed an atmosphere of academic freedom and was destined to fill a leadership-providing role in future society. Following up these recommendations, the Meiji governments established the framework for the development of a diverse multi-track post-elementary education system.

By contrast to elementary schools, the basic characteristics of secondary education might be summed up as selective, expensive, placing a distinct emphasis upon the academic type of curriculum, and treating boys and girls differently; indeed, these characteristics were to continue until the end of World War II. Upon these variations, the existing post-elementary schools were roughly classified into three categories. Firstly, the most prestigious but narrowest track led through middle school (*chūtōgakkō*) only for the male, entrance to which was by means of a severe entrance examination, and higher school (*kōtō gakkō*) into an Imperial University. What is mentioned particularly in the apex of this track is that for those who had succeeded in being accepted to Tokyo Imperial University or a few other selected universities an impressive career was especially guaranteed. Only five-year middle schools were regarded as so-called secondary education (*jinjyō chūtōgakkō*), as Mori expected that students in the middle schools would want to rise to the upper classes and not be left behind. Since Mori laid down the principle of having one middle school for each prefecture, most candidates at this time were expelled from a middle school education because places were quite limited. Only 8 percent of male students were advancing to this level in 1890. For academically able but poor children, even an offer of support from a sponsor had to be weighed against the immediate loss of labor and earning to the family. Consequently, most of the students who could afford middle school education were children from families who had been samurai in the Edo period. By 1890, 55 middle schools were attended by 11,620 students, but they were all male and came from the middle and upper classes.[10] In other words, the children of the general run of citizens would not be able to enter such schools.

Apart from the academic middle school, education beyond elementary school level was also provided in vocational and technical schools. Since there had been increasing demands for the post-elementary school courses since the 1880s, and the Technical School Code of 1899 was passed, the government tended to create these schools, known as *jitsugyō gakkō*, in response especially to local needs. However, these vocational types of schools were distinguished from middle schools, particularly in terms of curriculum, the main function, and social composition of student bodies. While the middle schools provided an academic type of education, this type of school placed a distinct emphasis on vocational, technical, and agricultural subjects. The main function of the schools was to train their students to be better workmen rather than the nation's leaders. Students from the schools entered employment in commercial business or became skilled artisans. The school was also inferior to the middle schools in some respects: For example, the number of students who were enrolled in the technical schools was only about one-third of those in the middle schools; and some of the schools had annexes that offered apprentice programs for workers. The government also established new types of vocational programs both at the primary and higher schools. Thus, by 1905 a complex pyramid of vocational and technical schools had developed that paralleled the academic track at the primary, secondary, and advanced levels. Since these were intended to mirror the occupational structure, they clearly reflected a hierarchy of strata with quite distinct prospects for income, power, and prestige.

Finally, there were also the national Normal Schools which were opened to the male and female graduates of primary schools who succeeded in passing the entrance examinations. Normal Schools, which aimed to train primary school teachers, particularly attracted youth who were from a lower socio-economic background and might not able to advance to the middle school track because of the lack of a free education. This type of school differed greatly from the academic middle schools; the Meiji government expected the schools to produce "patriot" teachers who were devoted to pursuing ultra-nationalistic schooling to establish Imperial Japan. The data from at least one Normal School indicated that by the early 1930s over 90 percent of students were from the commoner class.[11]

The Idea of an Educational Ladder

In Japan, if the first half of the Meiji era (1868–1890) concentrated on the establishment of universal elementary education, then the second half (1890–1912) saw the development of secondary and higher education. As the modernization of industry gathered pace from the last decade of the nineteenth century, the government began to introduce enlightened modernization polices such as the promulgation of a constitution and the establishment of representative political institutions based on the model of Prussia. At the same time, it followed the power politics of Western countries and aimed to regulate the nation under firm control, channeling popular energies into national development. Educational policies became an integral part of the effort to realize these ends. Monbushō acknowledged an urgent need to establish a national system of secondary education.[12] Four main elements influenced educational policies and reforms concerning secondary schools up to the end of World War II: (1) national integration as a reaction to external pressures from Western powers; (2) spiritual training based on the Confucian ethic, which emphasized the subordinate's duties toward the Emperor and a strong sense of patriarchal responsibility toward the commoners; (3) the need to develop a core of competent technicians to master modern technology and to foster industrialization and economic growth; and finally (4) rigid meritocratic selection of a national elite to meet the need for highly trained labor force.The compulsory elementary schools had been able to produce a small but sufficient number of diligent graduates for the middle schools by the first decade of the twentieth century, and therefore the government did not choose the American style of secondary education system, but the system prevailing in European countries such as England. As mentioned earlier, the secondary education system set up at the time in Japan was based on a dual system comprising an academic track and a non-academic track. Consequently, by the end of World War II, the Japanese school system consisted of five separate tracks or ladders which, once embarked on, determined one's length of formal education. Under this secondary education system, just over half the pupils went on to Higher Elementary Schools for two years, followed, for the boys during the war years, by part-time attendance at a Youth School for another two years. The other third of the school age population was destined for further schooling—20 percent of the age group went on to Vocational Schools for up to four years, qualifying them for semi-skilled occupations. Only one out of eight male pupils advanced beyond middle school, which finished at age 17; this percentage was even smaller for girls, a mere four percent.[13]

The Demand for Equal Opportunities in Education

The progressives' view, however, differed from the government's in their demands for a secondary education system. These progressives included members of the Japan Teachers' Union Enlightenment Association (*Keimeikai*) and some members of the Japan Labor Union and the Social Democratic Party. Most of them believed, at least in theory, in the existence of a fundamental clash of interests between different social classes and strove to move towards an egalitarian society. These progressives envisaged education mainly as the best tool for political and economic emancipation.[14] By 1910, the elementary education attendance rate had reached over 80 percent, and the progressives then concentrated on providing free state education, raising the school-leaving age, and promoting a scholarship system, most particularly secondary education for the children of lower social groups. It seems that the ideal of equality in education was adopted and the phrase itself used for the first time by the socialist groups, particularly by the members of the Japan Labor Union, in the process of emphasizing their demands for free state schooling. *Rōdō sekai* (Labor World), an organ published by the Japan Labor Union in 1898, formulated a specific resolution on educational matters, taking a stand on human rights. The resolution declared:

> We insist that education is a social and universal human right. Irrespective of rich and poor, all people in this civilized world have a right equally to receive education. It is a boon of civilized society and a public good of human society. Nobody should monopolize it as their private property. Therefore, the state should have a duty to establish public schools and bear the expense of providing them to the people.[15]

A similar resolution was presented as part of the Social Democratic Party's Declaration which defined the "equalization of life and education" as involving the opening up of educational opportunity to the workers. It ran:

> In order for people to receive education equally, the state should bear the expense of all educational costs. . . . Compulsory education should be until the end of Higher Elementary School, tuition charges should be totally abolished, and textbooks should be provided at public expense.[16]

The idea of fostering human dignity by promoting free secondary education was reflected in the resolution of *Keimeikai*, founded under the leadership of Shimonaka Yasaburō in 1919. In his book, *Education for Workers* (Ban'nin rōdō no kyōiku) of 1923, Shimonaka announced "The Four General Principles for Educational Reform" and put forward the following resolution:

> The right to receive education—right to learning—is a basic human right. Accordingly, based on the spirit that education is not an individual duty, but the right of people in society, and with a view to achieving equality of educational opportunity, we expect to realize public schooling from the elementary to university levels with (1) free tuition; (2) state-sponsored school supplies; and (3) guaranteed minimum living expenses.[17]

This seems to be the first time that the Teachers' Union applied the principle of equal opportunity to education. The notion of a "right to learning" implied more than the liberal perspective of equality, emphasizing the practical access to schooling, by providing, if necessary, compensatory financial aid. This would seem to be the first hint of what in the 1970s came to be called a policy of "Right to Learning" by the Japan Teachers' Union.[18] Thus, the Teachers' Union's first use of that principle in the domain of secondary education was significant as foreshadowing the way the Union of the future would follow in adopting the principle as a major goal of its educational policy.

Shimonaka was not the only one advocating such an idea of equality of educational opportunity. A more specific definition of the concept was made in the *Dictionary of Educational Studies* compiled by Abe Yoshishige, professor at Tokyo Imperial University, in 1936. Abe asserted:

> Free secondary education and tertiary education, in themselves, do not guarantee equality of opportunity in education. Earnings acquired by youths are a help to family finances and there are so many families which cannot make a living without these earnings. In order to achieve complete equality of educational opportunity, a state must provide financial support to families who have gifted children but cannot allow them to continue their education because of poverty. Therefore, such financial support must include living costs for the families, as well as scholarships.[19]

As the quotation demonstrates, Abe's definition of the concept of equal opportunity was not only focused on the legal, formal, and nominal provision of post-elementary education but also on the real, qualitative, and practical conditions for it. Acknowledging a practical hindrance which might prevent poor children from accessing secondary education, Abe further linked his ideas for achieving equality of educational outcome to the necessity for the provision of compensatory programs. This view was seen by the progressives at the time as the best means of achieving social construction and demolishing class privilege in education.

Nevertheless, it did not seem that the progressives' assertion of the radical notion of equal opportunity led them immediately to repudiate all the existing characteristics of secondary education. It is important to notice that Shimonaka and Abe did not reject the necessity for differentiation of children according to their ability, and like the Liberalists in the Meiji period, they interpreted equality of opportunity as applicable in two different ways: first, same access and second, different allocation of children, as represented in Abe's statement that "equality of opportunity does not mean requiring identical education. It means to give educational opportunity equally to all children and youths on the basis of their individual differences and needs in life."[20] For them, differences in children's abilities had to be allowed for beyond elementary education. Thus, for the progressives, the term equality of educational opportunity did not mean secondary schools (middle school) for all, nor a common secondary school, but various types of post-elementary education for all, suited to various abilities and future careers.

The time was not yet ripe for repudiating the multi-track secondary schooling system. Even though the progressives were aware of the probable danger of social discrimination arising from differentiation at the secondary education level, it seemed that the educational desirability of differentiation on the basis of children's ability from the national point of view was given a higher priority than the prevention of social discrimination. Indeed, Shimonaka had great respect for the imperial throne and stressed that his call for change was ultimately grounded in patriotism and loyalty.[21] The progressives understood and applied the principle of equal opportunity within the existing educational structure. However, considering the historical context of the pre-World War II period, when the establishment of an Imperial and militaristic education system was being consolidated and the period of middle schooling was required to be shortened in order to secure students' military service, the resolution of the progressives that the right to learning should be secured in a state education system, as well as imposing on the government a duty to provide financial support for poor children alongside release from tuition charges, seemed to be an inevitable practical step towards achieving equality of educational opportunity in post-elementary education.

Conclusion

To sum up, the trends in the pre-World War II concepts of equality of educational opportunity in Japan were firmly established by the end of the 1930s. On the positive side, whereas the children's educational opportunities were largely limited by their family background and economic situation in pre-industrial society, by 1910 elementary school had become universal for all children regardless of their social class and gender. In this respect, the concept of equality of opportunity was successfully transformed from the conservative perspective to the liberal perspective. However, with regard to secondary education, for the Japanese government a belief in equality of opportunity did not necessarily entail the rejection of a meritocratic approach. Indeed, it was quite the contrary: Since one of the motives of early espousers of the concept was the very need for fresh blood in the elite, the system recruited on merit from different social classes. Provision of state education was defined in terms of a functionalist view rather than in terms of a conviction of the egalitarian rights of individuals, and accordingly expansion of educational opportunity in secondary education was envisaged as necessary for the sake of national efficiency and desirable social reform. Thus, the whole mechanism of selection and the diversified education system was designed to produce an academic elite to stabilize the nation, a conventional concept in this period.

It can be concluded that as far as secondary education was concerned, the Japanese government subscribed to the "ladder of opportunity" as the concept of equality of educational opportunity in the pre-war period. This concept, which broke down the assumption that elementary and secondary education should relate to different social classes, was broadly supported. The original application of this notion stemmed from skepticism regarding the existing aristocracy of pupil bodies in secondary education and increasing support for meritocratic composition. Yet, equality in educational terms did not imply a belief that all abilities were equal or that all outcomes should be the same, but rather that equality of opportunity should be defined to provide different types of secondary schooling corresponding to children's abilities.

However, there still remained three crucial unsolved problems in the move towards a national system of secondary education, and these became the main issues for education reform by the outbreak of World War II. All three fall under the umbrella of equality of educational opportunity: (1) growing pressure on the secondary schools, which had insufficient accommodation even for all those children who qualified for a place in the academic types of secondary education; (2) a newly acknowledged need to give all different types of post-elementary school equal esteem and prestige; and (3) the existing inequality of educational opportunity between boys and girls in post-compulsory education. These unsolved problems became the focus and the prime aim of the post-war American Occupation's educational reform in Japan—to provide equal opportunity in secondary education.

Notes

1. Coleman et al., *Equality of Educational Opportunity*, 9–24; and Husén, *Social Background and Educational Career*, 27–39.
2. See Dore, *Education in Tokugawa Japan*.
3. Monbushō, *Gakusei 100 Nenshi*, vol. 2, 11.
4. See Hall, I., *Mori Arinori*; Lincicome, *Principles, Praxis, and the Politics of Educational Reform in Meiji Japan*; and Marshall, *Learning to be Modern*.
5. Motoyama, *Meiji Zenki Gakkō Seiritsushi*; and Marutani, *Fukuzawa Yukichi Kenkyu*.
6. Quoted in Marutani, *Fukuzawa Yukichi Kenkyu*, 145.
7. Kurasawa, *Gakkō Rei no Kenkyū*; Taniguchi, *Nihon Chūtō Kyōiku Kaikakushi Kenkyu*; and Yoneda, *Kindai Nihon Chūgakkōseido no Kakuritsu*.
8. Taniguchi, *Nihon Chūtō Kyōiku Kaikakushi Kenkyu*, 14–15.
9. Kokuritsu Kyōiku Kenkyūsho, *Nihon Kindai Kyōiku 100-Nen Shi*, vol. I.; and Yoneda, *Kindai Nihon Chūgakkōseido no Kakuritsu*, 21–31.
10. Kaigo, *Japanese Education*, 81.
11. Marshall, *Learning to be Modern*, 99.
12. Okada, "Equality of Opportunity in Post-war England and Japan," 47–57.
13. Ibid., 54.
14. Kurosaki, *Kōkyōikuhi no Kenkyu*.
15. Quoted in Kurosaki, *Kōkyōikuhi no Kenkyu*, 143.
16. Quoted in ibid., 145.
17. Shimonaka, *Ban'nin no Kyōiku*, 237–39.
18. Okada, "Equality of Opportunity in Post-war England and Japan," 285–86. See chapter 4 of this study.
19. Abe, *Kyōikugaku jiten*, vol. I., 464–66.
20. Ibid., 465.
21. Shimonaka, *Ban'nin no Kyōiku*, 237.

2

The Initial Position of the Concept of Equal Opportunity in Education, 1945–1950

In Japan, defeat in World War II and the American Occupation brought about a radical change in the post-war era. The hardships of the war and its ultimate futility prepared the Japanese people for a change of value orientations under the Occupation, and many enthusiastically endorsed democratization. Equality of opportunity was one of the main principles of the post-war education system, and it had been achieved through a series of debates on the process of the framing of Article 26 of the New Constitution and Article 3 of the FLE. The purpose of this chapter is to analyze the initial position of the concept of equal opportunity during the immediate post-war reconstruction period and to examine the notions of equal opportunity that were subscribed to by various groups for the first time. In order to do this it is especially necessary to analyze a series of debates that occurred during the process of these two significant articles in their respective pieces of legislations.

Educational Reform Under the American Occupation

Towards a More Democratic Education System

World War II finally ended when Japan accepted the Potsdam Declaration on 15 August 1945 and surrendered unconditionally to the Allied Powers. More than 2,300,000 military men had been killed or wounded and over 800,000 people had been killed or injured in air attacks. Japan's economy was a shambles. Japanese people were suffering direly owing to the food shortage after the defeat, and they were also in a mental state of confusion and lethargy.

In the sphere of education, under the Occupation Japan was required to transform a totalitarian state into a democratic one and to eliminate the foundations of the wartime education system in the Imperial state. However, education in the schools had been almost at a standstill since the final stages of the war: "Capitulation found 18 million students idle, four thousand schools destroyed, and only 20 percent of the necessary textbooks available . . . and more than one of every three institutions of higher education lay in ruins, thousands of teachers were homeless, hungry, and dispirited, and many of their pupils had been moved to safer areas."[1]

Post-war educational reform was undertaken by a U.S. Occupation Government headed by General Douglas MacArthur, the Supreme Commander for the Allied Powers (SCAP), who through his occupying army carried out policies of democratization, demilitarization, and decentralization of Japanese society.[2] Under SCAP, a General Headquarters (GHQ) was set up for the control of the Japanese government and a Civil Information and Education Section (CI&E) was established as one of the Special Staff Sections of the GHQ to be responsible for public information, education, religion, and other sociological and cultural problems of Japan. The Occupation recognized that a new orientation of the education system was an indispensable element in achieving its objectives, especially that of remaking Japan into a functioning democracy. Therefore, the first task for the Occupational forces was to remove those aspects of Japanese education that they considered anti-democratic or militaristic. The Supreme Command therefore issued Four Orders (*Yondai Shirei*) between October and December 1945 concerning the elimination of military and ultra-nationalist elements in teaching, the purging of war collaborators from the sphere of education, the separation of the *Shinto* religion and politics from education and the suspension of the courses in morals, Japanese history, and geography.[3] In addition, an order was issued that all ultra-nationalist or militaristic textbooks be destroyed and that all new textbooks be translated into English so that they could be evaluated by the CI&E.

While this negative side of CI&E's education reform was in progress, the Japanese side, too, however inadequate it was, was undertaking an active reform. Aware of the strong pressures from the Occupation, the Ministry of Education (MOE) and the Ad Hoc Committee (later renamed the Education Reform Council) began their task of preparing post-war educational programs in September of 1945. *The Educational Policy for Construction of a New Japan*, which was drafted by the Shidehara administration's Minister of Education, Maeda Tamon, was enacted on 15 September. Despite the fact that it still mentioned national polity or *kokutai* (corporate spirit of the nation), it talked of "education and its goals of serving the good of the country and, at the same time, constructing a peaceful nation by the eradication of militarism."[4] It emphasized "improvement of the education of the Japanese people, cultivating their ability to think scientifically, strengthening their desire for peace, and raising the general level of knowledge and virtue within our society."[5] Then the Ad Hoc Committee introduced the so-called inked textbooks (*suminuri kyōkasho*), which had the material on military matters inked out by the students themselves.

However, the existing educational system and ideology began to be strongly attacked by the CI&E as inadequate for the establishment of an equal society and even viewed as one of the major elements perpetuating the inequalities, while MOE's officials were in close touch with CI&E officers on such matters as ideological reform, the revision of textbooks, and the creation of a new education system to achieve greater equality of opportunity.

The U.S. Education Mission: Emergence of the New Concept for Equal Opportunity

During the Occupation period, the term "equality of opportunity" gradually emerged as a popular phrase indicating a long-term aim for a post-war education system, and widespread support for this idea could be found not only on the U.S. Occupation side but also on the Japanese side. From the perspective of tracing shifts in the leading concept of equality of opportunity in education, it is worthwhile to analyze how the American Occupation, Japanese political parties and groups at the center of the educational reform at that time interpreted this concept.

As soon as the U.S. Education Mission (USEM) started its work in March of 1946, the term "equality of opportunity" gradually appeared in post-war educational policies. The USEM, headed by George Stoddard and composed of twenty-six distinguished U.S. educationalists, designed and initiated a comprehensive reform—the democratization of Japanese education.[6] Its major contribution was to provide the Japanese with the necessary materials, advice, and encouragement to enable them to implement education reforms themselves, in accordance with their own requirements.[7] The report, completed by the USEM, contained very significant educational ideas which foreshadowed the trend in educational thought throughout the Occupation period. Repudiating the militarist and ultra nationalist aspects of the pre-war system elaborated by the Imperial Rescript (*Kyōiku-chokugo*), the USEM's Report proclaimed that "an equality of opportunity will create a new structure of education, open to all youth, alike to both sexes."[8] With regard to a new principle of "equality of educational opportunity," the USEM's Report proclaimed the following:

> The inalienable and universal rights of people are safeguarded largely through the process of education. Schools are established to supplement and enrich the experiences of people. That education is most desirable which results in the individual's attaining progressively throughout life his own best self. In a democracy, individual human beings are, we repeat, of surpassing worth. Their interests must not be subordinated to those of the state. *Educational opportunity, commensurate with*

individual ability, should be equally available for all persons regardless of sex, race, creed or colour. Minority groups should be respected and valued. . . . Intelligent citizenship, based on freedom of thought, communication, and criticism, should be an important outcome of education.[9]

In order to achieve greater equality of opportunity in education, the USEM made several recommendations, which constituted a prophetic blueprint for the move to end the existing parallel system of education. The members of the USEM exchanged various opinions and reached agreements that secondary education should be a natural continuation from elementary education, the compulsory schooling age should be raised to fifteen, secondary education should be free, and a coeducational public school system should be established. The overall goal was to create what was referred to as a 6-3-3-4 system based on a simplified U.S. model—six years in elementary school, three years in lower secondary school, and three years in upper secondary school in order to replace the multiple tracks of the pre-war system, which had required a career choice early in the student's schooling. There were also to be comprehensive upper secondary schools to which all students, male and female, were to proceed without taking an examination and where they would have freedom to choose their course or school subjects. The USEM's report recommended that each lower-secondary school graduate should be given an opportunity to attend an upper-secondary school that offered a wide array of curricula, including preparation for college. Further, the report looked forward to the establishment of the four-year universities above high school, and some two-year junior colleges.

As is clear from the above quotation and its recommendations, the USEM's Report put forward its notion of equality of educational opportunity as part of the social equality which post-war Japanese society should seek to achieve. The newly introduced 6-3-3-4 system was seen as the best means of achieving the reconstruction of society and of demolishing the class privileges of the pre-war secondary education system. The USEM firmly believed that without complete abolition of selection and establishment of a comprehensive upper secondary education system based on the U.S. model, the social class-bias in the pre-war middle school would be perpetuated. The USEM defined the concept of equality of opportunity as social integration of secondary schools. It is interesting to note that as compared with the 1944 Education Act in England, which had applied the principles to provide some new recruits for higher social positions, thus implying equality at the *starting* point in the educational race,[10] the USEM mainly used the terms "equality" or "equal opportunity" to produce a more desirable kind of society, therefore implying equality at the *finishing* point. Thus, for the USEM Report, the idea of fully developing a child's personal ability was much more important than allocating children into different types of schools according to their ability and the needs of national efficiency.

Political Debates on Equal Opportunity in Education

While the concept of equal educational opportunity was being transformed to signify eradication of social inequalities on the U.S. side, there was a noticeable development among Japanese political parties in their acceptance or interpretation of the principle of equal opportunity.

In November 1945, the conservative Japan Advancement Party (JAP) was set up under the leadership of Machida. It published *A Draft of the Post-War Education Reform* in May 1946, which specified that "equality in education can be realized for all pupils by the deliberate elimination of several handicaps arising from financial difficulties, sex discrimination, and so on."[11] It went on to insist on expansion of educational opportunity by saying that "all able children, irrespective of income, should be educated corresponding to their innate ability by expanding the present *Ikuei* scholarship."[12] Furthermore, it enumerated such definite policies as increasing the number of private schools and part-time evening schools for young people and the equalization of educational opportunity for both sexes.

In the same manner, the Japan Socialist Party (JSP), set up under the leadership of Katayama Tetsu on 2 November 1946, interpreted equality of educational opportunity as an extension of the length of compulsory education and national support for able children without financial resources.[13] Although the JSP had a very different political ideology from that of the JAP, as far as equality of educational opportunity was concerned, members of the JSP at the time concurred with the interpretation of the JAP. For the JSP, like the JAP, only able children should be helped on the basis of rational and relevant criteria, and equality of educational opportunity in this context meant equal cultivation of bright children.

The Japan Liberal Party (JLP), established in November 1945 and led by Hatoyama Ichirō, took a different view, seeing the concept of equality in terms of the relationship between national and private school. It was concerned with not only parity of prestige between the two types of schools but also provision of the same educational courses. The party announced an "Urgent Policy" on its founding day and pointed out that "in the pre-war period, the national universities enjoyed much greater advantages than the private universities did in terms of investment as well as prestige."[14] The JLP interpreted equality of opportunity as parity of conditions and esteem between national schools and private schools. However, the JLP's interpretation was not popular, and somewhat impractical, as it took no account of the financial difficulties of the Japanese government at the time.

Finally, the Japan Communist Party (JCP), most of leaders of which were imprisoned during the war, resumed its activity on 8 November 1945 under the leadership of its secretary-general Tokuda. Equality of opportunity was one of the outstanding concepts about which the JCP expressed its belief in *Cultural Policy*, which was adopted at the Fifth Rally in June of the following year. Severely criticizing the pre-war Imperial school system and the bureaucracy, it gave the party's account of the concept of equal opportunity in education as follows:

> Although every citizen takes on the burden of education, education is, in great part, given only to the children of the few who are the ruling elite. The majority of working class people who must be responsible for the future civilization are prevented from receiving education by various impediments. Therefore both the school system and the academic scholarship system must be reformed drastically so that every child can gain an opportunity to have a higher education corresponding to his or her ability and principles, regardless of class, occupation of parents, economic position, race, and sex.[15]

This resolution adopted by the JCP was of significance as being the first time that "equality of opportunity" was used in relation to education for working class people in the post-war period. Condemning the existing class distinction in education, the JCP thus defined equality of educational opportunity as involving the opening up of the highest levels of education to the workers.

It is important to notice that the principle of equality of opportunity in education was adopted and the phrase gradually came to be used not only by right-wing political parties such as the JAP and JLP but also by left-wing parties such as the JSP and JCP. However, it is very difficult to know exactly how much Japanese political parties at the time were really interested in the principle of equality of educational opportunity. It is fairly said that the notion of equality of educational opportunity envisaged by the political parties at the time was not enough to bring about social reconstruction or radical reform, as it seemed merely to emphasize equal access to schooling, no matter what sort of education such equal access might bring. In other words, the focus of this notion seemed to be a quantitative provision of educational opportunity rather than the qualitative conditions of the provision. Consequently, it seems that even if they acknowledged the urgent need to reform the education system, it would have been unlikely to bring about a radical social reconstruction of the kind which the USEM ultimately desired to achieve, but merely a gradual improvement by expanding the number of *Ikuei* scholarships.

MOE's Interpretation

On the other hand, the MOE, which had been working together with the USEM, also made vigorous statements about equality of educational opportunity in cooperation with the Ad Hoc Committee. A *Guide for the New Education* was published in May 1946 and contained a clearer interpretation of equality of opportunity in section 5, titled "The Need to Respect Children's Personalities Equally, and to Provide Educational Opportunity Suitable for their Individual Character," which read as follows:

> In democratic education, teachers must equally respect each child as an individual who has personality. They must not treat children as they are told to do by ruling elites and parents with the excuse that they are doing it for the nation and the families. . . . *It is the real justice in education to treat children differently corresponding to their ability just as parents treat a weak and a strong, a strong-minded and a timid child differently with consideration as they bring up their children.* In short, in democratic education, appropriate education should be provided for every individual as a human being who has individuality, while respecting them equally as a human being.[16]

The MOE proposed two clear but incompatible ideologies in the guide: In the name of equal opportunity, it suggested not only equal respect, but also allocation of children to different schools according to ability. It is important to notice that from the beginning the Japanese government and some members of the MOE began to match their belief in the principle of equal opportunity with the necessity for providing various types of schooling, while assuming a scheme of differentiation of the nation's children on grounds of difference in ability. The same may be said, no doubt, of Butler's tactic of the tripartite system in the English education system.[17] Analysis of rudimentary content of the equal opportunity in the various groups was undertaken using mainly just four elements for equality of educational opportunities as follows:

As will be discussed later in this chapter, as the reform of the educational laws and systems proceeded, however, conservatives and radical reformers started to debate the issue of whether educational opportunity should be given to all children according to their abilities or given regardless of their academic ability. Despite the fact that the concept of equality of educational opportunity was interpreted in a number of different ways by the USEM, various political parties,

Table 2.1. Rudimentary Content of the Equality of Educational Opportunity in the Various Groups

	USEM	JAP	JLP	JSP	JCP	MOE
By increasing scholarship	o	o		o	o	o
Based on ability		o	(o)	o		o
As social integration	o				o	
Regardless of gender difference	o	o			o	
Others			o			

the Ad Hoc Committee, and the MOE, their discussions during the first year were of significance in the sense that, distinct from the pre-war unenthusiastic attitudes, they advocated equality of opportunity as a guidepost for sketching the broad outlines of post-war educational policies. Their unprecedented support for equality of educational opportunity was explicitly reflected in the process of framing the New Constitution and the Fundamental Law of Education (FLE).

The New Constitution and Dispute over Equality of Educational Opportunity

Comprehensive discussions on the relationship between the new constitution and education were in progress in the 90th Imperial Diet (20 June–11 October 1946). Yoshida Shigeru became Prime Minister during the confusion after the general election in April. In his inaugural speech in the upper house on 21 June, he emphasized the necessity for social reform to include education by saying that "the content and the system of education would be reformed thoroughly in order to wipe out militarism and prevent it from recurring."[18] Tanaka Kotaro, the Minister of Education, also made a similar statement in the House of Representatives on 3 July to the effect that "education is very important and hereafter must be arranged in accordance with a democratic and pacifist spirit." One can infer from these quotations that concepts of democracy and the necessity of education as the best means to establish a democratic society were widely accepted by the Japanese government. However, while they regretted and criticized the pre-war education that took sides with the militarists, the leaders of the Japanese government kept making negative comments on the abolition of the Imperial Rescript. In fact, the conservatives had hoped to retain the Rescript, arguing that it could provide the symbolic axis for constructing a new future.[19]

Peoples' Right to Receive Education

Among the educational provisions in the Draft of the New Constitution, Article 24 illustrates most clearly how much the Japanese government emphasized concepts of equality and equal opportunity during this period. As to the process of framing the article, two issues were particularly focused on and discussed in the Imperial Diet: (1) the duty and the responsibility of the government to provide education; and (2) the offering of educational opportunities to all, especially at the secondary education level. As regards these two measures and their underlying values, the government, political parties, and radical reformers seemed to be of widely differing opinions. The principle of equal opportunity in education was explained in Article 24 of the Draft Outline of the Revised Constitution as follows:

All people shall have the right to receive equal education corresponding to their ability, as provided by law. All people shall be obliged to have all children under their protection receive *elementary* education as provided by law. Such compulsory education shall be free.[20]

What is noteworthy about the above quotation is that (1) compulsory education was not to be provided by the Imperial Rescript but by law; and (2) the right to receive education was approved in general. Yet it did not seem that the Draft's acceptance of the new notion of equal opportunity led immediately to a repudiation of all the traditional characteristics of the elitist education system. Elementary education was still distinguished from secondary education in this period in terms of curriculum, the social composition of the pupil population, and the length of schooling. Since the elitist secondary education was not available to all children in the pre-war educational system, the officials writing the Draft Outline could not easily specify secondary schooling as compulsory education. In fact, the government at the time had no clear definition of what compulsory education was to be in terms of when it should start or end, how long it should be, or what the content should be. Furthermore, contrary to the expectation of a majority of the members of the Diet, there was no provision in the Draft that the right of people to receive education should be guaranteed by the government.

Many criticisms and questions relating to the Draft were accumulating in the Diet. Analysis of the opinions revealed that some members of the Diet urged a more radical approach which sought to achieve equality of educational opportunity through administrative and structural changes in the education system. Behind this approach was their shared feeling that the state should do more to guarantee people's right to receive education. This type of perspective, advocating more state responsibility for providing education, was a part of the new ideology opposing the orthodox collectivist doctrine in the Meiji Constitution. In the pre-war education system, there was no principle laid down in the Meiji Constitution that said education was a right that people possessed innately.[21] Instead, it was regarded as something that was given to them by the Emperor, and therefore, as a duty of the people. Under the series of post-war social reforms, the gradual emergence of this new current of thought stemmed from a heightened awareness that sovereignty rested with the people, from the recognition of the changing role of the state, and from new ethical attitudes towards members of the new democratic society, all of which were emphasized by the Occupation. Thus, at the outset, conflicting and emotionally charged opinions were expressed regarding the obligation and duty of the government to guarantee the right of education for all the nation's people, an essential ingredient of the new democratic society.

For instance, criticizing the content of Article 24 in the Draft, MP Takahashi Eikichi of the JLP at the House of Representative's Special Committee asked for Revision of the Constitution dated 16 July as follows:

Equal opportunity in education appears in Article 24 . . . but, taking account of the present educational and social system, couldn't it, after all, mean lack of educational opportunities? Aren't equality, freedom, equal opportunity just mere slogans without substance? In short, our present society is full of educational inequality, handicaps, imbalance, and won't these problems still remain in the future even under this new constitution? . . . In other words, even if a child has intelligence and the right to receive an equal education, in the end he or she cannot enjoy the freedom of education without money for school fees. It means that equal education can never be provided until this issue is resolved. . . . Every citizen should have compulsory education. Therefore, the government should be responsible for providing it.[22]

Takahashi believed that without more state intervention in social and economic policies, poor children's educational opportunities would be under economic pressure. Advocating that the existing educational inequalities should be solved by supplying financial support for poor children and justifying his view that government should be obliged to guarantee to all people the right to receive education regardless of economic status, Takahashi insisted on putting forward the concept of equality of educational opportunity in the context of the existing social and financial inequality. Thus, political thinking was turning against the orthodox ideology of the people's duty to receive education: Instead, the positive concept of state responsibility for providing education began to emerge, particularly among political parties, regardless of their political doctrines. The post-war new democratic climate temporarily cooled the political tension over social policies including educational policy and provided a middle ground to force the government to admit the people's right to receive education. In order to achieve greater equality of opportunity, the parties opposed the obsolete system under the Meiji Constitution and claimed educational rights. This was a "Copernican change in the concept of national education which the people of Japan had never experienced before."[23]

The conservative government, however, did not accept the reformers' demand for a state guarantee of educational rights for all people, nor did it accept their emphasis on a positive state provision of education.[24] For instance, as to the government's obligation to provide education for all children, Tanaka, the Minister of Education, responded to Takahashi with a definite answer:

[In order to expand educational opportunity] it is necessary to manage the *Ikuei* scholarship system well and expand its scale in case there are able children who would like to receive a high level of education but cannot afford school expenses. And that is why I am asking for a budget five times larger than that of the previous year.[25]

In spite of the fact that conservative members of the same opinion as Tanaka considered it necessary to supply national financial support for poor but bright pupils, they constantly reiterated during the commission's inquiry that the right to receive education did not mean giving all people a concrete right to claim. It should be noticed that the conservative government at the time was not enthusiastic about a drastic reshaping of society, only about improving the devastated social and economic situation. In fact, the general climate of the nation up to the early 1950s was permeated by political and economic crisis and the consequent disorder and poverty. In other words, the nature of conservative educational reform implied "gradualism"—to be distinguished from an alternative radical socialism which was mainly concerned with rendering help to under-privileged members of society by means of legislation and with the removal of inequality due to privilege. All through the process of revising Article 24, conservative members were reluctant to discuss this issue, and the government favored a temporary solution by providing quite a small number of *Ikuei* scholarships to help able children only to receive secondary education. Behind this assumption, the notion of educational opportunity was interpreted by the conservatives to give bright children not only formal but also practical access to schooling by removing their economic handicap.

Dispute over Compulsory Education

The second and most important goal was to extend education for all to the secondary school level. More members of the Diet demonstrated a much greater interest in provision of compulsory secondary education for all than in the other goal of guaranteeing the right to education. Such a climate of opinion eventually made the government concentrate upon the secondary education issue rather than upon the tangled issue of the government guaranteeing the right of people to receive education. Just like the relationship between Senior School and Grammar School in British secondary school education at that time, in the pre-war Japanese education system, the Youth School received 85 percent of the nation's youth who finished elementary education, while on the other hand, the old Middle School intended for the elite maintained a great difference from the Youth School, being selective, expensive, and class-biased. Youth Schools were on a different track from proper middle schools and the door to the universities was open only to pupils from the latter. This problem had been at the center of the issue of reform in secondary education since before the war, and thus there was particularly fierce debate over the problem throughout the discussions.

However, the deliberations on the draft concerning this issue were hard going. On the one hand, the conservative government was not attracted by the argument that secondary education should be universal and compulsory, nor had its members abandoned their original stance of providing secondary education corresponding to children's ability. On the other hand, opposition parties and radical reformers in education demanded a stronger scheme which could make secondary schools fully accessible to all children regardless of their ability. For instance, at the Committee on 19 September, Tadokoro, a member of the House of Councilors, criticized the government's plan to limit compulsory education to the elementary education level as follows:

> There is no place for the term "equal opportunity" in Japan until the term is used to deny the elitist principle in secondary education which is similar to that found in European school systems. . . . Before the war any child regardless of social class could go to elementary school in Japan. . . . This means that equal opportunity is already promised for all. . . . Since the new meaning of educational opportunity should be considered to be about equality, it should be expanded to the secondary education level.[26]

In the same manner, M. P. Kimura of the JLP proposed a provision of universal secondary education for the nation's children regardless of their ability as the best means for achieving equality of opportunity. He asserted:

> Article 24 stipulates that all people shall have the right to receive an equal education corresponding to their ability, as provided by law, but in reality, I think that it is impossible to use the right under the present situation, even if such a right is given. . . . I guess that ability means intellectual ability of each individual, yet in reality, I think that intellectual ability is not shaped by education but in fact, largely depends on the financial status of the parents. . . . *I think that it might be good to delete the term "corresponding to their ability" from the new constitution.*[27]

Accessibility of secondary education for children regardless of their ability as proposed in the above sardonic statement was of historic significance. Kimura's view not only challenged the conventional elitist concept of secondary education, but also provided a powerful theoretical argument for universal secondary education for all, based on the principle of equality of opportunity. The fundamental characteristic of this new principle might be described as special emphasis on the term "equal education" proclaimed in Article 24 in the draft and later in Article 26 in the New Constitution and Article 3 in the FLE.[28] Thus all individuals should be given the same opportunity regardless of their academic ability, at least to the end of lower-secondary education, and the basis of the traditional and meritocratic nature of educational selection, by which allocation of children into differentiated secondary schools was assumed desirable, is condemned.

However, Minister of State Kanamori confirmed the conservatives' assumption as to the best workable solution to provide secondary education for all and replied to Kimura as follows:

> We do not intend to apply the notion of equality to the education system without limitation. . . . The purpose of the Article [24] is to ensure that no able child is not given the opportunity. . . . I am not going to delete the term "corresponding to ability" from the Article.[29]

It can be said that most conservatives at the time did not share the opinion of radical reformers regarding the concept of equality of educational opportunity. In fact, by the term "equality of educational opportunity" the conservatives did not mean secondary (old Middle) school for all, nor the comprehensive secondary school, but various types of secondary education for all, suitable for various abilities. Despite the advice of the USEM and the radical reformers of the Imperial Diet, who advocated the idea of the universal secondary school, the conservatives were not much interested in it, but generally assumed the suitability of the multi-track system as practiced in the pre-war period. While bitterly criticizing the contemporary militaristic nature of the pre-war education system, they did not want to abolish the prestige and advantages of the traditional Middle School and its advantages for effective selection of a national elite, but sought to expand the *Ikuei* scholarships so as to sweep away the financial obstacles for poor but able children. In short, the conservatives applied the principle of equal opportunity within the existing educational structure.

Enactment of New Constitution

As a result of repeated disputes over the issue, the term "corresponding to their ability" was finally incorporated into educational provisions in the new constitution as Article 26, which prohibits discrimination based on class, lineage, sex and anything but ability, and also under which the government takes a positive role in arranging scholarship systems for those who would otherwise be unable to receive secondary schooling in spite of their ability. At the same time, however, the government interpreted the provision as one that would play a role in taking away the opportunity to receive a complete education from people who have inferior ability and handicaps.

The Japanese Constitution was promulgated on 3 November 1946 after such disputes over its revision.[30] Prescriptions concerned with education formed an important part of Chapter III, "Rights and Duties of the People," of the New Constitution. In particular, Article 26 spelled out their rights and duties, as well as the duty of the state, in relation to educational opportunity. It stipulated that:

1) All people shall have the right to receive an equal education correspondent to their ability, as provided by law; and

2) All people shall be obliged to have all boys and girls under their protection receive ordinary education as provided for by law.

It was further decreed that compulsory education would be free. The new constitution aimed to sustain the right to an education as a fundamental human right of Japan's citizenry. Thus the conservative government had finally accepted part of the demands of radicals and directed the Committee members to draw up a new democratic version of the articles relevant to education.

The stipulation of the Right to Receive Education in Article 26 of the new constitution was there to confirm the supreme right to education as one of the fundamental human rights and a natural right. At that time, there was fairly general agreement that this article should be generally interpreted with emphasis put on the phrase "equal education" rather than on "correspondent to their ability."[31] Yet, as the disputes over the revised constitution clearly illustrate, the government was reluctant to interpret Article 26 in such a way, especially at the secondary education level. The words compulsory elementary education" in the draft of Article 26 symbolized the fact that the government, from beginning to end, took a stance to avoid as far as possible making itself responsible for actively considering the implications of equal education, especially the extension of compulsory education to the secondary education level, all of which would have required its financial support.

Thus, as the Imperial Diet debate on the bill shows, Article 26 was the outcome of a political compromise and therefore left some important gaps. The most noticeable weaknesses were: (1) the range of compulsory education was left undefined, and the definition of secondary education was unclear; and (2) that it did not extend to higher education. In addition to these weaknesses, the disputes over the definition of equal opportunity were hereafter focused on another weakness: Article 26 was ambivalent, merely juxtaposing recognized but possibly conflicting values (i.e., provision of secondary education for all children in the sense of equal opportunity versus allocation of it corresponding to their ability, without any precise examination of whether one principle could be congruent with the other in its application to educational matters such as the future pattern of secondary schools). As will be discussed in the following section, a more precise definition would eventually be given to equal opportunity in education through the process of framing the FLE.

Equal Opportunities for All: The Fundamental Law of Education

In August 1946, the Ad Hoc Japanese Education Committee which had worked out the post-war educational reform together with the American Occupation authorities was renamed the Educational Reform Council (ERC) and launched upon its new task of preparing more specific legislation to guide the implementation of educational provisions in the New Constitution.[32] The ERC played an important role in the drawing up of legislation for the FLE. At the third plenary session on 20 September 1946, Tanaka Kōtarō revealed a detailed plan of the FLE under the following headings: 1) principles and aims of education; 2) equal opportunity in education; 3) education for girls; 4) political education; 5) religious education; 6) school education; and 7) educational administration; and he also called for a discussion of science, physical and social education as supplementary issues.[33] At the same time, he argued that the spirit of the New Constitution—education based on democratic principles—should be reflected in the FLE, and stressed that old-fashioned militaristic and nationalistic educational policies should be eliminated. Both the process of formation and the disagreements over the FLE show that it was constructed in close relation to the New Constitution.

As mentioned in a previous section of this chapter, although the draft of the New Constitution had declared that "all people shall have the right to receive equal education correspondent to their ability, as provided by law," it had, however, left undefined who should be educated, and with what sort of education. When the ERC started its work, there was growing discontent with official policy on secondary education among radical reformers who became more conscious of the educational and social disadvantages of the existing limited opportunity for secondary education, and the bulk of opinion for educational reform towards "universal secondary education for all" was already waiting for the ERC's debates. Thus, from then until the enactment of the FLE, this basic question seemed to be the main topic of the discussions in the ERC. However, on this issue, ERC members' application of equality of opportunity to actual educational programs was not consistent, most probably due to the lack of consensus between the conservative group and the reformist group.

The issue of extension of the length of compulsory education and establishment of a new education system was discussed mainly at the ERC's second committee and fifth committee. How the pre-war secondary education system should be handled was the first problem the ERC embarked on. On the one hand, at the second plenary session, Morito Tatsuo of the JSP criticized the existing class-based secondary education system:

> Education in Japan was organized for the children of the rich or I should say the middle class, and most of the children who were below the middle class were accommodated in this Youth School. . . . The existing education system was established focusing on how education should be given from elementary school up to university to children of the middle class and above as the most important thing, and this is the main reason why the Youth School has been neglected.[34]

Recommending the great social advantage of the close association in a single type of secondary school of children differing in social background and intellectual capacity, Morito made the following significant statement:

> Under the new education system, the education which has been given to people of middle class and above should be given to working boys . . . by making the 6-year elementary schools and following 3-year middle schools compulsory and calling the latter "universal lower-secondary schools" which would combine the youth school

and the usual middle school in one. Wouldn't it be good if both the rich and the poor could study together under such an education system for ordinary citizens?[35]

It is noteworthy that the concept of equality of opportunity proposed by Morito contains an essential assumption, namely, that the idea of an 'educational ladder by *Ikuei* scholarship' is insufficient. Instead, Morito's intention was apparently equivalent to the idea of universal secondary education for all. Morito's concept involved acceptance of a clash of interests between different social classes and equality, which was understood in that context as the elimination of class distinctions in secondary schools. Both the manner of classifying whole groups of children in terms of their parents' social class and the terms used in the demand for the same right of access to secondary education and the same general (as opposed to vocational) education as that enjoyed by children of the middle class clearly show the underlying assumption on which Morito based demands for equality of opportunity. Thus, the concept of equality of educational opportunity began to be conceived of as all children's equal access to Middle School education.

On the other hand, as far as the conservatives were concerned, by the term 'equal education' in the draft they did not mean "equal opportunity for all" but equal treatment of those selected from all social classes. Diet member Ashida's comment at the 8th plenary session represented this conservative concept of equal opportunity as follows:

> Producing people who are likely to be useless despite the effort spent on them is the same thing as planting young plants which cannot bear aubergines. . . . There is no need to bother to try to push weak and useless people through the narrow gate. . . . [T]he right to receive education should be given only to people whose mind and body are really in good shape.[36]

A meritocratic view of equal opportunity is very clearly seen in the above quotation. With regard to the above provision of the draft, the conservatives, most of whom still assumed the desirability of selective and academic traditions in secondary education, repudiated the egalitarian interpretation of it, ardently insisting on an intellectually meritocratic one. Ashida's comment is typical of the denial by conservatives of any kind of discrimination but that on the ground of ability. To put it concretely, the concept of educational opportunity for them meant that any child who had ability could go on to higher or more prestigious schools and that educational opportunity was guaranteed only for bright children with the help of scholarship systems, etc., in order to attain it. Thus the conservatives merely claimed equal opportunity in education among bright children regardless of class. Conversely, their interpretation served to justify the idea that educational opportunity for children who did not have ability could be abandoned.[37] In this situation, social class, which had been the major factor sustaining the parallel system of the Youth School and the old Middle School would remain as a critical factor determining pupils' suitability or eligibility for the secondary school without any fundamental change of structure in the secondary education system.

This conservative assumption was, however, furiously attacked by several leading radicals in the ERC. In opposition to the conservatives' interpretations of equal opportunity, there appeared a new pressure to provide optimal opportunity to develop fully a child's personal ability. The radical reformers put emphasis on the term "equal education" in Article 24 of the draft of the New Constitution and arguments were made that educational opportunity should be given equally to children according to the level of their development in order to foster their individuality, yet it should not be the same education. For instance, at the third ERC plenary session, Kido Bantarō, president of the Education Research Institution and a leader of the reformers, criticized Ashida's interpretation of the concept of equal opportunity by saying:

> Education so far has made the ability of a child the central point in selection. *But the educator of the future has to consider how the individuality of each child could be developed and how it could be utilized for society.* In order to allow children to develop their individual abilities and respect others' individuality which is different from theirs, *educational opportunity should not be given correspondent to children's ability but equally to all children.*[38]

In addition, taking the same stance as Kido, Takahashi Sei'ichirō, a vice-president of Keio University at that time and a future education minister, addressed the 7th plenary session as follows:

> In order for children to develop their individuality as much as they can, all children equally have the right to have educational opportunity.[39]

As the above quotations illustrate, the radical reformers in the ERC proposed a new concept of equality of educational opportunity, with definite egalitarian characteristics: the term "correspondent to their ability" in the draft was interpreted as "correspondent to their aptitude"; and the meaning of "ability" was conceived of as "individuality." This new concept of equal opportunity was of historic significance in Japanese education in the sense that the traditional meritocratic concept supported by the government was challenged as being insufficient because it took for granted that only a few bright children could accede to a high level of education. Instead, this new egalitarian concept of equality of educational opportunity claimed the same right to receive education regardless of the difference in people's ability. This egalitarian view of "equal opportunity" was defined by the reformists in practical as well as theoretical terms.

Kawamoto Unosuke, principal of Tokyo Deaf School, further developed this viewpoint in connection with the necessity of providing education for the disabled. Emphasizing "esteem for human rights and humanitarian practice" as fundamental principles in the FLE, Kawamoto spoke out based on his firm belief that even disabled children could develop their abilities if they were educated "according to their handicaps." He insisted at the 3rd plenary session as follows:

> As far as our compulsory education is concerned, it is well known that it is in no way inferior in quality and so on to that of the world's greatest countries. But as far as our education for the disabled is concerned, it is far poorer than that of foreign countries. That is because we lack the spirit of esteem for human rights. . . . the government thinks that disabled people are after all, no use in building a strong fatherland even if education is given to them. . . . In the Japanese educational system I think that this is a major cause of the present situation, one most shameful for a so-called cultured state. By the New Constitution, let's extend the human right of education to the disabled too, under which they shall have the right to receive ordinary education *according to their handicaps*.[40]

As the quotation illustrates, the concept of equal opportunity was beginning to be applied to existing discrimination against disabled children. However, Kawamoto's interpretation implied a very significant element which gave the first hint of what, in the 1960s, came to be called *Gakushuken* or "the right to learning." As will be discussed in more detail later in this book, a group of educational law scholars began to set forth this new theory of the concept of equality of opportunity from the late 1960s.[41] Kawamoto's interpretation of equal opportunity "correspondent according to their handicaps" for disabled children was to be further developed by the educational law scholars to mean "according to their level of development" for all the nation's children. Thus, the new idea based on the egalitarian ground that educational opportunities should be given to all children corresponding to their aptitude was set against the meritocratic concept of equal opportunity. Taking these arguments into consideration, the former "correspondent to children's ability" provision was amended to "equally correspondent to children's ability and aptitude" in the draft outline of the FLE submitted by the ECR (29 November 1946 mid-term reference report) in order to broaden the opportunity for disabled children to receive education, too.

Considering its passive guidance and lack of interest in the matter of guaranteeing the people's right to receive education, the government rather easily approved of the idea that was to replace the complicated pre-war multi-track secondary education system with a single-track one, winning the agreement of both conservatives and reformers. After these discussions, a Secondary Education Reform Bill: (1) making three years of lower-secondary education compulsory; (2) making it full-time and mixed-sex; and (3) not approving any other kind of secondary school, was submitted at the ERC's 8th plenary session. All these provisions were approved, setting up a single-track education system. Educational opportunity was to be extended to all children by making secondary education compulsory and social justice was to be promoted for children of the different classes by newly establishing a single-track secondary education system at least at the lower-secondary level. However, this did not mean that all the problems of equal opportunity in education for young people were solved. The issue of making higher secondary education compulsory remained, and it was to be discussed continuously in the ERC.

The Bill of the FLE passed through all its stages in the ERC and became law on 31 March 1947. Together with provisions in the New Constitution, this law laid down the principles for the new system of education, in effect replacing the pre-war Imperial Rescript much as the New Constitution had replaced the Meiji Constitution. Proclaiming in its preamble that "we shall esteem individual dignity and endeavor to bring up a people who love truth and peace, while education aimed at the creation of culture, general and rich in individuality, shall be spread far and wide," the FLE was based on the idea that the principles of the New Constitution essentially rely upon the power of education to turn them into reality. It should be emphasized that the principle and concept of post-war education is rooted in law rather than the Rescript. Articles 3, 4 and 5 established the important principles of "Equal Opportunity in Education" for all children, irrespective of "race, creed, sex, social status, economic position, or family origin" (Article 3); and the duty of parents to provide their children with nine years of "Compulsory Education" (Article 4); "Co-education" (Article 5); and, finally, "the obligation of the State and local bodies to guarantee such educational opportunities" (Article 10). In a key provision the law also laid down that "education shall not be subject to improper control, but it shall be directly responsible to the whole people." Thus the FLE confirms one of the significant themes of educational reform during the Occupation: egalitarianism under which all people shall be given equal opportunities of receiving education.

It should be noted how the concept of equality of opportunity decreed in Article 3 of the FLE was generally understood at the time. The best account can be found in *A Commentary on the FLE*, edited by the MOE officials. The Commentary made several annotations to explain each article of the FLE. Concerning Article 3, "Equality of Opportunity in Education," the Commentary interpreted it as follows:

> The principle of equality of educational opportunity is inevitable to establish a democratic society. It [equality of opportunity] means that all people shall be given an equal right to receive education regardless of social status and economic position. No distinction shall be made, except based on their different individualities. However, equality of opportunity is not defined as being identical opportunity. . . . Since there is no doubt that there are individual differences in people, various kinds of educational opportunity should be given to all people according to their individual differences to develop their natural talents and individualities.[42]

Quoting the recommendations proposed by the USEM's Report, the Commentary interpreted equality of opportunity in terms of an egalitarian perspective on our explanatory model (see the introduction to this book). As the above quotation indicates, the MOE's interpretation of equal opportunity was different from that of the government and the conservatives and rather close to that of the reformists in the process of framing the constitution and the FLE. In the Commentary, it was understood as an offer of educational opportunity to all children in order to develop their individuality. The MOE's interpretation was firmly and clearly distinguished from the meritocratic nature of the concept of equality of opportunity that was supported by the conservatives in the government. In fact, it is noteworthy that the characteristics of compensatory education, which emerged in England during the 1960s, can be seen in Section 2 of Article II of the FLE.[43] Thus, criticizing the scholarship system which was given only to able people as an overly narrow interpretation, the Commentary says that the scholarship system should include financial support not only for children who receive higher education but also for all children who receive compulsory education if they have difficulty in going to school owing to poverty.

However, although there is fairly general agreement that the interpretation of Article 3 in the FLE given by the MOE's Commentary is based on the egalitarian perspective of equality of educational opportunity, it allows plenty of scope for conservatives to read it in terms of their own meritocratic perspective. As mentioned earlier, there was no consensus between conservatives and reformers with regard to the concept of equal opportunity in this article, and in the end there remained a great many compromises and vague abstractions that both conservatives and reformers could take advantage of. Thus, as will be discussed later in this book, we can find one of the origins of the fierce confrontation between conservatives and radical reformists over the interpretation of equality of educational opportunity in this ambiguous stipulation of the FLE.

Conclusion

Analysis of parliamentary debates on both the New Constitution and the FLE reveals that equality of educational opportunity was interpreted by MPs in three distinctive ways. First, equality of educational opportunity was conceived of as all children's free, compulsory access to secondary schooling. With regard to the lower-secondary education system, both conservatives and reformists accepted the egalitarian concept, which insisted on full development of a child's individuality. Based on this assumption, both agreed about providing a common secondary schooling for all children, regardless of difference in academic ability. Next, the concept was defined as closely related to elimination of class distinctions in education. This notion of equality was strongly advocated by the U.S. Occupation, most of the radical reformers in the National Diet, and some conservatives in the government. They criticized the pre-war elitist multi-track system and insisted on a growing contemporary egalitarian view of equality, which emphasized the need for social mixing of children at all levels of schooling. Thus, their demand focused on open admission and was aimed at helping children share the same or a similar experience throughout the education system, in order to establish a more homogeneous society. Finally, it was applied to the inequality between boys and girls. There is no doubt that girls' opportunities for secondary education were lower than those of boys in the pre-war education system. Under the Occupation's social reforms, the principle of equality of political rights between the sexes was being fought out, and as a result, women's suffrage was equalized with that of men for the first time in Japanese history. Parallel to this fact, equality of opportunity in education between the sexes was also introduced. Three major patterns of inequality of educational opportunity —between children of different ability, between children of different social class, and between children of different sexes—were criticized: and consequently three major criteria for determining whether children's educational opportunities were equal—ability, class, and sex—had been resolved. Thus, it seems reasonable to suppose that the time, in general, was socially ripe for accepting the principle of equal opportunity.

However, even though the conservatives in the government accepted several elements of the egalitarian concept of equality of opportunity proposed by the radical reformers, they did not totally abandon their espousal of the traditional meritocratic concept. They did not ignore differences in the ability of children, but recognized the need for providing education that was "correspondent to their ability." In this respect, the conservatives' view was fundamentally different from the egalitarian view. In fact, most conservative MPs' remarks on equality of opportunity in the National Diets seemed to reflect this meritocratic concept and the Ministers of Education were representative of them. Therefore, as Article 26 of the New Constitution and Article 3 of the FLE have already shown, they were the outcome of a political compromise and thus deliberately wove two contradictory ideas— "equal education" and "correspondent to children's ability"—into one allegedly compatible synthesis in the name of equality of opportunity. As will be mentioned later in this study, when a series of measures to reverse course in the education system were steadily put into practice during the 1950s, an intense struggle over the principle of equality of educational opportunity was touched off between the MOE as conservatives and Japan Teachers' Union (Nikkyōso) as reformists.

Notes

1. Hall, R., *Education for a New Japan*, 2.
2. For further details of these policies, see Suzuki, *Kyōiku Gyōsei*; Suzuki, *Nihon Senryō to Kyōiku Kaikaku*; Kubo, *Tai'nichi Senryō Seisaku to Sengo Kyōiku Kaikaku*; Nishi, *Unconditional*

Democracy, Education and Politics in Occupied Japan 1945–52, 187–96; Tsuchimochi, *Education Reform in Post-War Japan*; and Marshall, *Learning to be Modern*, 143–66.

3. See Yamazumi, *Nihon Kyōiku Shōshi*.

4. Monbushō, *Nihon kensetsu no kyōiku houshin* (The Educational Policy for Construction of a New Japan Shin. For an English translation, see Beauchamp and Vardaman, *Japanese Education since 1945*, 55–58.

5. Ibid.

6. For further details of tasks undertaken by the USEM, see Duke, *Japan's Militant Teachers*; Sato H., *Beikoku Tai'Nichi Kyōiku Shisetsudan ni Kansuru Sōgtōteki Kenkyu*; Kubo, *Tai'nichi Senryō Seisaku to Sengo Kyōiku Kaikaku*; and Tsuchimochi, *Education Reform in Post-War Japan*.

7. There are sharply divided opinions on whether the post-war educational reform in Japan was imposed by the U.S. government or initiated by the Japanese government. For detailed arguments see Hisaki, Suzuki, and Imano, *Sengo Kyōiku Ronsou Shiroku*, 56–67.

8. U.S. Education Mission (USEM), *Report of the United States Education Mission to Japan*, 6.

9. Ibid., 24 (emphasis added).

10. See Kang, *Educational Policy and the Concept of Equal Opportunity in England*, 142–61.

11. Japan Advancement Party, *Sengo kyōiku kaikaku an* (A Draft of the Post-War Education Reform), 4 May 1946. Most of the material relating to various political parties' educational policy in this section is derived from Sengo nihon kyōiku shiryō shūsei henshū iinkai, *Sengo Nihon Kyōiku Shiryō Shūsei*, vol. 1, 214–22.

12. Japan Advancement Party, *Sengo kyōiku kaikaku an*. The *Ikuei* scholarship system at the time was a system of financial support for able children only.

13. Japan Socialist Party, *I'ppan seisaku* (General Policies) section 9, "Culture" (Bunka), November 1945.

14. Japan Liberal Party, *Kinkyū seisaku* (Emergent Policies), November 1945.

15. Japan Communist Party, *Bunka seisaku* (Cultural Policy), February 1946.

16. Monbushō, *Shin kyōiku shishin* (A Guide for the New Education) May 1946 (emphasis added). English translation is quoted in Beauchamp and Vardaman, *Japanese Education since 1945*, 90–95.

17. Kang, *Educational Policy and the Concept of Equal Opportunity in England*.

18. Most of the material about minutes of the 90th Imperial Diet for making a New Constitution are derived from Shimizu, S., *Tuijō Nihonkoku Kenpō Shingiroku*.

19. For detailed arguments see Horio and Yamazumi, *Kyōiku Rinen*, 92–112; and Suzuki, *Kyōiku Gyōsei*, 159–89.

20. *Kenpo kaisei souan yōkō* (The Gist of Draft for Revising Constitution) (emphasis added).

21. See Hirahara, *Gimu Kyōiku/Danjo Kyōgaku*.

22. The 14th Committee on Revision of Imperial Constitution, 16 July 1946.

23. Kobayashi, *Society, Schools and Progress in Japan*, 55.

24. See Suzuki, *Kyōiku Gyōsei*, 246–325; and Horio and Yamazumi, *Kyōiku Rinen*, 398–438.

25. The 14th Committee on Revision of Imperial Constitution, 16 July 1946. This issue was also discussed in debates held by the Educational Reform Council (ERC) to formulate the FLE. Similarly, with regard to this issue, it was a speech by Ashida Hitoshi, a member of the House of Representatives, which represented clearly the opinion of both the government and the conservatives at that time. See the 8th plenary session of the ERC, 1 November 1946.

26. A Special Committee of the House of Councilors, 19 September 1946.

27. A Committee of the House of Representatives, 17 July 1946 (emphasis added).

28. See Iizaki, *Kyōiku no Kikaikintou, Kyōikukihonhō Bunken Senshu*, vol. 3; Munakata, *Kyōiku Kihonhō*; and Suzuki, *Kyōiku Gyōsei*.

29. A Committee of the House of Representatives, 17 July 1946.

30. This New Constitution was promulgated 3 November 1946 and went into effect 3 May 1947. For an English translation see Beauchamp and Vardman, *Japanese Education since 1945*, 97.

31. Munakata, *Kyōiku Kihonhō*; Iizaki, *Kyōiku no Kikaikintou, Kyōikukihonhō Bunken Senshu*, vol. 3; and Horio, *Gendai Nihon no Kyōiku Shisou*.

32. The power to set the agenda for the council was given to a nine-member steering committee with three each selected from among CI&E personnel, the MOE officials, and the ERC itself. Between September 1946 and June 1952, the whole group met, on average, twice a month, and its subcommittees once or even twice a week. A full list of members of the ERC is given in Monbushō, *Kōyku sa'sshin shingikai yōran* (A Handbook of the Educational Reform Council), June 1952.

33. The 3rd plenary session of the ERC, 10 September 1946. The minutes of the ERC used in this chapter are collected from various sources and translated into English by the present writer. See Monbushō, *A Handbook of the Educational Reform Council*; Suzuki, *Kyōiku Gyōsei*; and Sugihara, *Kyōiku Kihonhō*.

34. The 2nd plenary session of the ERC, 13 September 1946.

35. Ibid.

36. The 8th plenary session of the ERC, 1 November 1946.

37. See Suzuki, *Kyōiku Gyōsei*, 333; Munakata, *Kyōiku Kihonhō*, 104–32; and Horio and Yamazumi, *Kyōiku Rinen*, 339.

38. The 3rd plenary session of the ERC, 20 September 1946 (emphasis added).

39. The 7th plenary session of the ERC, 18 October 1946.

40. The 3rd plenary session of the ERC, 20 September 1946 (emphasis added).

41. Useful information on the development of "the right of education" is given in Nagai, *Kenpō to Kyōiku Kihonken*; Kaneko, *Kokumin no Kyōikuken*; Maki, *Kyōikuken*; and Horio, "Chūkyōshin Kaikaku Kōsō to Kokumin no Gakushū Kyōiku Ken."

42. Monbushō Hourei Kenkyukai, *Kyōiku kihonhō no kaisetsu* (A Commentary on the FLE), 76. For further details on the commentary of the FLE, see Tanaka, *Kyōiku Kihonhō no Riron*; and Arikura and Amagi, *Kyōiku kankei hō II*.

43. Takakura, *Kyōiku ni Okeru Kousei to Fukousei*, 11. However, this interpretation was not realized for a long time until educational law scholars insisted on it from the late 1960s.

3

THE DEVELOPMENT OF THE NEW PERSPECTIVE ON EQUAL OPPORTUNITY IN EDUCATION, 1951–1959

While the democratic reconstruction of post-war Japan led by the United States was being carried out, the international environment surrounding Japan was changing. In 1947, the Truman Doctrine and the Marshall Plan were announced and anti-communist sentiment in the United States was on the rise. It was the beginning of the so-called Cold War. In 1950, the year in which the Korean War began, the Second U.S. Education Mission, led by Willard Earl Givens, visited Japan and submitted a report to the GHQ/SCAP. Praising the success of the democratization of post-war education reform over the previous five years, the report said that "one of the best weapons to counter communism in the Far East was Japan's well-educated electorate."[1] In the midst of a consequent worldwide "Red Purge," the San Francisco Peace Treaty was signed on 28 April 1952, and Japan became independent. This chapter is concerned with analyzing the development of the concept of equal opportunity that unfolded during the 1950s. Although this period can be defined as one of growth and consolidation, during which successive conservative governments were concerned about putting into effect the Occupation reforms in education, it was also a period which contained the germs for repudiation of the concept's definition of the previous period.

The Modification of the Democratic Education System

Reverse Course

From the beginning of Japan's independence in 1952 and until 1960, the education system passed through a period of so-called "reverse course," or the reassessment of Occupation policies after independence.[2] Independence gave the conservative government a free hand to modify the legislative legacy of the Occupation according to the domestic conservative ideology of the day. Indeed, a re-examination of the American-style educational reform had already begun towards the end of the Allied Occupation.

Both General MacArthur and the conservative camp began to keep strict watch on the movement of the progressive forces in the country, including the Japan Teachers' Union (Nikkyōso: JTU).[3] Their major new concern—in the developing Cold War climate—was "International Communism" which led to suspicions about the susceptibility of the JTU to left-wing influence. By 1947, 95 percent of elementary school teachers had joined the newly established JTU.[4] Faced with a dangerous trend towards union radicalism, in 1948 MacArthur decided to remove the JTU's right to strike, which was regarded as a "social weapon in the present impoverished and emaciated condition of Japan."[5] Subsequently, the government enacted legislation which spelled out that the JTU would not be an agent for collective bargaining: Teachers would no longer be allowed to strike, and the political rights of teachers to run for office and to campaign would be strictly restricted. In 1947, the Occupation carried out a red purge that led to the imprisonment of 1,200 teachers.[6] Further, after the ineffectual performance of a coalition government including the JSP, the Occupation Authorities developed greater respect for Japan's conservative political leaders.

Advisory Committee for Ordinance Revision

Educational policy was formulated in this political context. In spite of the fact that most Japanese approved of the new post-war educational reform, which stemmed from the idea of equal opportunity based on a democratic education system, the American Occupation's reform gradually came to be criticized by conservative political parties; it was modeled on a foreign system based on a different historical and cultural tradition and was, they felt, doing considerable violence to Japanese values and traditions. Accordingly, during the 1950s there occurred a trend or movement in Japan to revise the post-war education system and policies with an eye to curbing what were widely viewed as excesses. Five important changes in post-Occupation Japan in the field of education were pushed through by the conservative government to restore national identity and put power back in the hands of the MOE. These were:[7]

1) diversification of the 6-3-3-4 system;

2) returning to the pre-war system of government preparation and publication of all textbooks;

3) revising the school board system;

4) creating a system for rating teacher efficiency; and

5) setting up moral education as part of the core curriculum.

These moves to reorganize the new education system inevitably took on an acutely political character in the nation's political climate, marked as it was by a sharp polarization into conservative and progressive forces. In fact, the final moves of the American Occupation served to push the two opposing sides in the education debate even further apart; a kind of tit-for-tat relationship came to exist between the conservative authorities, who sought a return to the nationalistic system of the pre-war days, and the progressives, especially the JTU, who wholeheartedly supported the democratic principle of education decreed in the New Constitution and the FLE.[8] JTU found itself pushed into a defensive position as it struggled to guard the Occupation reforms.

From the early 1950s the Japanese conservatives began to scrap a number of American-initiated reforms and modified others to more closely fit a traditional Japanese model. Education did not escape the conservative government's reassessment. Right at the beginning, the government set up the Advisory Committee for Ordinance Revision (Seirei shimon iinkai, ACOR) in 1951 as a private advisory body to Prime Minister Yoshida.[9] In November, the ACOR issued a set of *Recommendations for Educational Reform* which touched upon problems fundamental to post-war education reform. In the process of urging the "reverse course," the preamble of the ACOR's recommendation decreed:

> The reform of the educational system carried out after the end of the war contributed in no small measure to rectifying the defects of the past educational system and to establishing a democratic educational system. Nevertheless, not a few points of the reform were obviously incompatible with the actual state of affairs in Japan since the reform was modeled after various systems of a foreign country largely different from our country in internal conditions and thus hastily sought to attain an ideal form of education. These points should be fully re-examined so that the educational system may be improved in a rational manner commensurate with Japan's national strength and international conditions in order to achieve a true effectiveness in education.[10]

Exactly the same view would be stated in the years that followed by three successive conservative education ministers in three successive cabinets of Prime Minister Yoshida (the ministers were Amano Teiyu, Okano Kiyohide, and Odachi Shigeo).[11]

With regard to equality of educational opportunity, an extremely controversial issue over which the conservatives and progressives did battle during this period of the "reverse course" was the area of the school system. As noted in chapter 2, the Occupation reforms introduced following World War II greatly increased the egalitarianism of the single-track 6-3-3-4 system by extending compulsory education (in which students were educated as equals) from six to nine years. Ever since, there have been at least some conservatives who have wanted to restore earlier selection. Some of these conservatives were motivated largely by a desire to erase Occupation influence on the system.[12] The ACOR's recommendation called for the "diversification" of the single-track uniformity of the post-war education system as one of its main purposes. The two major reasons which brought about such diversification in emphasis were: (1) the belief that the government should "establish a flexible education system capable of meeting the needs of actual society" while maintaining the 6-3-3-4 school system as a matter of principle; and (2) the belief that the government should "revise the existing education system in which too much emphasis is placed on ordinary education, attach greater importance to and strengthen vocational education and thereby improve and rationalize the contents of education" with a view to meeting the needs of society and industry for people with certain skills.[13] Thus, on a fundamentally important issue—the pattern of secondary education—the ACOR's Recommendations proposed the following three main schemes as alternative possibilities:[14]

Analysis of the initial discussions about each of the three schemes shows that the ACOR members were particularly concerned about three basic premises: (1) the desirability of earlier selection in pursuit of "utilitarianism"; (2) the necessity for preserving some sort of elite course similar to the old middle school/higher school track; and (3) a newly acknowledged need to give all children equal opportunity to receive the same length of compulsory education. The ACOR's three alternative schemes reveal that the division of opinion on the pattern of secondary education hinged upon the difference in various interest groups' emphasis upon any particular one of these three premises.

For example, Schemes B and C were especially supported by conservatives and or industrial circles (Zaikai), both of which were dissatisfied with the inefficiency of vocational education for industrial and economic reconstruction. These two schemes also gained some support from conservatives and or industrial circles because under them it would be possible to continue the tradition of the old Middle schools and make a more accurate classification of pupils' abilities for the Middle or the vocational schools. Thus both conservatives and the industrial groups wanted to move away from the newly established 6-3-3-4 single-track system (Scheme A) towards a pre-war multiple-track system.

However, these conservative-supported schemes were attacked by those who emphasized equal opportunity, since they would have serious repercussions on the egalitarianism of the post-war education system. For instance, progressive groups, especially the JTU, supported Scheme A as the best device for satisfying most of the requirements of the three basic premises. They strongly opposed the further diversification of secondary education not only at the lower secondary

Scheme A

(Basic Type)

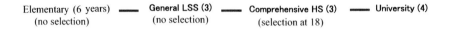

Elementary (6 years) —— General LSS (3) —— Comprehensive HS (3) —— University (4)
 (no selection)   (no selection)   (selection at 18)

Scheme B

(Special Case I)

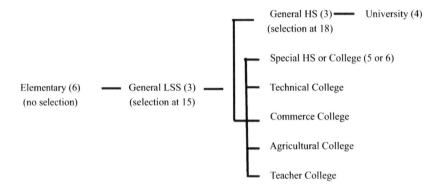

General HS (3) —— University (4)
(selection at 18)

Special HS or College (5 or 6)

Elementary (6) —— General LSS (3) —— Technical College
 (no selection)   (selection at 15)

Commerce College

Agricultural College

Teacher College

Scheme C

(Special Case II)

General Middle School (5 or 6)

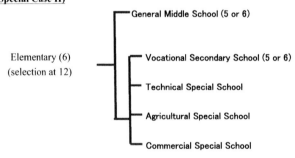

Elementary (6)   Vocational Secondary School (5 or 6)
(selection at 12)

Technical Special School

Agricultural Special School

Commercial Special School

Figure 3.1. Three Main Schemes in ACOR's Recommendations
Note: LSS = Lower Secondary School
HS = Higher School

but also the upper secondary level. Since they thought that diversification of the 6-3-3-4 system would lead to the danger of a return to the class-based multiple-track system of pre-war Japan, they opposed all efforts to increase that diversity through such means as the establishment of "new-type lower and higher secondary schools" and the creation of specialized course.[15] Most progressive groups urged that as many students as possible be given an academic secondary education in order to put off the need for selection in the system. They supported efforts to extend "equal education" through the upper secondary school as seen in Scheme A. Asserting the idea of "upper secondary school for all" as one of its top priorities, they proposed that the period of compulsory schooling be extended to include at least some upper secondary education and that the traditional hierarchical system in upper secondary education be replaced by regional comprehensive secondary schools which would admit students on an equal basis within a small district without resorting to competitive examinations.[16]

Despite the failure to reach an agreement on which type of education system was suitable for an independent Japan, however, the ACOR's Recommendations in the early 1950s were of significance in the sense that the egalitarian nature of the concept of equal opportunity introduced by the Occupation and gradually put into practice began to be challenged by the conservatives' version of the concept. Although the conservatives and the industrial circles supported the idea of expansion of educational opportunities in principle, they felt that the unitary structure of the 6-3-3-4 system was overly standardized. They strongly criticized the system on the grounds that, in its attempt to keep everyone on the road to university as long as possible, it would end up training too many mediocre generalists and not enough well-trained workers and specialists. They advocated a return to the multiple-track pre-war system whereby those students not bound for university would be given a more practical education. With regard to the concept of equality of opportunity, therefore, the ACOR's recommendations reaffirmed that different types of secondary education would be needed to meet the differences that existed among children, and thus reiterated the logic of education corresponding to ability which had been strongly supported by the conservatives since the Occupation reform.

The Emergence of the Counterattack

However, the ACOR's advocacy of diversification of secondary education and its reluctance to recommend a universal 6-3-3-4 system provoked severe criticism from the progressives. The attack came in the first place from an academic group led by fifteen educationists of the Education Department in Tokyo University who, now that demands for "secondary education for all" had been fulfilled, were most concerned with defending and maintaining the democratic principles of the New Constitution and the FLE and strongly advocated the

6-3-3-4 system as the only solution to realize such principles. When the ACOR asserted the meritocratic concept of equal opportunity, this group, headed by Munakata Seiya, Miyahara Sei'ichi, and Katsuta Shū'ichi, severely opposed it, insisted on more egalitarianism in the secondary education system in terms of academic perspective:

> The ACOR's Recommendation shows complete indifference to the establishment and expansion of human rights to be brought about by education. Its total lack of any mention of evening school education ignores education for working youths. In addition, it does not mention the general scholarship system at all. It completely ignores special education. In short, the concept of equal opportunity in education cannot be found here. The aim behind the recommendation is to foster social stratification using the school system. Making a distinction between ordinary education and vocational education definitely leads to a return to the multi-track school system from the single-track one, and it looks as if a military-style hierarchy of soldier, lower ranked officer, and officer is to be adopted to differentiate schools to satisfy the values of commercialism. This is to say that children of poor families should merely be society's slaves and lackeys.[17]

It is noteworthy that the Tokyo University group reaffirmed the significant aspects of the egalitarian concept of equal opportunity at the same time the great social advantage of the close association in a single-track school system of children differing in social background and intellectual capacity was recognized.

Furthermore, disappointment at the ACOR's lack of concern with these issues and angry protest against its endorsement of diversification of the secondary education system were voiced by many other progressives. For instance, the ERC also warned against the ACOR's recommendations by saying that "the ACOR's memorandum could not win its immediate support because it threatens to destroy the democratic principle of equality of opportunity."[18] Hiratsuka Masunori, the dean of the Education Department of Kyushu University, did not agree with separating the lower secondary school into two different streams either; he said that "the pre-war vocational education system ignored the significance of general education which is the most important thing for human beings to develop their ability. Therefore not only students but also teachers in such schools suffered from an inferiority complex."[19] Fujita Nobutaka, an editorial writer of the *Mainichi Newspaper* also advocated that "the single track 6-3-3-4 system should be kept, in order to realize the democratic principle within it. Introducing a vocational education track at the secondary education level will bring the danger of establishing an apprentice system within the system."[20] Kido Bantaro, an ex-member of the ERC, as noted in chapter 2, made the critical comment: "The single-track education system is inevitable to achieve the democratic principle of equality of educational opportunity. We must accept nothing less than the establishment of a complete general secondary school."[21]

In short, some opponents used equality of opportunity to defend the 6-3-3-4 system against the attack in the ACOR's recommendations. As noted before, their reactions to this issue in general centered on the basic assumption of the FLE and other legal bases for the new educational system, which stressed "the non-cognitive and non-utilitarian goals of education: independence, individualism, self-actualization, friendship, peace," etc.[22] Further, the social and educational opportunities presented by the idea of the 6-3-3-4 system were strongly asserted as of great importance in principle. Thus, repudiating the introduction of vocational education into the secondary education level, most of the progressive groups simply expressed their support for the 6-3-3-4 system, which in fact provided a justification of the egalitarian assumption of equal education for all regardless of their academic ability.

The MOE's Initial Stance Regarding the 6-3-3-4 System

It must be noted that the MOE's attitude toward secondary education at the time was not so much different from that of the reformers. By equality of opportunity the MOE meant the same thing as the reformers—all children's equal access to ordinary secondary schools. In fact, the MOE's position at that time could be described as ambiguous. While its officials seemed to sympathize with the conservative government's advocacy of ability-based diversification, they were not initially hostile to the universal 6-3-3-4 system. For instance, the MOE published *The Reasons for Preserving the 6-3-3-4 System*, which stated:

> This new school system [6-3-3-4] was implemented as the significant educational policy for establishing a peaceful Japan and the system begins to be realized by the efforts of the people of the whole nation. Therefore, any retreat from this system would mean a betrayal by the government of the great expectations of the nation's people. Further, there is a danger of its being used by some political parties [the Japan Communist Party].[23]

As noted, this type of opinion is typical of the criticisms of the ACOR's recommendations by the people who desired the advancement of post-war democratic education. Thus, although the MOE had accepted the necessity of improving the education system to meet national needs, its fundamental stance as regards the 6-3-3-4 system remained unchanged throughout the early 1950s, a period which was for the MOE one of uncertainty, demonstrating its own two polarized commitments—one to the meritocratic concept of equal opportunity, the other to the increasing support of the egalitarian concept.

However, although the ACOR's utilitarian approach to secondary education was not immediately dealt with, the conservative government and the industrial groups began to make use of this recommendation. The MOE and the JTU enjoyed a honeymoon period because of the budget for the 6-3-3-4 system they had secured, but after the ACOR's recommendation, matters moved to a new phase, one of confrontation between the MOE and the JTU.[24]

Consolidation of the Logic of "Education Corresponding to Children's Ability" by the Industrial Sector

Zaikai's Demands for 'Diversifying' 6-3-3-4 System

In tracing the shift in the major concepts of equal opportunity in education, the 1950s mark a significant turning point. A new purpose was proposed which contained the germ of the repudiation of the egalitarianism of the Occupation policies and reinterpretation of the meaning of equal opportunity: national economic development. The Korean War and Japanese independence had both direct and immediate impacts upon this change. These events in the early 1950s contributed to restoring Japanese confidence not only politically but also economically. In fact, the Japanese economy had regained its pre-war level by 1955 and thereafter the economic demands of industry significantly determined educational policies.[25]

The first initiative to reconsider the post-war education system and to repudiate the validity of the egalitarian concept of equal opportunity after the ACOR's recommendation came from the Zaikai (industrial circles). The Zaikai is generally considered to include the Federation of Employers' Associations (*Nikkeiren*); the Japanese Committee for Economic Development (*Keizai Dōyūkai*); and the Japanese Chamber of Commerce and Industry (*Nisshō*). Shoppa argues that these groups of the Zaikai were and still are involved in various spheres of policy making and, on the education issue, their views were taken very seriously by the conservative political parties and MOE bureaucracy.[26] During the 1950s, when the Japanese economy completed the reconstruction phase and entered upon a period of full-scale growth, the Zaikai began to give a relatively greater priority to educational policy. Unified in their pursuit of utilitarianism, they had always sought to pursue the educational policies which would best help the nation continue its economic advancement. The Zaikai pursued this aim, encouraging the expansion of secondary schools and the diversification of this level in favor of greater emphasis on science and vocational education. In this sense, it was no wonder that the Zaikai became very outspoken in their criticism of the 6-3-3-4 system.

The Zaikai's admiration of a diversified education system was first publicly expressed in Nikkeiren's *Recommendation for Reconstruction of the New Education System* of 1952. Taking a highly critical view of the Occupation's educational policy, it insisted as follows:

> In the new educational system which started after the war, there were fundamental and sweeping reforms of the nation's traditional structure. . . . But since these

reforms were performed hastily and even without preparation for them, and, furthermore, ignore our nation's circumstances, recently there are a number of criticisms against various failures resulting from the new system. Looking at the future of the nation, we, the employers, feel urgency for reconsidering the system. . . . At upper secondary education level, vocational and commercial education should be given corresponding to children's intellectual ability.[27]

There were complaints from industry about the quality of the graduates entering the work force. Nikkeiren as well as other members of the industrial groups were nostalgic for the pre-war multi-track system and wanted to reinstate elitism in the secondary school system by creating inferior tracks. Viewed from these perspectives, Nikkeiren urged the MOE to increase the number of vocational upper secondary schools and to revise its curriculum to reflect the needs of industry.[28] At the same time, it also urged a fundamental review of post-war university education to improve studies in special fields that had direct relevance to industry.

In 1954, Nikkeiren issued another recommendation intended to reinforce its earlier memorandum. Recognizing the need for increased training in engineering and science at the compulsory education level, Nikkeiren's *Recommendation for the Improvement of the Current Education System* asserted:

> At present about half of the lower secondary school graduates immediately get a job and become members of society, and the majority of almost half of these who enter the world of industry become general skilled workers. Since the foundation of the success of Japanese science depends on exhaustive vocational and science education in their childhood, such education in elementary and middle school should be stepped up and expanded, and therefore with the renovation of vocational and science education given at the teacher training institutions something should be done to change citizens' recognition of science education and to raise their interest in it.[29]

The same view was echoed in 1957 in another recommendation by Nikkeiren, which supported the conservative authorities' firm belief in the logic of "education corresponding to children's ability" by emphasizing the necessity for economic and industrial efficiency. Nikkeiren issued *Our View Concerning the Improvement of Science and Technical Education*. It declared:

> We insist that in order to make education more effective and efficient, the single-track system found in lower and middle-level schools should be replaced with a dual-track system. In the middle and higher level schools, we believe there should be a division between academic and vocational programs. (It is also necessary in the academic programs to distinguish between humanist and science courses of study.) *The separation of students into academic and vocational tracks should be engineered in accordance with each student's abilities, specific characteristics, and appropriate lifelong agenda.*[30]

The above quotation is especially significant, for it shows Nikkeiren crudely pressing for the validity of the meritocratic concept of equal opportunity: education corresponding to pupils' different academic ability. Nikkeiren did not ignore differences in the abilities of children, but saw a need for differentiation of children on the basis of proven merit. Equality of educational opportunity, in this way, began to be defined by the Zaikai as offering the same possibility of access to differentiated tracks—general or vocational—for every child at the outset according to his ability. This definition foreshadowed the way in which the principle of equal opportunity would be interpreted in the next three decades, reflected particularly in both the Central Council on Education (CCE) and the Economic Deliberation Council (EDC), as will be seen in chapter 4 of this book. Thus, in this respect, Nikkeiren's view of equal opportunity fundamentally distinguished itself from the egalitarian view supported by the progressive groups since the post-war education reform.

In short, the unified opinion that the Zaikai urged in their recommendations to the MOE during the two decades from 1951 generally adopted human capital theory, which assumes that there is a close relation between investment in schooling and economic growth. Not surprisingly, the industrial groups' main concerns with the principle of equal opportunity arose from their position as employers seeking a labor force which would meet their employment needs' human capital theory. They criticized the post-war single-track system for being totally unresponsive to changing business demands for workers with skills needed in growing sectors of the economy and called for reforms designed to force secondary and higher schools to respond to employers' needs for specialized, productive and disciplined workers. Thus, they wanted the nation's children to be separated into various tracks earlier in their school years, sorting them by ability and training them to meet the specific needs of the economy.[31]

Central Council on Education

In response to Nikkeiren's repeated demands for separate allocation of the nation's children into a diversified education system, the newly established CCE, a permanent advisory body to the Minister of Education, and the Liberal Democratic Party (LDP) issued a series of recommendations.[32] Since the end of the Occupation period, it had gradually become accepted that the Courses of Study, which were published by the MOE in 1947 and considered to be the standard for curricula throughout the school system, should be reviewed and revised in such a way as to make them more suitable for the Japanese education system. In 1958, the CCE published "On the Renovation of Primary and Lower Secondary School Curricula" and shortly after, proposals for the upper-secondary schools. Stressing the division of courses at the lower secondary school level into ordinary and vocational, it asserted:

We need to be clear about the reason why lower secondary school is the final stage of our children's compulsory or free education. During the third year (the ninth and last year of compulsory schooling) much more time should be made available for teachers to give guidance on appropriate courses for future study and on the proper career paths for the individual student to pursue.[33]

This quotation illustrates that the existing conditions and curricula of lower secondary schools, based on common and standardized subjects, were regarded as inadequate as a model to be followed uniformly for all future secondary schools. Instead, the CCE's report evinced a strong belief in the need for early selection of the nation's children at the compulsory education level. It also shows that the CCE's acceptance of the principle of equality of opportunity was not accompanied by any significant change in its attitude towards the diversified system of secondary education, which had been strongly emphasized by the conservative political parties and the industrial sector since the early part of the decade. Therefore, the CCE's report strongly recommended that the 6-3-3-4 system be augmented by two new tracks: (1) a 6-6 track, which would replace the lower secondary schools and upper secondary academic track with six years of vocational training; and (2) a 6-3-5 track, which would shunt lower secondary school graduates immediately into advanced technical training. It was from the standpoint of giving the same priority as the Zaikai to the need for more rigorous and extensive training of students and making improvement of technical and vocational education at the lower secondary education level a reality that the CCE defined as equality of opportunity, and its definition was in consequence consistent with the conservative interpretation of the doctrine of education corresponding to children's ability. The CCE, which had a large majority of conservatives and business officials, assumed that the "diversified" secondary education system would realize its notion of equality of opportunity. Thus, the CCE's several recommendations at that period affirmed conservative support for defining equality as "diversification of the education system" or "separation of the nation's children at an early stage of their life" rather than social integration of them at the secondary education level.

The Birth of the Liberal Democratic Party:
The Process of Dismantling the Democratic
Principles of Post-war Education Reform

Meanwhile, the Zaikai were not merely concerned with "labor force" training and other economic imperatives; they also demanded political stability. The political situation in the mid 1950s was characterized by a merger of political parties as a result of a continual confrontation between the conservatives and progressives. On the one hand were the conservatives who had a commitment to anti-communism and a willingness to be allied with the United States in the Cold War and who regarded education as a political tool for national solidarity and stability. On the other hand were progressives, who formed a hard-core of anti-government forces and obstructed the conservatives' educational policies.[34] In October 1955, the Japan Socialist Party (JSP) put an end to the split between left and right which had lasted since 1951 and re-attained unity. In November of the same year, the two main conservative parties, the Japan Liberal Party (JLP) and the Japan Democratic Party (JDP) were merged to make a new party called the Liberal Democratic Party (LDP) in response to the urging of the Zaikai in order to oppose the socialist ideology supported by the JSP. It was the beginning of the so-called "55 system."[35] The pretext for the coalition of conservatives was to create a British-style political situation with two dominant parties, conservative and labor. However, their real intention was to find a way to prevent the JSP, with its socialistic slogans, from coming to power.[36]

From 1954, having rejected the reformers' proposal of preserving the egalitarian characteristics of the single-track education system, the conservative governments diverted the major focus of their emphasis away from diversification towards other issues: regaining central control of education policy, restoring national values to a central place in the system, and weakening the reformers' power, especially that of the JTU.

The government's strategy, as it developed, was as follows: First, the early efforts of the conservative government and the CCE were intended to destroy the co-operative spirit of the JTU. Since the JTU had been the main force blocking conservatives' efforts to re-establish pre-war patterns, it had naturally become a corollary of these policies that the JTU must first be weakened. The first attempt of the CCE to do so was in the Two Education Bills (*Kyōiku nihō*) of 1954, which consisted of measures to maintain the political neutrality of teachers, and which prevented teachers from participating in any political activities (except voting) and from advocating political positions in their classes.[37] The JTU was also barred from disseminating political literature. Further, in 1958, the LDP suggested the *Teachers' Efficiency Rating Plan* whereby all principals were encouraged to rate their teachers each year on the basis of efficiency ratings devised by the MOE, punishing those who performed poorly. Teachers who received a low rating would be in danger of losing pay increases or of being sacked. The JTU therefore regarded the enforcement of the teachers' efficiency rating system as the next stage in the conservative government's plan to extend its power and control back down into the schools themselves, while at the same time making a direct attack upon the union. Thus, the conservative political parties' educational policy was in those early years largely subsumed in their broader political campaign against the JTU. In fact, the conservative authorities wanted to weaken the JTU because of its prominent role in building up electoral support for the opposition, the JSP.[38]

Secondly, the LDP was much more active in seeking to reverse the U.S. Occupation's excesses in the area of democratic control. The LDP and the MOE realized that regaining central control of education policy was a prerequisite for any measures to undo the 6-3-3-4 system it might want to take. Japan had little experience with the American idea of local autonomy and the MOE did not see central control (under a democratically elected government) as contrary to the FLE provision that education be controlled "by the whole people." Equally important, however, was the fact that both the LDP and the MOE saw centralization as a way of countering the JTU influence. In 1956, the LDP laid the Three Education Bills (*Kyōiku sanhō*) before the Diet. The Bill Concerning the Organization and Functions of Local Education Administration was passed, helping the government to take direct control of educational policy by greatly weakening the Occupation-imposed system of local autonomy. The bill abolished the system whereby local school boards were elected, instead providing for board members to be appointed by prefectural governors and mayors. At the same time, MOE's powers were to be enhanced by making the local boards subject to ministry demands. Despite the vocal and unified protests of the JTU, the bill was passed. Thus, this modification was one of the stepping stones in the direction of the centralization of power in the control of national education.[39]

Finally, having established strict national standards, the only remaining step in the LDP's effort to regain control of education was to exert direct influence over the school curriculum and textbooks. Under the Occupation reform, textbooks were allowed to be published by private publishers and selected for use by local boards, with the MOE having only the authority to issue certain minimum standards. From the middle of the 1950s, however, the LDP and the MOE began to argue that this system led to the JTU disseminating communist ideology disguised as democratic values.[40] In 1958, the MOE replaced the previous Course of Studies and made its curriculum mandatory by means of The Enforcement Regulations for the School Education Law under which the curriculum of all elementary, lower secondary, and upper-secondary schools should be revised in accordance with the standards that the MOE would draw up.[41] The most controversial change was the reintroduction of a moral education course to be taught for one hour per week in elementary and secondary schools. At the same time, the systematic teaching of history and geography was revived within the area of social studies. Thus, LDP nationalism was concerned primarily with the goal of restoring national values to a central place in the post-war system.[42]

In short, as the predominant party from its founding in 1955, the LDP had consistently played an important part in the education policy-making process. Its role did not change dramatically over the following decades. From the beginning, concerned almost exclusively with the destruction of the JTU, the LDP increased its involvement in the process to the point that it was exercising influence over virtually all aspects of educational policy-making. In this context, the LDP's definition of equality of opportunity was made to justify its traditional decision to favor the diversification of the secondary education system in terms not only of the need to segregate the nation's children according to their academic ability at an early stage in their life, but also of a response to the economic and political pressures to rebuild the curricula to augment Japan's response to the emerging and potential economic and political imperatives on both the domestic and the international scenes. Throughout the 1950s, the LDP maintained this standpoint, and justified its assertion by saying that the 6-3-3-4 system had lowered academic standards and was not suitable to foster the nation's elite.

Dispute over Equality in the JTU

The conservatives' intense antagonism to the single-track 6-3-3-4 system was matched by the degree to which the JTU and the JSP developed their support for it. While the reverse course was being implemented, the JTU involved itself in the wider struggle that was going on between the conservative government and the progressive opposition. As noted before, this situation came to be known as the "1955 system" and proved to be the defining arrangement of Japanese politics until the LDP lost control of the Lower House of the Diet for the first time in 1993. From the early 1950s when the conservative government in partnership with the CCE and the industrial sector attempted to destroy the egalitarian nature of the Occupation reform, the JTU began to fight back by establishing educational committees in almost every city, town, and village, and by co-operating with the JSP and other unions to turn the public against the government.[43]

While the opinions of conservatives and progressives about the structure of secondary education were becoming polarized, the JTU had gradually developed its own interpretation of equality or equal opportunity based on egalitarianism in opposition to the meritocratic one supported by the conservatives. For instance, in A Code of Ethics for Teachers issued in June 1952 and justifying "secondary education for all corresponding to children's individuality," the JTU unanimously adopted the following resolution:

> Equal opportunity in education and respect for the dignity of the individual as guaranteed by the Constitution are today still dead letters. The youth of today are severely restricted in their educational opportunities because of the social and economic limitations placed upon the individual. It may be said in particular that no serious consideration has been given to educating either the multitudes of working young people or mentally and physically handicapped children. Children are not being guaranteed equality of conditions for life and growth either within or without the schools. We have reached a point where eighteenth-century individualism no longer opens the way to the development of the individual. Today social procedures must be followed in order to create equal opportunities in education.[44]

The above definition implied more than the meritocratic concept of equality, not only emphasizing the need to remove artificial barriers against children's access to formal schooling, regardless of difference in financial conditions and class, but also suggesting widening the definition of equality, which had been discussed merely as equality of opportunity among able children by the conservatives and the Zaikai during the period. It is important to note that the JTU assertion of the concept of equal opportunity was essentially continuous with the idea of the progressives since the latter viewed the unaltered 6-3-3-4 system as a crucial means in the larger process of social equality. Here one can see the JTU's firm repudiation of the meaning of equal opportunity favored by the conservatives, which was in essence meritocratic.

The JTU's Definition of Equal Opportunity

In his recent study, Kariya Takehiko, one of the more famous educational sociologists in Japan, explored the development of the concept of educational equality that unfolded between the 1950s and the 1960s in the JTU.[45] This section analyzes the kinds of equality in education that the JTU achieved during this period in compliance with Kariya's suggestions.

Kariya's analysis of the discussion records in the JTU's annual meeting—*Zenkoku kyōiku kenkyu shūkai* (ZKKS) compiled in *Nihon no kyōiku* (Japanese Education)—and a series of the JTU's official reports during the period demonstrates that the JTU began to apply the principle of equal opportunity especially to two major concerns: (1) realization of the impossibility of achieving parity of esteem between different streams in lower secondary school: on the one hand, a general course leading to an academic type of upper secondary schools, and on the other, a vocational course leading to working or various types of special schools; and (2) recognition of evidence of the contemporary social class composition of the academic stream of lower secondary education and those entering academic-type upper secondary schools.[46] Thus, from the early 1950s, the JTU began to seriously concentrate on the issue of equality, by opposing streaming and social bias in children's scholastic attainment. The JTU's proposals concerning these issues contained a new definition of equal opportunity and both provided a significant basis for repudiation of the logic of "educational opportunity corresponding to children's ability" and contained the germ of its own perspective of equal opportunity.

Parity of Esteem in the Different Streams in Lower Secondary School

Moved by the first consideration, for instance, some members of the JTU began from the early 1950s to call for the abolition of streaming in the third grade of lower secondary school as the best means of providing children with equal opportunity.[47] Although it is well known that nowadays the Japanese mixed-ability system in the compulsory years treats all children equally, streaming within the lower secondary school level was very common at that time. In the streaming system, classes were organized into two selected groups according to ability, and each group was labeled as "academic" or "vocational," with the academic stream regarded as superior in intellectual ability and the vocational stream as inferior. According to Kariya, by the mid 1950s, not only many upper secondary schools, but also some lower secondary, and even a few elementary schools had adopted this class streaming system.[48] Research on the streaming system carried out by Murata in 1955 found that the number of schools using the streaming system was more than 445.[49]

It is interesting to note that the JTU at the time regarded the streaming system as a means to realize "democratic education," although as will be seen later, it began to strongly oppose this system as a root of discrimination in the early 1960s. However, the practice of streaming within the compulsory lower secondary school came to be a source of difficulties in pupil discipline and a strain on teachers, and it gave rise to a feeling of inferiority among pupils in vocational courses. Therefore, some members of the JTU gradually started to criticize this streaming system, especially at the lower secondary level. For instance, the JTU asserted that dividing pupils into two different tracks—one for the brightest who would go on to an academic upper secondary school, the other for the less able who would leave school or go on to a vocational special school—produced self-fulfilling prophecies in terms of children's behavior and attainment. One member of the JTU insisted at the 1952 ZKKS as follows:

> On the one hand, students [at lower secondary school] tend to choose the academic course if at all possible. On the other hand, students who are going to specialize in the vocational course feel themselves inferior. . . . In the case of teachers, they are annoyed by the pressure caused by having to teach students in both academic and vocational courses. Although the post-war education system is said to be a single-track system, it is not true in reality in view of these situations in schools. I have a feeling that these problems are basically impossible to solve as long as the negative attitude Japanese people have towards vocational education remains.[50]

As this shows, some teachers of the JTU began to link the issue of educational inequality to a sense of inferiority of the students in vocational streaming in lower secondary school and to the social disparity of esteem of the vocational type of upper secondary schools to which they were later going. To put it another way, "an ideal education system for the JTU meant that no pupils felt such 'inferiority' at any level of schooling."[51]

Despite the fact that the conservative government and the industrial sector emphasized the need to develop a vocational type of school for national development during the period, vocational courses and schools faced difficulties in attracting pupils because of their poor image. Since the leaving qualification determined employment, career patterns and earning, it was evident for the JTU that, so long as children were segregated into the two different types of streaming and school, pupils on the vocational track, most of whom were children from poor families, would perpetually suffer from an inferior label, which stemmed from the lower academic status of their schools, and from the expected divergent types of career for which the courses and schools would prepare them. Parents also expressed their fears about the insecurity which in the past had been attached to industrial employment and hence colored their view of vocational schools. Thus, the JTU did not believe that parity of esteem between different streamings and schools could be achieved merely by the conservative government's efforts to get rid of the stigma attached to vocational education by providing the same quality of equipment and highly trained teachers.

The JTU eventually concluded that without abolishing the streaming system, parity of esteem would be impossible to achieve, as would equal opportunity. Its members' idea of the integration of pupils of different classes was thus seen as more attractive and the only solution for the prestige problem. In 1958, many teacher groups from various prefectures expressed their firm belief in abolishing the streaming system, using the term "discriminatory education" (*sabetsu kyōiku*) to describe it. This was the first time that the JTU officially used the term to criticize the streaming system. It was suggested that the immediate effects of such discriminatory education were to:[52]

1) establish an uncomfortable relationship between pupils in the academic stream and those in the vocational stream;

2) create, once again, elitist schools at the compulsory lower secondary education level;

3) cause misallocation of pupils to different kinds of schools at an early stage of their life; and

4) arouse strong resistance from parents of pupils.

Kariya argues that, from the late 1950s the JTU gradually developed its own notion of "discriminatory education" (*sabetsu kyōiku*) in order to criticize the existing disparity of esteem between the two different streams in lower secondary school.[53] The JTU believed that 'discriminatory education' meant an education system which "gave birth to the sense of inferiority of pupils in the non-academic stream of the streaming system and the non-academic schools of the school system."[54] Therefore, the JTU linked the sense of equality in education with a refusal to accept inferiority among pupils in vocational courses. As will be mentioned in chapter 4, beginning in the 1960s, the JTU often used the term "discriminatory education" as its official slogan against the meritocratic concept of equal opportunity put forward by the LDP, CCE, and the Zaikai.

Equality of Educational Opportunity for Different Social Strata

A yet more powerful criticism voiced by the opponents of streaming in secondary education concerned the question as to whether or not the expansion of the secondary education system had promoted equality of educational opportunity for different social strata. The JTU's discontent with the class bias of children's scholastic attainment in secondary schools had been expressed earlier than their dissatisfaction with disparity of esteem among schools. As early as the 1950s, the JTU voiced its concern about the scholastic achievement of children and published a "White Paper on Education" which pointed critically to several factors that caused the low academic attainment of children from poor families. Examining all the children in the highest grade at 55 schools in Tokyo, including 706 children in lower secondary schools and 1,406 in elementary schools, the JTU's white paper revealed that:

> Especially the children who have no father are in the worst condition. A family income of less that 7,000 yen a month is true for 53—that is 33.5 percent of them—in the case of elementary schools, and 32—that is, 33.7 percent—in the case of lower secondary schools. No decent home discipline can be expected of a family in such a wretched state. . . . The worst situation occurs in the case of the children who live in rented rooms. It fosters the habit of loafing around outside their homes. It is clearly shown in the increased number of run-away cases of children in these days. . . . Here it was found that the scholastic achievements are vitally connected with the economic conditions of the family, educational environment (qualifications and experience of teacher and sex of teacher), facilities at school and cultural environment (urban and rural). It is concluded that economic conditions are the most important factors in determining the degree of scholastic achievement.[55]

In the white paper, the JTU said it had found that performance in the examinations was shown to be highly dependent on the environment provided at home. In the case of children from economically disadvantaged homes, this could be detrimental. Furthermore, the social class bias in children's scholastic attainment was also mentioned for the first time in the ZKKS in 1952. One JTU teacher reported on children who did not take upper secondary education:

> Some students cannot go to upper secondary schools because they do not have enough time and money, and due to the problem of distance from school. They lack the will to study because of the influence of social environment. Further, there are undoubtedly defects in the present education system. They do not enter the

higher levels of schooling due to all these reasons. . . . In general, many pupils from the lower strata suffer from bad economic conditions. They know they are regarded as thick-witted and, expected to behave badly, they play their roles with corresponding stupidity. . . . [56]

In 1956, ZKKS reaffirmed these findings, particularly with respect to the influence of "poor economic conditions, social stratification, and local feudalism on children's educational prospects."[57] As these quotations indicate, the JTU acknowledged that social origins and family environment influenced children's scholastic attainment in school and consequently their performance on the entrance examination to upper secondary school. Some reports published by the JTU during the period found that, while the number of pupils who attended the upper secondary school had gone up during the period, there had been no great increase in the percentage of pupils from poor families going to such schools. Poverty was in fact an issue of great seriousness at the time. For instance, a piece of research by Moriguchi Kenji threw light on the issue of social bias in children's scholastic attainment.[58] Moriguchi conducted a survey that revealed the relation between children's opportunity to go to upper secondary school and social stratification.

Although the government's "Economic White Paper" declared that "we are already out of the post-war period," poverty was nevertheless still much in evidence during the 1950s. There were a lot of students who could not go to school due to financial difficulties even if they had brilliant ability. Thus, the JTU linked its understanding of educational inequality to the factors which hindered children from poor families from taking schooling. In other words, the JTU applied the principle of equal opportunity to the issue of difference of scholastic attainment between different social classes. Therefore, it was natural for the JTU to deal with children's social background as an issue of educational inequality.[59]

Political Debate about the Class Issue in Scholastic Achievement

While the JTU was arguing in public that the class-based difference in children's scholastic attainment was contrary to the principle of equal opportunity, it must, however, be noted that there was very little political debate about the class issue in scholastic achievement between the political parties at that time. In contrast to the English educational situation of the same period, it was rare for the political parties in Japan in those days to link the principle of equal opportunity to the social class bias in children's educational achievements.

For instance, analysis of the electoral manifestos of the various political parties in the 1950s shows that political parties' advocacy of the principle of equal opportunity in education was generally related to three major issues: First, the conservative political parties, the JDP and JLP, applied the concept of equality of educational opportunity to promote the development of special education for the disabled and school education in remote rural areas.[60] As already mentioned in the early part of this chapter, since the conservative political parties and the industrial sector desired to diversify the single track 6-3-3-4 system and expand the number of vocational secondary schools, they might be reluctant to deal with the class issue and turned their attention to other issues in education.

Secondly, as opposed to the educational policies of the conservatives, both left and right, JSPs saw preserving the 6-3-3-4 system as the best means to achieve equal opportunity.[61] It strongly insisted on some measure of financial support in order to establish the 6-3-3-4 education system immediately throughout the country. However, although both JSPs justified their demand for the 6-3-3-4 system in the name of equal opportunity, it must be noted that the demand was not accompanied by absolute rejection of the necessity of differentiation between children. One conclusion, therefore, may be drawn at this point: the JSPs' advocacy of the 6-3-3-4 system in the name of equal opportunity was pursued merely from the perspective of remedying formal access to secondary education, rather than from any firm belief in the egalitarian concept of equality.

Thirdly, the JCP required the government to bear the whole educational expense for the nation's children.[62] Considering the economic difficulties at the time, this party's educational policies seemed to be empty political slogans.

In short, Japanese educational policies formulated to promote equality of opportunity over the period reflected a distinctive characteristic; in contrast to other educational issues, over which battles between conservatives and progressives raged, such as the textbook and moral education controversies, regaining central control of education, and government policies perceived as being anti-JTU, the social class issue in education did not attract much attention from the public or politicians. Further, the relatively small proportion of public spending devoted to education up to 1960 testified to only a mediocre interest of government in education.[63] It is natural that educational reform to promote equality of opportunity had to be restricted within the limits of available financial resources. Thus, the educational policies implemented during this period reveal, on the one hand, a lack of initiative to introduce a more fundamental reform for educational equality, and on the other hand, a lack of enthusiasm for settling the issue of class in education.

Conclusion

With regard to the issue of equality of educational opportunity, the dispute over diversification of the single-track 6-3-3-4 system illustrates the struggle between the conservatives and progressives in the period of reversed course. The 6-3-3-4 system based on the American model came under attack from the moment it was put forward as the model for Japanese schooling in the closing years of the Occupation. The three groups examined in this Chapter—the conservative political parties and Zaikai on the one hand, and the JTU on the other—represented such different perceptions, such different needs and different interests that fast reorganization of the system became impossible. The conservative groups were represented by the LDP (from 1955), the Zaikai, and older-generation MOE bureaucrats, all of whom wanted to secure diversification of the single-track system by establishing a vocational type of secondary school and were eager to weaken the power and solidarity of the JTU, which was a major group defending the current level of egalitarianism. In the various demands for the diversification of the 6-3-3-4 system, one viewpoint stands out. It was mainly from a perspective of emphasizing national economic development that the LDP (from 1955), the Zaikai, and older-generation MOE bureaucrats put forward their request. With recovery from the post-war situation of economic devastation, the first priority they saw was the urgent need to effectively train both a national elite and a skilled workforce for industry and so they applied their declared criterion of efficiency to educational reform policies. They believed that there was a necessary and close link between educational reform and national efficiency, and that, of all the factors impairing efficiency, the lack of a suitable education system was the most serious. It was in this context that such conservatives counted education as of crucial importance and saw it in essentially utilitarian terms. Their viewpoint was based upon two major assumptions: One was that all forms of social organization must contribute to the development of Japan; the other was that a diversification of what was seen as the overly standardized 6-3-3-4 system would increase national efficiency in terms of developing industry and commerce. These assumptions underpinned their view that the meritocratic concept of equal opportunity should be applied, which to them signified the same as education corresponding to children's ability.

The fiercest opponent of these conservative groups was the JTU. The JTU had emerged as a major force defending the 6-3-3-4 system, maintaining the system's emphasis on equality of educational opportunity. The strong obstruction from the JTU eventually prevented any change from taking place. In reality, the two reasons identified above were the main ones which prevented the conservatives' diversification plan from receiving the Diet's approval. Firstly, the JTU realized that parity of esteem between academic-type and vocational-type streaming within the lower secondary school and between such streams in upper secondary schools could not be achieved because the latter still had a poor reputation from the pre-war period. Thus, in the late 1950s the JTU gradually came to insist that equal opportunity should mean the possibility for the nation's children to have an academic schooling, not a vocational one, at the secondary education level. Secondly, the meritocratic concept of equality of opportunity supported by the conservative groups raised the question of whether real equal opportunity in education was achieved. Since the JTU understood the class bias in the scholastic attainment of children, which was affected by various factors such as parental income, occupation, and academic background, they worried that diversification of the 6-3-3-4 system would result in a system like the pre-war multi-track education system which did not pay enough attention to the class issue and put poor children at a disadvantage. Thus, during the 1950s, the JTU did not hesitate to use the class issue in education to oppose the conservatives' plans for diversification of the single-track system. However, as will be clear in chapter 4, the JTU grew unwilling to deal with the class issue in education, and even regarded mention of it as discrimination, as Japan's rapid economic growth improved the living standard of the nation's people in the 1960s.

Notes

1. For further details of the Second U.S. Education Mission, see Sengo Nihon Kyōiku Shiryō Shūsei Henshū Iinkai, *Sengo Nihon Kyōiku Shiryō Shūsei*, vol. III, 95–192; and Kuroha, *Gakkō to Shakai no Shōwashi*, 129–30.
2. Schoppa, *Education Reform in Japan*, 38–52.
3. In December 1945, two major teachers' unions, the Japan Teachers' Union (JTU) and the Japan Educators' Union (JEU), were emerging to promote democracy in education in Japan and also to campaign for a fivefold salary increase for teachers. In the process of resisting the "reverse course," JTU involved itself in the wider struggle that was going on between the conservative government and the progressive opposition. See, in particular, Duke, *Japan's Militant Teachers*; and for a recent analysis of the schism in the JTU that occurred, see Aspinall, *Unions and the Politics of Education in Japan*.
4. Thurston, *Teachers and Politics in Japan*, 43.
5. Duke, *Japan's Militant Teachers*, 63.
6. Nishi, *Unconditional Democracy, Education and Politics in Occupied Japan 1945–52*, 250.
7. See in particular Kyōiku no sengoshi henshū iinkai (1986), *Kyōiku no sengoshi*, vol. I, 179–257; Schoppa, *Education Reform in Japan*, 36; and Yamazaki, *Jimointō to Kyōiku Seisaku*, 90–113.
8. Schoppa, *Education Reform in Japan*, 38–52.
9. The Advisory Committee for Ordinance Revision (ACOR) was created on 1 May 1951, at the suggestion of the Supreme Commander for the Allied Powers by the Cabinet of the Japanese government as an informal advisory committee which was to review the Ordinances that had been issued by the Japanese government under the Occupation, and to recommend to the Prime Minister the policies and means for enactment necessary after the abolition of the Ordinances. The ACOR held its first meeting on 14 May 1951 and completed its work by the end of that same year. Its eight members included lawyers, economists, journalists, businessmen, and one educator. See Kobayashi, "From Education Borrowing to Educational Sharing: the Japanese Experience." In *Cultural Identity and Educational Policy*, ed. Colin Brock, 111 n. 11.
10. Seirei shimon iinkai (Advisory Committee for Ordinance Revision), *Kyōiku seido no kaikaku ni kansuru tōshin* (Recommendations for Educational Reform), 2 July 1951 (English translation quoted in Amano and Aso, *Education and Japan's Modernization*, 71–72).
11. Yamazaki, *Jimointō to Kyōiku Seisaku*, 103.
12. Schoppa, *Education Reform in Japan*, 43–46.
13. Seirei shimon iinkai (Advisory Committee for Ordinance Revision), *Kyōiku Seido no Kaikaku ni Kansuru Tōshin* (Recommendations for Educational Reform).

14. The diagram is adapted from the ACOR's Recommendations.

15. Yomiuri shinbun sengoshi han, *Kyōiku no Ayumi*, 418–32.

16. In fact, the 1946 USEM's Report recommended establishing the comprehensive type of upper secondary school without selection. However, it had been postponed because of the economic difficulties. This will be discussed in chapter 4.

17. Tokyo daigaku kyōikugakubu kyōju dan, *Iwayuru seirei shimon iinkai no 'kyōikuseido kaikaku ni kansuru tōshin' ni taisuru iken* (Opinions against Report Concerning on Reform of Education System Proposed by So-called ACOR), 22 December 1951. The full list of members of the group is available in Sengo Nihon Kyōiku Shiryō Shūsei Henshū Iinkai, *Sengo Nihon Kyōiku Shiryō Shūsei*, vol III, 209–10.

18. A plenary session of the ERC, 28 November 1951.

19. *Monbujihō*, Number 894, February 1952: 2–31.

20. Ibid.

21. Ibid.

22. Cummings, *Education and Equality in Japan*, 59.

23. Monbushō, *Rokusansei o sonzoku seshimurubeki riyu* (The Reasons for Preserving the 6-3-3-4 System), 14 August 1951.

24. Aspinall, *Unions and the Politics of Education in Japan*, 39–56.

25. Shimahara, *Adaptation and Education in Japan*, 127–45.

26. Schoppa, *Education Reform in Japan*, 120–48.

27. Nikkeiren, *Shin kyōiku seido saikentōni kansuru yōbō* (Recommendation for Reconstruction of the New Education System), 16 October 1952. A series of the Zaikai's reports and recommendations about the education system during the period are available in Yokohama kokuritsu daigaku gendai kyōiku kenkyusho, *Chūkyōshin to Kyōiku Kaikaku*; see Shimahara, *Adaptation and Education in Japan*, 129.

28. Thereafter, the MOE conducted a large-scale survey on the supply-demand problem of university graduates for three years from 1954. It forecast a serious oversupply of graduates majoring in law and liberal arts and a shortage of those from the natural science and engineering departments.

29. Nikkeiren, *Tōmen kyōiku seido kaizen ni kansuru yōbō* (Recommendation for the Improvement of the Current Education System), 23 December 1954.

30. Nikkeiren, *Kagaku gijutsu kyōiku kōshin ni kansuru iken* (Our View Concerning the Improvement of Science and Technical Education), 25 December 1957 (quoted in Horio, *Educational Thought and Ideology in Modern Japan*, 334 (emphasis added)).

31. Kyōiku no Sengoshi Henshū Iinkai, *Kyōiku no sengoshi*, vol. III, 23–53; and Horio, *Educational Thought and Ideology in Modern Japan*.

32. *Chūō kyōiku shingikai* (Central Council on Education: CCE) was originally founded in 1953. Its role is to make recommendations to the minister on vital educational policies, including legislative measures, curriculum revision, and similar policy matters. Its members are appointed by the minister, to whose influence they are likely to be amenable. In fact, members of the JTU and other academic associations that are critical of government policy have never been appointed to the CCE. Therefore, although it is a highly influential agency, it does not represent a wide spectrum of educational views. A series of the CCE's reports and recommendations at the time are available in Yokohama Kokuritsu Daigaku Gendai Kyōiku Kenkyusho, *Chūkyōshin to Kyōiku Kaikaku*.

33. Chūō kyōiku shingikai, *Shōchūga'kkō gakushū shido yōryō kaichō an* (On the Renovation of Primary and Lower Secondary School Curricula) (quoted in Horio, *Educational Thought and Ideology in Modern Japan*, 344).

34. For further details of Japan's general political history, see Tanaka, *Sengo Nihon Seijishi*; Watanabe, *Sengo Nihon no Saishōtachi*; and Kitaoka, *Jimintō*.

35. See in particular Tanaka, *Sengo Nihon Seijishi*, 122–72.

36. Yamazaki, *Jimointō to Kyōiku Seisaku*, 1–4.

37. Chūō kyōiku shingikai, *Kyōiku no chūritsu no iji ni tsuite* (About the Maintenance of the Neutrality of Education) and *Kyōiku no seijiteki chūritsusei iji ni kansuru tōshin* (A Report Concerning to Maintain the Political Neutrality), January 1954. These two laws can be seen in Beauchamp and Vardaman, *Japanese Education since 1945*, 136–40. Measures introduced under the Occupation had already restricted the political rights of teachers at the local level. Now the government wanted to extend such limits to the national level as well.

38. For further details regarding the issue of the teacher's efficiency rating system, see Duke, *Japan's Militant Teachers*, 141; Thurston, *Teachers and Politics in Japan*, 207; and Aspinall, *Unions and the Politics of Education in Japan*, 60–63.

39. For more details on the process of reformation of educational administration, see Ota, *Sengo Ninon Kyōikushi*, 205–68; and also see Takahashi, *Sengo Kyōiku Kaikaku to Shidō Shuji Seido*, 293–300.

40. For instance, the LDP published a pamphlet titled *Ureubeki kyoukasho no mondai* (Issues about Lamentable Textbooks) in 1955. It denounced the existing system for opening the door to the influence of the radical JTU. This was followed by a Textbook Bill of 1956 which aimed at giving MOE much more control over textbooks. However, this bill failed in the Diet.

41. Before this law, the 1956 revision of the School Boards Law had given the MOE the power to revise and standardize the curriculum.

42. In fact, in 1949, even before the Occupation ended, Prime Minister Yoshida Shigeru advocated the creation of an educational statement on morality that would replace the discredited Imperial Rescript. The following year Amano Teiyu, then minister of education, provoked charges of a rebirth of militarism by proposing that national holidays be celebrated by raising the rising sun flag and playing the national anthem. He also echoed Yoshida's call for a new ethical code to replace the discredited Rescript. Kyōiku no Sengoshi Henshū Iinkai, *Kyōiku no sengoshi* vol. I, 179–97.

43. Smethurst, *The Origins and Policies of the Japan Teachers' Union 1945–56*, 148; and Aspinall, *Unions and the Politics of Education in Japan*, chapter 3.

44. Nikkyōso (Japan Teachers' Union), *Kyōshi no rinri kōryo* (A Code of Ethics for Teachers), June 1952 (quoted in Beauchamp and Vardaman, *Japanese Education since 1945*, 131–32).

45. Kariya, *Taishū Kyōiku Shakai no Yukue*, 160–97.

46. Nikkyōso, *Nihon no kyōiku* (Japanese Education), various years.

47. Nikkyōso, *Nihon no kyōiku* (Japanese Education), vols. I, IV, and V.

48. Kariya, *Taishū Kyōiku Shakai no Yukue*, 53–[XX. PLEASE INCLUDE LAST PAGE; FF IS DISCOURAGED]

49. Murata "Sengo no nōryokubetsu ga'kkyū no hensen."

50. Quoted in Kariya, *Taishū Kyōiku Shakai no Yukue*, 160–61.

51. Kariya, *Taishū Kyōiku Shakai no Yukue*, 162.

52. *Nihon no kyōiku*, vol. VII. See Kariya, *Taishū Kyōiku Shakai no Yukue*, 164.

53. Kariya, *Taishū Kyōiku Shakai no Yukue*, 165.

54. Ibid.

55. Nikkyōso, *Kyōiku hakusho* (White Paper on Education), 1 May 1950 (quoted in Beauchamp and Vardaman, *Japanese Education since 1945*, 125–26).

56. Kariya, *Taishū Kyōiku Shakai no Yukue*, 166.

57. Ibid., 168.

58. Moriguchi, "Shin'gaku no kitei sho'inshi ni kansuru ichikenkyu" (A Study Concerning Some Elements to behind Proceeding to High School), 128–49.

59. However, as will be examined in chapter 4 of this book, the JTU gradually began to see the viewpoint that children's social background was linked to educational inequality as taboo,

as Japan achieved high economic growth in the 1960s and the level of people's living conditions rose.

60. For instance, see JLP, *Jiyūtō bunkyō shin seisaku taimo* (Liberal Party's A New Grand Designing Plan for Education), 13 November 1954; and JDP, *Bunkyō seisaku* (Education Policies). These educational policies of the various political parties are available in Nihon Kyōiku Ga'kkai, *Kakutō no Bunkyō Seisaku.*

61. The right JSP, *Bunkyō seisaku* (Education Policy), 10 November 1954; and the left JSP, *Tōmen no sho'seisaku* (Policies for the Present), January 1954.

62. The JCP, *Kyōiku bunka seisaku* (Policies for Education and Culture).

63. See in particular *Monbujihō*, various years.

4

The Development of the Concept of Equal Opportunity under the High Economic Growth Period, 1960s–1970s

From the early 1960s to the mid 1970s, Japan experienced rapid changes not only economically but also socially. In 1960, Ikeda Hayato was appointed as Prime Minister by the party in power, the LDP. Ikeda completed the formation of his cabinet immediately and announced a policy aiming for high economic growth and development of human resources. It was the beginning of the so-called "heyday of economic development." In fact, by the 1960s, Japan's industrial output had skyrocketed to more than double the 1955 figure, making the country number four among capitalist nations. Educational policy during the 1960s and the early 1970s was consciously designed to foster economic development. As noted in chapter 3, there was little doubt that since the middle of the 1950s the interests of industrial circles had been extremely influential in shaping educational policy. The role of education shifted towards the training of the human resources required by the expanding economy and the emergence of new scientific and information technologies. Schools were expected not only to teach the basic skills more efficiently, but also to train the nation's children in the skills of the new technologies. In this way, the theories of human capital and investment in education became officially accepted bases for determining the direction of educational policy and investment in training scientists and technicians as strategic manpower to speed economic growth, and came to receive priority. This chapter examines the notions of equality of educational opportunity that the various groups achieved under the high economic growth and educational expansion period.

The Official Announcement of the "Ability First" Principle

The 1960s marked a phenomenal expansion of the Japanese economy. The annual rate of economic growth reached as high as 18.3 percent and stayed well above 10 percent throughout the period. Japan had become one of the leading industrial countries of the world and efficient adaptation to the international economy became more urgent. Consequently, the Japanese government and the industrial sector demanded a larger and larger skilled labor force and even more of the schools.

The LDP's reactions to the issue of manpower and educational expansion in line with its attempts to promote and sustain rapid economic growth were immediately reflected in its official political slogans. In order to meet these new labor force demands, the LDP government led by Ikeda announced the National Income Doubling Plan (NIDP) in co-operation with the Economic Deliberation Council (*Keizai shingikai*: EDC) as the coordinating body for overall government economic planning. The government plan, in effect, required an annual growth rate of about 7 percent.[1] In order to accomplish its goal, the EDC gave top priority to educational policy. Setting the Improvement of Human Abilities and Encouraging Education in Science and Technology as one of its five objectives, it specified:

> Considering the swift progress of science and technology, the sophistication of the industrial structure and the prospective trends of labor, it is essential to take up positively in the context of economic growth the problems of developing human abilities, involving education, training and research, which have so far tended to be considered separately from economic problems. Further development in economics and social welfare depends largely on the effective use of the human resources of the nation.[2]

As is clear from the above quotation, the new plan stressed the importance of education as an investment in developing human resources. Early on, the EDC had identified secondary education, especially the upper secondary school level, as a critical factor in human resource development. Although it recognized the long-term need for overall improvement in general secondary education, it insisted on the necessity of extending science and technology education in the short term, pointing out that "sufficient numbers of scientific technicians and skilled labor should be secured so that economic growth will not be impeded by lack of human resources" and suggesting the setting up of an immediate plan for "the improvement of training schemes for scientists and engineers."[3]

In short, the LDP government and the business sector realized the significance of investment in education, which had played a major part in the rapid growth of the Japanese economy in the past, and came to see as necessary the mapping out and enforcing of educational policies in organic relation to economic policies. Further, they required a new system of criteria to evaluate the ability of the nation's youth in accordance with those changing economic conditions: They strongly emphasized "ability" or "merit" in both employment and education.[4] The conservative government defined children's ability in purely economic terms. Thereafter, as will be seen later in this chapter, such phrases as "Nōryokushugi" (ability first) were frequently used not only in business and politics, but also in a series of reports by the CCE in the 1960s and the 1970s. These phrases became popular within the conservative groups as a principle to evaluate the effectiveness of equal opportunity in education.

MOE's Response to the Government Plan

Meanwhile, the MOE moved quickly to respond to the government's plan. During the period, the MOE became more favored by the government and more willing to implement educational policies which equated rapid economic growth with the development of human abilities. The NIDP required the production of an additional 170,000 scientists and engineers. It planned to meet this need with a seven-year plan that added 16,000 places annually, but it was subsequently replaced by a four-year plan to increase the number of students which added 20,000 new places yearly. Among specific examples of methods the NIDP employed in the creation of these additional places were the inauguration of the five-year technical school system, combining three-year secondary education and two-year higher education, to provide an institution for training practical intermediate-level technicians[5] and a large-scale policy of expanding the natural science and engineering departments at universities.[6] As a result of investment in these priorities, the number of students in technical schools rapidly rose as follows:

Table 4.1. The Quantitative Expansion of Technical Education in Japan[7]

	Number of Students			
	1960	1965	1970	1972
Graduate	1,537	4,457	12,607	14,476
Undergraduate	81,684	158,006	283,674	308,322
Junior colleges (2 years)	8,116	14,203	21,799	22,322
Technical colleges (5 years)	3,375	22,208	44,314	47,853
Technical high schools (3 years)	305,687	565,270	565,508	541,412

The establishment of the five-year technical school system is notable as the creation of a new education system parallel with the formal 6-3-3-4 system. There is no doubt that founding such schools represented demolition of the single-track education system. A multi-track system with a technical education component became a reality in response to the LDP's and the business sector's demands. Araki Masuo, the Minister of Education of the day, did not deny this fact but asserted as follows:

> Apart from the 6-3-3-4 system, I have a plan to establish another system, a "6-3-5" system as a completely discrete thing. Of course, I fully understand the importance of equal opportunity in education, but the concept of equal opportunity in education is not solely attained by the 6-3-3-4 system, but it must be considered from the viewpoint of the young people studying in schools. In this sense, I believe that the present 6-3-3-4 system is a splendid system which should be preserved because school education is completed through the 6-3-3-4 system, but at the same time, I consider that it would be pleasurable for some children who might find leaving school through the soon-to-be-implemented 6-3-5 school system useful and appropriate because of their family circumstances because this will lead to greater educational opportunity for them and therefore I submit this bill for creating the higher technical college.[8]

As this illustrates, it is noteworthy that the MOE's attitude toward the 6-3-3-4 system suddenly changed with the trend of the economic situation at the time. In the same way as the conservatives, the MOE accepted the EDC's definitions and views of education, and it modified the purpose and orientations of schooling in terms of them.[9] The egalitarian concept of equality of opportunity embodied in post-war reforms was in fact being seriously eroded. The MOE related the principle of equality of educational opportunity to diversification of the single-track education system.[10] In other words, the principle of equal opportunity was translated into the establishment of a variety of types of secondary school "corresponding to the different abilities of the nation's children,"—"diversification" of the education system called *tayōka* in Japanese.[11] However, the MOE seemed to place more importance on the development of the nation's economy than on the development of individual children.

Strong Misgivings of the JTU

On the other hand, there were strong misgivings among progressive groups, especially the JTU, about the idea of education as an investment. They were worried that the MOE's "utilitarian view of education implicit in the idea was too narrow and one-sided, and that it would encourage one to judge the effects of education solely by its contribution to industrial efficiency."[12] They did not want to regard education as simply a tool for economic growth and the interests of industry.

The opponents argued that the proper role of education should be to develop *zenjin kyōiku*, a term used long before the post-war education debates to describe education to create "whole people."[13] Underlying the opponents' critique was the assumption that education was concerned with the well-being of individuals as well as with that of society and abilities to meet industrial needs. Thus, the concept of equal opportunity was interpreted from an egalitarian perspective by the progressives, as "equal education corresponding to children's individualities."

Economic Deliberation Council

However, the conservatives' educational policies of the 1960s for rapid economic development and the consequent demand for manpower reached its peak in the EDC's 1963 report, *Policies for Developing Human Abilities in Pursuit of Economic Expansion*.[14] This report was worthy of note as the first candid statement by the economic planners of their view of education, and its proposals contained a new definition of equal opportunity, which eventually provided a significant basis for repudiation of the logic of *zenjin kyōiku*. Setting the keynote for subsequent economic and educational policy formation, the document proceeded from the observation:

> The scale of our entire economic structure will be greatly expanded in the wake of technological innovations and the changes in our industrial structure that will inevitably follow. This will necessitate a new economic and occupational structure, one within which the quantity and quality of the labor power required by industry will no doubt change more than it has up to this time. Accordingly, the structure and scale of educational training will have to be reformed and balanced by future manpower requirements for the cultivation of all types of workers.[15]

With the widely supported idea of "education for manpower," the EDC's 1963 report contained three important ideas and suggestions that exerted influence on educational policies thereafter.

First, the report introduced the new term *Nōryokushugi* (ability first) or the meritocratic principle of equality of educational opportunity. This was the first time in the post-war history of Japanese education that the term was used and that the meritocratic principle was justified officially for the development of national talent. The Manpower Policies Committee, set up within the EDC to consider policy to promote human ability, emphasized the importance of *Nōryokushugi* as follows:

> *The principle of equal opportunity means that educational opportunity is given equally among people who have equal ability.* Following this interpretation, the principle of ability first (*Nōryokushugi*) must be applied. Selection by ability is not discrimination. . . . [T]he principle is not to have identical conditions going on to the higher

grade and the senior class in the given educational courses but to have a flexible education system correspondent to people's ability.[16]

It was a significant shift in official statements that the meritocratic principle was demanded and justified in the name of equal opportunity. This new concept of equality of opportunity, married to the principle of *Nōryokushugi*, appeared in the EDC's 1963 report to substantiate essentially anti-egalitarian criticisms of the post-war education reform based on the FLE and the 6-3-3-4 system. Under "the imperative to reorganize both society and education on the basis of a new formulation of ability" in order to resolve the problem of securing the talents and capacities required to successfully realize the aim of high economic growth, it was a logical conclusion for the EDC's report to condemn the post-war education reform on the ground that "it is established based on the principle of standardized egalitarianism and has many problems finding, observing and systematically expanding the diverse abilities and aptitudes of people."[17] After this important report, the conservative groups such as the LDP, the MOE, the CCE and the business sector gradually fortified their concept of equal opportunity through reliance on the principle of *Nōryokushugi*.

Secondly, under the ideology of ability first, the EDC's report demanded *tayōka* or "diversification" of the education system in order to discover highly talented children at an early age and to serve the aims of economic growth. As noted before, these education policies were gradually demanded from the 1950s by the industrial community and consistently advocated over the next few decades by the Ad Hoc Council (*Rinkyōshin*) and the CCE. The elements of diversification were described in the EDC's report, from which the following was taken:

As a part of the thorough emphasis on achievement orientation in education, a problem has arisen in relation to the training of highly talented manpower. Here highly talented manpower refers to human competence that can play a leading role in various fields concerned with the economy and promote economic development. Despite the fact that education is well developed, there is no sufficient readiness to train these talented human resources and to offer unique education programs . . . Corresponding to the demand to accomplish the ideology of ability first in education and society, the nation's people should take appropriate educational opportunities corresponding to their different abilities and aptitudes and be evaluated by their real merit.[18]

The EDC's report took a controversial step in seeing equality of opportunity as being something to be achieved partly through the diversification of a single-track educational system. In other words, the principle of diversification favored by the conservatives was not the same as the egalitarian principle of "equal education corresponding to individualism." To provide adequate opportunities, the EDC insisted, for pupils whose abilities were varied and who should contribute to economic development, lower secondary schools were expected to give appropriate career orientation and classify children for allocation to diverse educational systems corresponding to their ability.[19] Upper secondary schools also adopted a multi-track education system and provided different types of curriculums. Thus, in order to cope with the shift in the industrial structure, the EDC especially suggested that curricula in both lower and upper secondary education should adopt technical, commercial, and vocational subjects.

Thirdly, the EDC's espousal of ability first and diversification marked the peak of the argument for the meritocratic notion of equality, and in consequence the official definition of equality of educational opportunity was entering a new phase. After the publication of the report, these two elements were effectively integrated and became a new slogan, "diversify by ability," which was frequently used by conservative groups. With the EDC's support for "diversify by ability" and the conservative government's acceptance of its recommendations, the egalitarian concept of equal opportunity decreed in the New Constitution and the FLE—"equal education corresponding to individualities"—was evaluated as *aku-byōdō* or "excessive egalitarianism."[20] It is interesting to note that, as examined in chapter 2, the same phrase in Article III of the FLE, "according to their ability," which was originally understood as an expression of the principle of individuality, not as meaning diversification, was used by the conservatives in order to justify their meritocratic concept of equal opportunity. Indeed, equal opportunity began to be interpreted in terms of children having the same access to different kinds of schools, which would directly affect the economic development of Japan. Under this new interpretation, a diversified secondary school system was seen as one of the most significant steps "to meet the needs of industrial society."[21] Moreover, the major criterion for assessing equal opportunity in state education shifted from the development of the individual to state instrumentalism. As Shimizu argued:

> Education does not possess its own objectives. What determines educational objectives are the forces actually existing in society. Under the framework of high economic growth, national educational policy should be formulated in accord with the shifting of concern from quantitative to qualitative issues and from political to industrial interests. . . . Speaking straightforwardly, the pursuit of Japan's economic growth through educational policy formation means cultivating superior-quality labor power. Educational policies must work to make the school system serve as the supplier of the desired work-oriented competencies.[22]

This shift culminated in the EDC's 1963 report's advocacy of diversify by ability as the major yardstick for evaluating inequality in education and the ensuing conclusion that the meritocratic principle of equal opportunity should be realized for national development. Thus, it is noteworthy to see that the gloss on equality which had been supported since the Occupation period by the conservatives and the business sector—diversification of education corresponding to children's ability—became an official definition of educational policy directly related to economic development and emerged as one of the most important criteria in evaluating equality in education. The meaning of equality of educational opportunity became increasingly mixed with the meritocratic idea of opportunities and, from that time on, a shift in the main notion of equality could be traced.

Assessment of the Nation's Children for Economic Development: The Nation-wide Scholastic Achievement Test

The issues of children's ability and the utilization of that ability began to be a subject of heated discussion from the early 1960s when the NIDP was announced. As noted before, the principle of ability first (Nōryokushugi) was formulated and given a privileged position in the educational policy of the LDP government and the business sector, for high economic growth and labor force development was the central link between the economy and education. At that point, the most urgent task for the conservatives was how to systematically control the different kinds of abilities of the nation's children to achieve these goals. In order to respond to these political and economic demands, the MOE proposed a systematic use of the Scholastic Achievement Test (SAT) for measuring the nation-wide distribution of talent to provide the data required for the establishment of an effective workforce. The SAT was administered in five subjects (Japanese language, mathematics, science, social studies, and English) to all second-year and third-year lower secondary school students. The practice became more general after the implementation of the 1958 Course of Study which gave the MOE strong administrative power. The MOE issued A Plan for Developing Human Capital and the Reform of the Examination System in 1960 in which it enumerated the main aims of the SAT.[23]

The SAT was designed to serve two important functions. Firstly, the test was to forge a new relation between education and the manpower training policies desired by the LDP government and the business sector since the early 1960s in line with the NIDP. The SAT was adopted to "discover outstanding talent at an early age and cultivate it through an appropriate form of education."[24] More frankly, it was implemented "to distinguish able children and poor learners at [the] compulsory education level to meet the demands of economic development."[25] There is no doubt that the MOE used it as one of the major means to apply the principle of Nōryokushugi, and this began to attract attention. In other words, the MOE desired to put the meritocratic principle into practice in the education system to foster national talent. The MOE expressed this intention clearly in another report:

It [the SAT] should be useful data to identify the number of able children who were impeded from taking further schooling due to their financial conditions . . . and to improve the policy for expanding and strengthening the *Ikuei* scholarship system [scholarships only for able children].[26]

As this indicates, the principle of equal opportunity in education was interpreted by the MOE as equal access only for able children to move on to a higher level of schooling regardless of their financial situation. Thus, it is clear that the liberal concept of equal opportunity, which had remained submerged in the MOE during the Occupation, in general envisaged the objectives of the SAT only as giving advantages to able children for the sake of Japan's economic development. The students in the lower secondary schools were being ranked through the SAT and thereafter distributed among a wide variety of upper secondary schools which were themselves marked by considerable difference in quality.

Moreover, the SAT was designed to serve as an important link in the policies the MOE had implemented as a part of its attempt to impose greater control over the contents of education, the production of textbooks, and the organization of classroom instruction. Having thoroughly transformed the character of the 1958 Course of Study, the MOE decided to institute the new test to strengthen its control over the intellectual growth of the nation's children and "to test the loyalty and commitment of teachers to the aims and values which the State sought to impose under the guidance of its administrative expertise."[27] In addition to providing a way to measure the extent to which teachers were actually following the government-amended curriculum, it also provided a way to test their loyalty to the MOE in general. Indeed, as Horio has argued, "the teacher's attitude to the testing provided a source of very useful data for the Teacher Evaluating System."[28] Now through this new system for controlling teachers, the MOE attempted to bring the remaining loose ends of educational freedom within the purview of its administrative control.

In short, the MOE's purpose in introducing the SAT on a national scale was mainly to serve an important function in the implementation of these industrialization policies by tightening state control over the educational administration and by making it more responsive to the manpower requirements of the Japanese economy and industry.

"Improper Control" on Education Administration

However, the MOE's advocacy of the SAT raised severe criticism from the JTU and its supporters. Analysis of these criticisms demonstrated that their reasons for opposing the test seemed to stem from three major concerns. First, the JTU maintained that the MOE's SAT test constituted "improper control" in violation of Article X of the Fundamental Law of Education. Since the JTU held the position that the MOE only had the right to administer education and not the right to decide on the curriculum nor to conduct the SAT, which would lead to further curriculum diversification,[29] they were strongly opposed in principle to the extension of the MOE's control over assessment of the varied abilities of the nation's children and the content of school curriculum. The JTU supported this opposing stance on the grounds that Article X of the FLE decreed that "education shall not be subject to improper control, but shall be directly responsible to the whole people." In a question to Minister of Education Araki Masuo as to the enforcement of the SAT, the JTU stated:

> In the pre-war period, as education was controlled by the state, Japan had the Sōchō Scholastic Achievement Test implemented throughout Japan by the military regime, but the test focused on making education policy (including revision of educational content with reference to the results of the survey inquiring into the diffusion or degree of penetration of nationalistic and militaristic ideas through education) a means to sustain and strengthen military power. If an educational test is needed, school teachers who are actively engaged in teaching should devise the test according to the child's individuality, ability, and progress in class work . . . and should utilize it to improve educational conditions. The SAT which the MOE is now trying to impose, ignoring the opinion of schoolteachers who are in charge of everyday teaching, is no different from the test in the pre-war period. Does it mean state control of education and can the SAT be understood as a test for the development of human resources with the ultimate purpose of attaining the policy of high economic growth set by Prime Minister Ikeda?[30]

Calling for the involvement of classroom teachers in the process of creating any testing instrument, the JTU was apprehensive about a crisis of teachers' educational authority and autonomy and demanded limits upon the state's intervention in the education process. Thus, the JTU feared that results of the SAT would not be used solely for improving the quality of education, but would be used against the teachers.

Skepticism about the "Academic Ability" Measured by the SAT

Apart from the issue of improper control as an administrative matter, another criticism of the SAT was that it ran counter to the conventional belief about the academic ability of children. Among its opponents, skepticism was expressed about how reliable the SAT was in measuring whole ability. Against the authorized definition of "ability" made largely on the basis of five subjects of the SAT, the Education Society of Japan cast doubts on the rationale that the SAT was to be used for evaluating pupils' ability. Various criticisms were amassed as follows:[31]

1) The academic potential of children is unlimited, and a test taken only once is not sufficient to predict the development of children's ability in the future;

2) judging the ability of children just from the limited number of five subjects is to ignore other elements of their academic ability. The assumption that the mere accumulation of knowledge alone is true academic ability casts doubts on the scientific basis of the SAT; and

3) the limited number of five tests is against the principle of *zenjin kyōiku* (the proper role of education is to develop whole person) stipulated in the Constitution and FLE.

Furthermore, the JSP, the most powerful opposition party at that time, announced its firm opposition from the same perspective:

> The SAT with five subjects lays stress only on academic knowledge for university entrance exams. It is undeniable that the purpose of the test is to select an academic elite for national development . . . Compulsory education will more and more lean toward the pursuit of academic knowledge and the lower secondary schools will just be preparation for upper secondary schools. This means the collapse of the secondary education system. Enforcing only five subjects with the ostensible aim of examining pupils' academic ability will result in undermining such subjects as music, physical education, domestic science, and vocational education.[32]

What was clear from the above two quotations was that the ability the SAT attempted to measure looked at only a part of children's ability—the part that consisted of knowledge useful for the economic growth of the nation. Since the conservative camp might avoid investing in areas with bad scores, teachers and the JTU felt that the SAT itself would produce unhealthy competition among teachers, among students, and among schools.[33] They feared that such competition would be detrimental to the egalitarian principle of equal opportunity, which they saw as equal opportunity in education corresponding to children's individuality.

Stigmatization of Children of "Poor" Ability

The opposition further objected on the ground that the SAT could be used to stigmatize children of poor ability or make invidious comparisons between able children who would go on to receive upper secondary education and less able children who would leave the lower secondary school to work. For instance, recognizing the enforcement of the SAT as a series of education policies developed in response to the demand from industry, Miki Yoshio, MP of the JSP, made the following statement at the 39th Special House of Representatives' Education Committee in the Diet:

The JSP is wondering if this test has the hidden motive of restructuring the Japanese workforce by dividing technicians into unskilled workers and middle-level workers. I find the idea very dangerous. It is because making separate classes according to children's ability in lower secondary schools brings discrimination in education. . . . It is an invidious task to distinguish children into groups who will leave school to work and who will take upper secondary education at this stage, said an 8th grade school teacher responding to my question. . . . The parents want their children to join the group who will prepare to advance to upper secondary school and parents whose children are taken into the group who will leave school to enter the workplace are strongly discontented . . . children have come to hate being allocated to the group who will leave school.[34]

The JTU attacked the SAT from the same point of view:

The intention of a small number of people who control the world of industry to create a sense of discrimination in children by the SAT, to divide them into groups who will take upper secondary education and who will leave school to work, and to raise children who are to enter the workforce as mere labor without complaining about anything are reflected in the SAT. For teachers who teach and learn directly with children every day, this policy aiming to discriminate and decide children's lives by a single mechanical and oppressive test cannot be allowed to pass.[35]

The above quotations indicate that the opponents regarded the SAT as fostering a sense of discrimination between children at birth, and at the same time they blamed such discrimination for creating submissive workers under the capitalist system. They believed that the test result would be used to divide children against each other. As discussed in chapter 3, the issue of equality in education was, here as well, linked to a sense of inferiority as well as discrimination among children who had to give up taking upper secondary education in order to work. As will be seen later in this chapter, this sense of discrimination concerning poor learners' feelings of inferiority would lead to the formulation of a new concept of egalitarianism in the JTU when the conservatives attempted to diversify the upper secondary system in the mid 1960s.

Nevertheless, beginning in October 1962 the MOE ordered the school boards to direct their administrations to carry out the second test. The JTU recognized the urgent need for political and legal countermeasures. These took the form of a collective protest in which teachers in many regions of the nation refused to handle the test materials when the time came to implement them. The resulting disruption had varying consequences according to the local balance of power within each prefecture and depending on the willingness of ordinary teachers to support the JTU's action.[36] By 1962, most prefectural boards had agreed to the JTU's main demand that the names of students not appear on the answer sheets nor the test scores on their academic records. In response, the MOE brought suit against those teachers who refused to cooperate, charging that they had failed to execute their proper educational duties. This move gave the opposition the chance to test the constitutionality of such central control in court.[37] Between 1962 and 1976, there were seventeen separate judgments.[38] In ten cases, the national test was found to be illegal, but in seven cases it was declared legal. This resistance by the JTU produced changes in the policy of the MOE concerning the administration of the test. Teachers who refused to obey the directives regarding testing were within their rights, and consequently the MOE had to settle for sampling schools rather than attempting to test the whole nation annually, thus foregoing the use of the results to punish or reward schools.

The Emergence of the Counter-Part-Theory to the "Ability First" Principle

From the early 1960s, the people's demand for post-compulsory education for their children developed into a powerful social pressure seeking the expansion of equal opportunities. This demand was based on the post-war baby boom, which started in 1947 after a multitude of soldiers and civilians returned from overseas. By 1953, a new flood of children reached elementary school age and by 1959 the population bulge was beginning to be felt at the lower secondary level. In 1962 and 1965, respectively, it began to affect the demand for upper secondary and university education. The rapid growth of the Japanese economy during this period provided the economic conditions necessary for meeting such a strong demand for higher education. After the nine-year compulsory education system was enforced almost without complaint, upper secondary education entered a stage of steady development in the latter half of the 1950s. In fact, the ratio of those entering upper secondary schools to the total graduates of lower secondary schools increased steadily.

It is worth pausing here to recapitulate on the development of the upper secondary system since the Occupation reform. As noted in chapter 2, the new upper secondary school system was planned by the 1946 USME and then established by the Japanese government. Unlike the pre-war secondary education system, the new system was modeled after the comprehensive high school system of the United States on the basis of kōkō sangensoku or "three principles of upper secondary school": the small school district system, co-education, and comprehensive system.[39] Although the upper secondary school was not compulsory, all students continuing their education were able to matriculate at such schools without selection or tuition costs. In the post-war educational reform period, however, the disastrous state of the nation's finances made it impossible to provide all young people with the educational opportunity to go to upper secondary schools and there was no option but to put screening into practice. Yet the MOE

Table 4.2. Percentages of Boys and Girls Entering Upper Secondary School[40]

	Boys	Girls	Total
1950	48.0	36.7	42.5
1951	51.4	39.6	45.6
1952	52.9	42.1	47.6
1953	52.7	43.7	48.3
1954	55.1	46.5	50.9
1955	55.5	47.4	51.3
1956	55.0	47.6	51.3
1957	54.3	48.4	51.4
1958	56.2	51.1	53.7
1959	57.5	53.2	55.4
1960	59.6	55.9	57.7
1961	63.8	60.7	62.3
1962	65.5	62.5	64.0
1963	68.4	65.1	66.8
1964	70.6	67.9	69.3
1965	71.7	69.6	70.7
1966	73.5	71.2	72.3
1967	75.3	73.7	74.5
1968	70.7	76.5	76.8
1969	79.2	79.5	79.4
1970	80.6	82.7	82.1

submissively agreed with these principles of the new upper secondary education. For example, the MOE issued *A Desirable Guideline for Administration of the New Lower and Upper Secondary Schools* in 1949, which insisted as follows:

> The new lower and upper secondary schools must be based on a belief that they are founded in order for the nation to educate not a selected minority but as many young people as possible. The new lower and upper secondary schools should never have the idea that selecting the candidates for admission is desirable. . . . Even if they have to, we must consider it as *undesirable and done only for lack of an alternative* and as a makeshift system which can be replaced as soon as the economy has recovered making it possible to provide students who wish to study at the new lower and upper secondary schools with appropriate facilities.[41]

The MOE fundamentally maintained the above policy until the mid 1950s. However, as Japan's economic growth, begun after independence, was regained, this ideal of the new upper secondary school gradually started to fade. As already examined in chapter 3, the U.S. vision of comprehensive upper secondary schools with all the students in a district enrolled did not materialize due, in part, to resistance from the outset by the conservative government and industrial circles which believed that most youth should be tracked into vocational training at an earlier age. During the 1950s, the MOE (and the CCE after 1953) revised the original Course of Study in 1951, 1955, and 1960 so that the curriculum of the upper secondary schools could be diversified in response to the demands of the business sector. Consequently, there was a gradually stepped-up specialization of the system in the ordinary course giving preparatory education mainly to those pupils wishing to advance to universities and in the vocational course giving terminal education to those planning to take up occupations upon graduation. Thus, by the 1960s, graduates of lower secondary schools who wished to continue their education needed to be directed into one track or the other on the basis of severe entrance examinations. On the other hand, parallel with those changes, a movement was formed by parents, children, and teachers demanding the opportunity for all to go to upper secondary schools; this movement promoted measures such as increasing the number of upper secondary schools and abolishing harsh examination systems.[42] This was the start of the so-called Zen-nyū (upper secondary school for all) movement.

Upper Secondary School for All: Zen-nyū Movement

Equality of opportunity was again referred to in all the renewed arguments for and against the premise of zen-nyū, which the JTU used not only to respond to the demands from parents who desired their children to have upper secondary education, but also to justify its intention to abolish the severe competition among students to enter these schools. At the JTU's annual conference (ZKKS) in 1959, its members decided on a policy for the zen-nyū movement for the first time. It insisted that:

> Taking a stance of equal opportunity in education, the abolition of entrance examinations in lower and upper secondary schools and 'zen-nyū' [upper secondary school for all] should be required in order to promote a normal development of curriculum. We demand a substantial increase in the education budget in order to obtain the establishment of an increased number of upper secondary schools.[43]

However, it was mothers who became the real main power promoting this movement. They feared their children might not be able to enter upper secondary school as the children of the post-war baby boom reached the age to go to upper secondary schools. This feeling among mothers made the campaign for an increase in the number of schools—the zen-nyū movement—more and more earnest.[44] For instance, in this atmosphere, the National Debate Council on the Issue of Upper Secondary Education for All was formed in 1962 with the JTU, mothers, and labor unions as the leading forces. Criticizing the government's timid educational budget to cope with the anticipated sharp increase in the number of students who would be going to upper secondary schools, it declared:

> The extreme shortage of upper secondary schools creates distinctions between children who will go to upper secondary schools and those who will leave school to work, and destroys education in lower secondary schools. The demand of citizens with the slogan of "upper secondary education for all our youth" is a natural consequence in order for us to live in an era of rapidly-advancing technical innovation. Furthermore, the number of students who will be going to upper secondary schools will increase by about 0.5 million between 1963 and 1965. The government turns a blind eye to this situation. . . . Measures to be taken to cope with this dramatic increase are delayed, and this will unavoidably create a lot of students unable to go on to the upper secondary schools. This situation cannot be left as it is.[45]

As a result, the demands to increase the number of upper secondary schools strengthened among citizens from the early 1960s, and those movements, with upper secondary education for all as their principal demand, rapidly expanded nationwide. Thus, equality of educational opportunity was defined by the JTU and many parents as closely related to upper secondary school for all.

These nationwide movements worked, putting powerful pressure on the government, and the government and the MOE started to develop a policy to build many upper secondary schools to increase the number from 1961.[46] However, the MOE did not accept the demands of the *zen-nyū* movement, as proclaimed by the JTU and many parents. The MOE issued its own pamphlet in 1961 criticizing the *zen-nyū* movement from the following three points of view:[47]

The *zen-nyū* movement of upper secondary education for all:

1) gives the impression that it is chosen as a slogan by the JTU in order to motivate the general public to involve itself in political struggle supporting an extreme ideology;

2) by ignoring the differences in children's ability, is likely to end up creating a large number of students who cannot keep up with the class—so called *ochikobore*; and

3) promotes a decline in the academic ability of children among state upper secondary schools, and is causing the escape of excellent students to private schools.

This pamphlet was also made to clearly express the intention of vigorously fostering the idea of diversify by ability, which was supported by the conservative group as mentioned earlier. Criticizing JTU's *zen-nyū* movement which was based on the *kōkō sangensoku,* as a kind of purely mechanical equal opportunity in education and as an armchair proposal, the MOE described how it saw equal opportunity in education as follows:

> The idea of equality of education is certainly an important principle as shown in the third article of the FLE, but it is not the general intention of the FLE itself to adapt it mechanically to upper secondary schools as the JTU has. At the same time, the FLE stipulates "education corresponding to children's ability." In order to form a system able to give education to all the lower secondary school graduates who have different levels of ability . . . establishing schools to provide ordinary and special education based on the present upper secondary education system is not enough, and a plan to create a variety of educational institutions other than that must be formulated.[48]

Furthermore, in the same pamphlet the MOE publicly announced an important change in its way of thinking about the entrance examinations of upper secondary schools. As explained earlier, although the MOE considered the entrance examination for upper secondary schools as "an undesirable harm" and hesitated to implement it during the period of post-war education reform under the Occupation, the same MOE insisted in the pamphlet that "the educational case to select appropriate students to receive a certain level of upper secondary education and to provide them with appropriate education is needed according to the principle of equal opportunity in education," and mentioned that the MOE did "not anticipate unrestrictedly allowing any student to go to the upper secondary school just because the student wants to."[49] The fundamental attitude of the MOE toward the entrance examination for upper secondary schools was further confirmed by a circular produced in 1963.[50]

Thus, the ideologically-charged transformation contained in the concept of diversify by ability generated by the conservative group permeated the MOE's educational policies for upper secondary education in this period. Taking their cue from the NIDP, the MOE, working closely with local education boards, implemented the meritocratic principle of equal opportunity to diversify the upper secondary education system in line with the demands of the business sector and allocated the nation's children to different kinds of schools corresponding to their academic ability. In brief, the measure taken by the MOE to cope with the rapid increase in the number of upper secondary school students was, at the same time, a measure to train technicians.[51]

The CCE's Attitude

If the EDC's report of 1963 was the first official declaration clearly proclaiming the imperative to reorganize Japanese society on the basis of the new formula known as *Nōryokushugi* (the ability first principle), two substantial reports issued by the CCE in 1966 and 1971 were the concrete expression of the principle in the realm of education. Once again, the term of 'ability first' had been given a privileged position in the national policies for high economic growth and manpower development. In the opening paragraph of the 1966 report (The Expansion and Adjustment of Education in the Final Stages of Middle-Level Schooling), the CCE explained its basic philosophy, declaring that:

> For development in the new era, the exhaustive reinforcement of equal opportunity in education is desirable. At the same time, it is today's important national task to provide our young people, who have the greatest part in forming national society and in taking responsibility for its economic as well as social development, with opportunities which enable them to give full scope to their more enriched individuality and ability based on compulsory education.[52]

Exactly the same view was echoed in the preamble of the 1971 report. In essence, these two reports presented no arguments that had not already been made by the EDC in 1963. There is no doubt that the CCE inherited the task of educational reorganization in line with the principle of diversification by ability. By the mid 1970s, the emphasis had moved even further towards concerns over the system and curriculum on upper secondary school in general. In fact, the 1966 report recommended that "the curricula and forms of upper secondary education should be diversified to meet the demands of society as well as individuals, varying according to their abilities, aptitudes, future careers, and local conditions."[53] Also, the 1971 report asserted as follows:

> Diversification of the curricula of the upper secondary schools enables students to choose courses suited to their particular abilities and interests. In this context, while the courses are diversified, it should be made easier for individual students to transfer from one major to another as their abilities develop and their interests change. The system should also be structured so that students may advance to schools of a higher grade from various courses.[54]

Besides the proposals for upper secondary school, another prime aim of these reports was to change the 6-3-3 system at a structural level. This was not new, as the previous chapters have shown. However, the 1971 CCE report, referring itself as "the third major educational reform" in Japan's history, differed from its precursors in that it actually proposed *sendōteki shikō* (experimental pilot projects) to determine which alternatives might best serve the national interest. The possibilities that were suggested are as follows:[55]

1) Experiment with ways to improve the effectiveness of primary education by establishing an institution that provides continuous education for youths

from the ages of four and five through what is now the lower years of elementary school.

2) Establish an institution that provides a consistent program of secondary education as an experiment to find solutions to the problems caused by the current division of secondary education into upper and lower schools, and introduce educational guidance as well as diversified courses so that students can plan their courses according to their abilities and interest.

3) In addition to the two experiments above, other experiments such as linking the upper grades of elementary school with the lower grades of lower secondary school and the upper grades of lower secondary schools with upper secondary schools should be attempted.

4) Extend the idea of the educational program offered at present in the technical colleges, i.e., a consistent set of courses covering both secondary education and the first stage of higher education, to other subject areas and educational establishment.

The 1971 report recommended fundamental changes in the articulation of the various levels in the present system. This included a plan to introduce 6-6 system (other alternatives designed in that period were: 6-4-4, 5-4-4-4 and 6-3-5) that might exist alongside the 6-3-3 system to benefit the academically gifted students. Indeed, some of the council members actually argued for ability-based rather than age-based promotion, insisting that the brightest should be permitted to move up faster. This idea would lead to a concept of called "liberalization" (jiūka) of the system proposed by the Ad Hoc Council on Education during the 1980s (see chapter 5).

In short, equality of educational opportunity, in the proposals of the two CCEs, began to be defined as the same possibility of access for each student to a "gifted education" (esai kyōiku) in the upper secondary schools (differentiated curriculum, teaching method and treatment) according to abilities, personalities, and interests. This definition foreshadowed the way in which the principle of equality would be interpreted over the next two decades, reflected particularly in both the Ad Hoc Council on Education and the CCE's report of the 1990s. The 1971 report included a proposal for a credit-based system that allowed for gifted students to move more quickly through the system than their peers. Two other CCE proposals also concerned "gifted education" aspects.[56] In addition to streaming between upper secondary schools, the CCE sought to establish streaming within individual schools. The idea that students at top academic upper secondary schools should be given freedom to choose courses matching their abilities and interests was viewed by some as elitist. Many progressive observers suspected that even though students would supposedly be given freedom to choose the courses that they liked, they would in actuality be separated by ability; this would become an elitist tracking system.

As part of this report, the CCE made another important recommendation, titled On the Image of the Ideal Japanese, which covered ideal moral and ethical qualities of the national culture.[57] This was the first official and open criticism of the democratic principles of the FLE of 1947. Kosaka Masa'aki, an eminent philosopher and chairman of the sub-committee which drafted the statement, explained the announcement of the recommendation by saying that the ideals of a welfare state could not be actualized only by material wealth produced by the development of human capabilities, but also required high moral standards in the people, created by the improvement of human quality.[58] In the face of the startling economic development of the period and constant change in the pattern of society, the conservatives wanted a stable pattern of cognitive and motivational orientations to be internalized in the nation's youth. The recommendation talked of necessary personal qualities and abilities, each individual's sense of membership within the family and within society at large, possession of the proper form of patriotism, respect and love for the Emperor as the symbol of Japan, and the promotion of excellent national characteristics. Thus, the significance of the CCE's recommendation on the "Ideal Japanese" lies in its implication that the conservatives should attempt to strengthen national integration and promote effective economic expansion and competition through traditional institutions and ideology.

In short, the CCE's reports of 1966 and 1971 advocated the diversification of upper secondary school in line with the EDC recommendation of 1963 and did not approve of the original U.S. version of a comprehensive high school enrolling all children in a district. Once again, the *Nōryokushugi* doctrine (education corresponding to children's ability) played a central role in the claims of those who repudiated the egalitarian principle of equality of educational opportunity supported by the JTU and many parents: upper secondary education for all. Based on the assumption that children's intelligence or ability is a characteristic determined wholly by inheritance,[59] the MOE as well as the CCE justified the selection system for upper secondary education.

JTU's "Sabetsu = Senbetsu Kyōiku" (Discrimination = Selection by Ability)

However, the series of recommendations on upper secondary education from the MOE and the CCE in the period caused a heated dispute on the equality of educational opportunity; the main reason for the criticism lay in the definition of children's "ability." It was already becoming clear that the CCE's proposals would make the educational system subordinate to industrial requirements and become part of a system for selecting and developing ability to assist industry.

Under these educational conditions, while protesting against CCE's recommendations on the grounds that its educational policies on upper secondary school had too narrow a utilitarian view and were too confidently based on ability measured by the entrance examination, the JTU developed a new interpretation of ability or intelligence that would mark an important turning point in the process of JTU's official definition of equality. As Kariya's study acutely points out, this new interpretation of the meaning of ability and intelligence first appeared at the JTU's annual conference on education in 1958.[60] Criticizing intellectual ability testing (which takes the inheritable character of intelligence for granted) as a part of the diversify by ability policy which the MOE was trying to promote at the time, the JTU unanimously adopted the following resolutions:

> . . . it is doubtful that IQ tests can predict children's future intelligence with precise accuracy and can, in this sense, be valued as a predictive test on the basis that intelligence is innate. MOE, taking it for granted that IQ is constant throughout life . . . sees children's expanding potential as something fixed and labels them superior or inferior, making their future predestined. This does more harm than good.[61]

In Kochi prefecture where the "upper secondary education for all" movement started, teachers who supported such movements commented: "What is academic ability? Can it be examined easily by a paper test? Is it right to make a simple link between the exam result and ability to receive upper secondary education?"[62] In the education periodical called *Kyōiku*, one lower secondary school teacher insisted that "all children, at least almost all children, are innately endowed with the ability to get full marks, and therefore if this ability is not taken full advantage of, education cannot be said to be being given properly."[63] These statements clearly show that the JTU, assuming children's unlimited potential in intelligence and academic ability and not seeing their intelligence as something fixed, opposed the idea of screening students according to their intelligence and academic ability. Skepticism about children's intelligence and academic ability as a basis to judge their superiority or inferiority emerged as an important point of issue in the criticism of the policy of diversify by ability promoted by the conservatives in the educational system.

In addition to this, the JTU, critical of the idea of ability determined from birth, developed a different view which did not accept the ability measured at schools as true ability or academic ability.[64] Naturally such skepticism about the assessment of children's academic ability and intelligence affected the screening system at lower and upper secondary schools. As was mentioned in chapter 3, there were some cases in the 1950s where a streaming class system based on children's ability was adopted. However, as a lot of reports revealed that the distinction between the ordinary and the vocational courses among lower and upper secondary schools was just making students in the vocational ones feel inferior, the JTU began to view such a system as discrimination after the late 1950s. Moreover, in the early 1960s, not satisfied with criticizing diversified education, which was only causing a sense of discrimination among children, the JTU began to go further, acutely criticizing the division of children between different kinds of schools or courses based on the unreliable achievement tests or entrance examinations. To sum up, the JTU started its attack against the principle of diversification by ability, as recommended by the conservatives, from the viewpoint of the unreliability in defining children's ability. Thus, adding the sense of inferiority among students and the new definition of ability, the JTU formulated a new attack on inequality called "*Sabetsu = Senbetsu Kyōiku*" (discrimination = selection by ability).[65]

It should be noted that, according to Kariya, in the JTU's "*Sabetsu = Senbetsu Kyōiku*" it was taboo to link ability with social stratification. In other words, the JTU was reluctant to think that the low academic attainment of poor children was caused by their family background or social stratification. For instance, their attitude was observed strikingly at the 10th ZKKS in 1961 in an argument concerning what determines children's careers. When the teachers' group in Chiba prefecture found that the determinants in children's career choices were related to social environment and children's innate nature, they proposed a hypothesis in their report as follows:

> Although it may be the natural consequence of poverty and unstable life-style to lower children's academic grade at schools, are the different levels of intelligence among children which result from their standard of living, as revealed in this survey, a result of a vicious circle where poverty causes poor intelligence, and poor intelligence leads to poverty?[66]

Objection after objection was raised against this report:[67]

1) With regard to intelligence and standard of living, it raises problems to think that poor people have poor intellectual ability (Gunma prefecture);

2) The report mentions a vicious circle of poverty and poor intelligence, but before that, the meaningfulness of the IQ tests must be examined (Kyoto prefecture);

3) The IQ tests have a kind of mystique. Intelligence is not something innate. Intelligence does not reflect social differences [but way of teaching] (Osaka).

It is noteworthy that although, as seen in chapter 3, many teachers in the JTU did not hesitate to consider the relationship between poor learners and their families, and their economic and social environments during the 1950s. They began to regard mention of the relationship itself as discrimination, as pressure from the conservatives to diversify the education system and allocate the nation's children to different schools based on their ability for the sake of economic development was getting stronger during the 1960s. Based on these assumptions that all children's ability is equal, academic ability is not whole ability, and ability is not inherited, but acquired in the society, the JTU established its own concept of equality, the "Sabetsu=Senbetsu" principle, which can be expressed in the following formula:

> The "Sabetsu = Senbetsu" Principle: Discrimination (creates a sense of inferiority in students) + egalitarianism (equality in ability) + a taboo (on linking low ability and class).

Thus, the unique sense had formed among the JTU that it is taboo to mention and deal with the issue of class in the debate on equality of educational opportunity.

Kyōikuken: Right to Learning

The JTU's espousal of the "Sabetsu = Senbetsu" principle reached its climax in the argument for the egalitarian notion of equality of educational opportunity by the mid 1970s when the Committee for Evaluating the Education System, organized by the JTU, published two significant reports—*Nihon no kyōiku wa dōarubekika* (How Should Japan's Education Be?) in 1971 and *Nihon no kyōiku kaikaku o motomete* (Manifesto for a Revolution in Japanese Education) in 1974. In opposition to the ability first principle which "brought about sharp and cold rivalry among children," these two reports declared the *Kyōikuken* or "the right to learning"[68] as follows:

> The right to learning is one of the fundamental human rights like the right to life, development, the pursuit of happiness, and work. It is also inseparable from academic freedom and the pursuit of truth. *The people's right to learning is first to secure full development of children and youth as one of their essential needs.* With help and instruction in family, school, and community children are expected to grow and choose spontaneously their future course in life. If children are deprived of their right to learning, they may become too ignorant to demand their right when grown up, and sometimes it can be harmful to society. Thus, the children's right to learning is a pre-condition to all the other human rights.[69]

These two reports emphasized the importance of the right to learning, demanding that education based on the ability first principle not be one of cutthroat deviation but one of education with standards based upon responding to the developmental needs of each individual. In this context, we find that the JTU claimed that the drives towards equalization and individualization of educational opportunity should be the moving force behind educational reform for upper secondary education. Furthermore, both reports linked *Nōryokushugi* with nationalism in order to criticize the educational policies of the conservatives, which were based upon thoroughly responding to the need to tailor the education system to the technological changes in economic development during the 1960s. The reports asserted that:

> Educational policy in present-day Japan is based on the ability first principle . . . and easily linked with narrow nationalism. As for textbooks, dangerous nationalistic ideas have been brought into the content of education in accordance with Japan's development as a "powerful nation." Such attempts are aimed at diverting children's attention from the vices of present Japan, and infiltrating in their minds false and illiberal nationalistic ideas that Japan is the leader of Asia and a supporter of the free world without harboring any doubt for already-established economy, politics and culture. Education based on this ability first principle and nationalism naturally promotes the principle of strong managerial control and centralization in education. Such a concept is revealed in the idea that "the State has the right to educate children."[70]

It can be said that the fundamental issue here was whether the right of education is for the development of the individual or for the good of the state. The new concept of *Kyōiku-ken* began to be utilized as a counter-theory to the right of the State to educate people, to conduct education, to decide on its contents, and revise the education system for national development. In other words, in this situation the debate battlefield concerning the equality of opportunity between the conservatives and the JTU shifted from the social class issue—conflicts between rich families versus poor families over the opportunity for upper secondary school—to a somewhat abstract issue: conflicts between state instrumentalism and personal development in relation to the right of education.

After all, there are many possible reasons for the apparent lack of success of the CCE's reform proposals, in large part because there was no agreement within either the MOE or the conservative group on how to implement multi-tracking. Moreover, these proposals, many of which would have been expensive to implement, were issued just as Japan was being hit by the 1970s oil shock; the government did not have the resources it would have needed to respond to them. Although the Progressives opposed these proposals and the conservatives themselves had difficulty agreeing on them, de facto tracking at the post-compulsory level was already widespread by the time these proposals were issued. About a third of the nation's high schools were focused on college prep with no vocational offerings; another third had become almost exclusively focused on vocational subjects such as agriculture, business and shop. Only a third of the nation's upper secondary schools had offerings in both areas. By the mid 1980s nearly half of all upper secondary schools stressed pre-collegiate studies and only about a quarter of all such schools could have been called comprehensive.

Conclusion

Educational policy during the 1960s had adapted to respond to pressures generated by the LDP government and industrial circles for economic expansion and political stability. They regarded schooling as a powerful instrument of adaptation, necessary for Japan to advance in international economic competition. Perhaps the single most influential educational document of this period was the EDC's Report of 1963, which argued that it was imperative to reorganize both society and education on the basis of *Nōryokushugi* (the ability first principle). The report outlining NIDP included a special target of an 86,000 increase in the number of technical upper secondary school students. In 1966, the CCE went further in proposing such an emphasis on vocational upper secondary education as part of an official policy of "diversify by ability." Arguing that education should be given correspondent to children's ability, as required in Article III of the FLE, the CCE pointed to the need to consider the establishment of a mechanism for providing special training for students with special talents. It was the first time since the war that the MOE had called for elite education in such clear terms. Thus, the CCE as well as the MOE criticized the post-war single track 6-3-3-4 system as excessive egalitarianism and justified selection in the early stages of children's lives. The MOE, therefore, strongly opposed the JTU's egalitarian concept of equality of educational opportunity such as the upper secondary education for all movement.

On the other hand, progressives, led by the JTU, opposed most of these proposals both because they saw them as reflecting a business influence that was too narrow and utilitarian, and because the proposals to emphasize diverse tracks threatened the egalitarian concept of equal opportunity of the post-war 6-3-3-4 system. The JTU opposed, as discriminatory, the *Nōryokushugi* favored by conservatives. With the demands from many parents who wanted their children to go to upper secondary school, the JTU began to conduct the *zennyu* movement (upper secondary for all). Based on the assumption that children's abilities were not inherited, but acquired in their social conditions, the JTU formulated its own notion of "selection = discrimination" as a counter-principle against the *Nōryokushugi*. However, this new principle contained an element of reluctance to deal with the social class issue in education. Thus, because of the JTU's negative attitude toward dealing with class inequality in education, the social class issue began to disappear from the main area of the educational debate in Japan.

Notes

1. Keizai Shingikai (EDC), *Kokumin Shotoku Baizō Keikaku* (National Income Doubling Plan).
2. Keizai Shingikai (EDC), *Jinteki Nōryoku no Kōjō to Gijutsu no Koushin* (Improving Human Abilities and Encouraging Education in Science and Technology), in part II of the *Kokumin Shotoku Baizō Keikaku* (National Income Doubling Plan).

3. Keizai shingikai (EDC), *Shotoku Baizō Keikaku ni Tomonau Chōki Kyōiku Keikaku Hōkoku* (Report of Long-Term Educational Plan Accompanied with National Income Doubling Plan).

4. See in particular Hisaki, Suzuki and Imano, *Sengo Kyōiku Ronsou Shiroku*, vol. III, 401–13.

5. In 1962, the government passed legislation creating a system of nineteen technical colleges. These institutions, offering a five-year curriculum in a variety of industrial (and sometimes merchant marine) studies, were open to graduates of the lower secondary school. As of May 1983, there were 62 technical colleges with a total enrolment of 47,245 students, of whom 97.2 percent were male. Monbushō, *Outline of Education in Japan*, 13.

6. Monbushō, *Kokuritsu Kōgyō Kyōin Yōsei no Se'chi Touni Kansuru Ringi Sochi Hōan* (An Emergency Bill Concerning Teacher Training in National Technical Schools.

7. Kobayashi, *Society, Schools and Progress in Japan*, 96.

8. The Education Committee of the House of Representatives, 26 April 1961. The same view was expressed by Naitō Tosaburō, the vice-minister of education. See *Monbujihō*, No. 1016, April 1962.

9. In fact, the MOE issued *Kyōiku hakusho* (White Paper on Education): *Nihon no Seichō to Kyōiku* (Japan's Development and Education), on 5 November 1962. The title indicated that MOE was approaching education from the perspective of its links with policies designed to stimulate economic growth.

10. See *Monbujihō*, no. 993, May 1960; *Monbujihō*, no. 999, November 1960; *Monbujihō*, no. 1008, July 1961; and *Monbujihō*, no. 1016, April 1962.

11. During the 1980s, Nakasone Yasuhiro, a conservative LDP prime minister, used the same term in order to reform the education system in accordance with New Right ideology. For further details of Nakasone's educational reform during the 1980s, see Schoppa, *Education Reform in Japan*, 211–50; Goodman, *Who's Looking at Whom?*; Hood, *Japanese Education Reform, Nakasone's Legacy*; and chapter 5 of this book.

12. Kobayashi, *Society, Schools and Progress in Japan*, 104.

13. A typical expression of this assumption can be seen in Umene, *Nihon no Kyōiku Dōarubekika*; Umene, *Nihon no Kyōiku*; and Horio, *Gendai Nihon no Kyōiku Shisou*.

14. Keizai Shingikai (EDC), *Jinteki Nōryoku Seisaku ni Kansuru Tōshin* (Policies for Development of Human Abilities and in Pursuits of Economic Expansion). Useful information on the report is given by Inui, *Nihon no Kyōiku to Kigyō Shakai*, 38–76.

15. Keizai Shingikai (EDC), *Jinteki Nōryoku Seisaku ni Kansuru Tōshin*. This paragraph is quoted in Horio, *Educational Thought and Ideology in Modern Japan*, 345.

16. Keizai Shingikai (EDC), *Jinteki Nōryoku Seisaku ni Kansuru Tōshin* (emphasis added).

17. Ibid.

18. Ibid.

19. See Shimizu, *20 Nen Go no Kyōiku to Keizai*. Shimizu Yoshihiro was an educational sociologist at Tokyo University who took part in the EDC's policy-making.

20. The term *aku-byōdō* (excessive egalitarianism) has been often referred to by the conservative groups, particularly the LDP, to justify their firm belief in the Nōryokushugi principle. This view was reflected clearly in the article written by Asu no Kyōiku o Kangaeru Kai (Association for Considering Education in Future) which was set up in the LDP in the late 1960s with "Ko'kka Hyakunen no Tameno Shin-Kyōiku Sengen" (A Declaration of New Education for the Nation over the Next 100 Years), in *Bungeishunjū*, 92–126.

21. *Bungeishunjū*, 92.

22. Quoted in Horio, *Educational Thought and Ideology in Modern Japan*, 347.

23. Monbushō *Jinzai Kaihatsu Keikaku no Ritsuan to Nyūgaku Senbatsu Seido no Kaizen* (A Plan for Developing Human Capital and Reform of the Examination System).

24. Monbushō, *Jinzai Kaihatsu Keikaku no Ritsuan to Nyūgaku Senbatsu Seido no Kaizen* (A Plan for Developing Human Capital and Reform of the Examination System).

25. Kyōiku no Sengoshi Henshū Iinkai, *Kyōiku no Sengoshi*, vol. III, 56.

26. Monbushō, *Shōwa 36 nendo zenkoku chūgakkō i'ssei gakuryoku chousa ji'sshi yōkō* (Outline for Simultaneously Implementation of Nationwide Scholastic Achievement Test for Secondary School on Shōwa 36).

27. Horio, *Educational Thought and Ideology in Modern Japan*, 215.

28. Ibid.

29. For detailed arguments, see Kaneko, *Kyōiku-hō*. General explanations of the Japanese educational administration system are available in Kida, *Kyōiku Gyōseigaku*; Ichikawa, *Kyōiku Gyōsei no Riron to Kōzō*; and Uehara, *Kyōiku Gyōseigaku*.

30. Nikkyōso (Japan Teachers' Union), *Gakute Ji'sshi ni Kansuru Monbudaijin Eno Shitsumonsho* (Questions towards Minister of Education on Implementation of the Scholastic Achievement Test).

31. Kyōiku no Sengoshi Henshū Iinkai, *Kyōiku no Sengoshi*, vol. III, 62.

32. JSP, *Nihon Shakaitō no Gakuryoku Tesuto ni Taisuru Hihan to Taido* (Japan Socialist Party's Criticism against the Scholastic Achievement Test), 8 September 1962.

33. Thurston, *Teachers and Politics in Japan*, 210; and "Kyōiku no Mori" (Woods of Education), in the *Mainichi shinbun*, June 1965–March 1968.

34. The 39th Special Diet in House of Representatives on Educational Committee, 6 October 1961.

35. Nikkyōso (Japan Teachers' Union), *Watashitachi no U'ttae* (Our Complaint), 7 October 1961.

36. For example, in Iwate, Fukuoka, Hokkaido, Kyoto, and Kochi most schools did not administer the test. In other prefectures such as Aichi, Kanagawa, and Hyogo, disruption was less significant. See in particular Thurston, *Teachers and Politics in Japan*, 212.

37. See Marshall, *Learning to be Modern*, 191–92.

38. For further details of these trials, see Kaneko, *Kyōiku Hōgaku to Kyōiku Saiban*; and Kobayashi and Kaneko, "Kyōku Hanrei 100 Sen," *Jurist*, no. 41.

39. See in particular Kokumin Kyōiku Kenkyūsho, *Kokumin kyōiku* (National Education), vol. 10; and Hisaki, Suzuki, and Imano, *Sengo Kyōiku Ronsou Shiroku*, vol. 3, 108.

40. These figures are cited in Kyōiku no sengoshi henshū iinkai, *Kyōiku no sengoshi*, vol. III, 119.

41. Monbushō, *Shinsei Chugakkō Shinsei Kōtōgakkō Nozomashii Un'Eino Shisin*, 9, 112–13 (emphasis added).

42. Hisaki, Suzuki, and Imano, *Sengo Kyōiku Ronsou Shiroku*, vol. III, 100–22.

43. Nikkyōso (Japan Teachers' Union), *Kōkō Nyūshi Haishi, Zen'in Nyūgaku Undō no Hōshin* (Abolition of Entrance Examination in Upper Secondary School, A Policy of Upper Secondary School for All Movement).

44. See Kyōiku no Sengoshi Henshū Iinkai, *Kyōiku no Sengoshi*, vol. III, 122; and Komori, *Kōkō Seido Kaikaku no Sōgōteki Kenkyu*.

45. Zen-nyū Zenkyo, *Kōkō Zen'in Nyūgaku Mondai Zenkoku Kyōgikai Seimei*.

46. MOE's plan was that state schools should accommodate 0.67 million public and 0.43 million private out of 1.12 million students, which was the expected additional number of students, and that about 200 new state schools should be built. State schools agreed to increase the number of classes and the class sizes in order to meet the increase in the numbers of students; Kyōiku no Sengoshi Henshū Iinkai, *Kyōiku no Sengoshi*, vol. III, 85.

47. Monbushō, *Kōtōtgakkō Seito Kyūzō Taisaku to "Kōkō Zen-Nyū Undō" no Kahi* (A Measure for Suddenly Increasing the Number of Upper secondary School Students and Advisability of Upper Secondary School for All Movement).

48. Ibid.

49. Ibid.

50. Monbushō, *Kōkō Nyūshi Seido Kaisei Shōrei* (A Ministerial Ordinance to Reform the Entrance Examination of Upper Secondary School).

51. These strategies were experimentally worked out in Takaoka City in Toyama prefecture which was designed by the government as a New Industrial City based on a series of economic development plans. For further details of the 3-7 system and parents' opposition to the plan, see Tsukasaki Mikio and Tsukasaki Masako, *Kyōiku no Kikai Kintou Towa*.

52. Chūō Kyōiku Shingikai (Central Council on Education), *Kōki Chūtō Kyōiku no Kakujū Seibi ni Tsuite no Tōshin* (The Expansion and Adjustment of Education in the Final Stages of Middle-Level Schooling). The full content of this Chūō Kyōiku Shingikai (Central Council on Education) report is available in Sengo Nihon Kyōiku Shiryō Shūsei Henshū Iinkai, *Sengo Nihon Kyōiku Shiryō Shūsei*, vol. VIII, 70–83.

53. Chūō Kyōiku Shingikai (Central Council on Education), *Kōki Chūtō Kyōiku no Kakujū Seibi ni Tsuite no Tōshin* (The Expansion and Adjustment of Education in the Final Stages of Middle-Level Schooling). The full content of this Chūō Kyōiku Shingikai (Central Council on Education) report is available in Sengo Nihon Kyōiku Shiryō Shūsei Henshū Iinkai, *Sengo Nihon Kyōiku Shiryō Shūsei*, vol. VIII, 70–83.

54. Chūō Kyōiku Shingikai (Central Council on Education), *Kongo ni Okeru Gakkō Kyōiku no Sōgōteki na Kakujū Seibi no Tame no Kihonteki Shisaku ni Tsuite* (Basic Ministry of Education Guidelines for the Reform of Education) (quoted in Beauchamp and Vardaman, *Japanese Education since 1945*, 220).

55. Chūō Kyōiku Shingikai (Central Council on Education), *Kongo ni Okeru Gakkō Kyōiku no Sōgōteki na Kakujū Seibi no Tame no Kihonteki Shisaku ni Tsuite* (Basic Ministry of Education Guidelines for the Reform of Education) (quoted in Beauchamp and Vardaman, *Japanese Education since 1945*, 219).

56. Schoppa, *Education Reform in Japan*, 204.

57. Chūō Kyōiku Shingikai (Central Council on Education), *Kitaisareru Ningenzō* (On the Image of the Ideal Japanese).

58. Kosaka Masa'aki, *"Kitaisareru Ningenzō" ni Tsuite* (Concerning on the Image of the Ideal Japanese) (quoted in Sengo Nihon Kyōiku Shiryō Shūsei Henshū Iinkai, *Sengo Nihon Kyōiku Shiryō Shūsei*, vol. VIII, 53–57).

59. Horio, "Chūkyōshin Kaikaku Kōsō to Kokumin no Gakushū Kyōiku Ken."

60. Kariya, *Taishū Kyōiku Shakai no Yukue*, 153–97.

61. Quoted in Kariya, *Taishū Kyōiku Shakai no Yukue*, 176.

62. Ibid., 186.

63. *Kyōiku*, May 1962, 28.

64. This opinion is clearly reflected in the concept of *gakurekishugi* or "degreeocracy," considered later in this book.

65. This term is introduced by Kariya, *Taishū Kyōiku Shakai no Yukue*, 156.

66. Ibid., 177.

67. Ibid., 177–78.

68. There are many books that deal with *Kyōikuken*. See Kaneko, *Kokumin no Kyōikuken*; Nagai, *Kokumin no Kyōkuken*; Iizaki, *Kokumin no Kyōikuken*; and Namimoto, *Kyōiku Seisaku to Kyōiku no Jiyū*.

69. Nikkyōso (Japan Teachers' Union), *How to Reform Japan's Education: A Report of Nikkyōso—Council on Education Reform*, 38 (faithfully quoted from the contemporary translation) (emphasis added).

70. Ibid., 24.

5

From Human Capital to Market Values in Education, 1980s–Present Day

The two decades that followed the EDC's Report of 1963 were years of commitment to expansion of the education system as a part of the government's policy of public welfare and investment in public service. The demand for education and for general access to various sorts of high schools backs up the assumptions of two different reports of the CCE on secondary education (1966 and 1971), which regarded investment in education as a condition of economic growth. These decades showed the value placed on the development of human capital by government intervention and on the maximization of the ability of the nation's children by enhancing their opportunities and capitalizing on their talent.

This period came to an end in the 1980s with the appointment of the Ad-Hoc Council on Education (*Rinji kyōiku shingikai*), comprising both neo-liberals, who called for decentralization, and neo-conservatives, who called for tough steps towards centralization in order to recover the glorious days of the pre-war education system; both strands shared the view that government intervention and investment in education, as well as in other public services, should be decreased, calling for abolition of the welfare state and adoption of the market economy system in all public services. This had a direct effect on restructuring the education system during the 1980s. The Nakasone administration, from 1982 onwards, adopted an explicit policy of fostering market conditions in education and encouraging entrepreneurship in schools to raise private funds as well as the view that schools should be regarded as "cost centers."

Thus, whereas chapter 4 concentrated on the internal factors within the school system, which stimulated criticism and the campaign for government policies to diversify the secondary education system and curriculum, the aim of this chapter is to describe the various factors and ideology of the campaign at the macro level against the whole collective approach to social problems and the consequences of the new movements and ideas that finally brought an end to the human capital approach and were the basis of a new construction of education.

The Ad-Hoc Council on Education: *Rinji kyōiku shingikai*

More responsibility on the part of the individual, a more active role of private institutions in education, greater contribution to the community, and budget cuts for education, social welfare, and agriculture were all recommended in the 1980s by the second Ad-Hoc Council on Administrative Reform (*Rinji Gyōsei Chōsa-kai* or *Rinchō*). They distributed five reports in July 1983 outlining the context of the proposed reforms, which, in the realm of education, focused on self-study. These same proposals stated that minimizing class sizes, and making compulsory education budget cuts, etc. were not necessarily going to solve the problems within the education system, but would rather celebrate individual differences among students, which was what was needed to be done in order to improve the current situation.

The Ad-Hoc Council on Education (*Rinji kyōiku shingikai* or *Rinkyōshin*: AHCE) inherited the same belief in the mid-1980s.[1] The AHCE, which was set up in August 1984 as a supra-cabinet advisory committee to Prime Minster Nakasone Yasuhiro, embarked on discussion of education reform from a long-term perspective, rather than relying on the MOE's permanent CCE. To the end, the council made few concrete proposals, but was highly influential in setting an agenda for subsequent policy through its focus on key directions for education, notably internationalization (*kokusaika*), information technology (*jōhōka*), life-long learning (*shakai kyōiku*), and perhaps most fundamentally, a move towards liberalization (*jiyūka*).[2]

One of the declared purposes of the AHCE's proposed educational reform was to diversify the strictly egalitarian 6-3-3-4 system. This reconstruction of the system aimed to re-establish the high standards of attainment of the pre-war middle school, in order to select national elites effectively and triumph in international industrial competition. To achieve these goals, the AHCE advocated the adoption of market principles in education. In this regard the two key terms, *jiyūka* (liberalization; later replaced with *koseika*; individualization) and *tayōka* (diversification) came out of the council's deliberation process. As a matter of fact, these terms hold the key to tracing the concept of equal opportunity in education during this period and after. The *jiyūka* involves proposals for increasing competition in the compulsory sector of the existing education system. *Tayōka* meant ability-streaming and the introduction of elitism into the system. When seen in the context of the events that occurred during the deliberation of the council, it becomes possible to understand how these two ideologies could be joined together.

Jiyūka: Liberalization

The terms of liberalization and diversification were already seen before the council set to work from 1984. Nakasone together with Mori Yoshirō, the Minister of Education, became involved in the education reform debates in early 1983 and was very earnest about introducing these principles into the education system. In June 1983, Nakasone established a private commission, the Group for Discussion of Culture and Education (GDCE, *Bunka to Kyōiku ni Kansuru Kondankai*), for making blueprints of future reform in the education system based on these key words. For instance, the GDCE published "A Memorandum of Basic Concepts for Promoting Education Reform" in February 1984. This memorandum stated that "irrespective of different ideological standpoints, it is important to deny uniformity of schooling, to reconsider authorization of educational policies, and to introduce liberalization and diversification into fields of education as the principle of competition."[3] Similar viewpoints were also described in a report titled "Seven Recommendations to Revitalize School Education," proposed in March 1983 by the Kyoto Group for the Study of Global Issues (*Sekai o Kangaeru Kyoto Zaikai*, KGSGI), chaired by Matsushita Kōnosuke (president of National Panasonic) and many other leading businesspeople, as well as right wing academics and government figures.[4]

Two market ideas were now being discussed with regard to the education system. The idea was put forward that the school system would achieve better standards and greater efficiency for the same recourses if it was driven not by the educational authorities such as the MOE and the CCE but by consumers—in this case, parents. The idea was to establish a direct link between liberalization and diversification of the school system by extending education choice for parents and children, not in the egalitarian school system but in a flexible one. In the election campaign on 10 December, Nakasone finally showed his commitment to education reform with the declaration of the Seven-Point Proposals which were:[5]

1) to consider changing the present so-called 6-3-3 school education system;

2) to revise the upper secondary school examination system and discontinue reliance on test results as the main yardstick of students' academic success;

3) to revise the university entrance examination system;

4) to promote extracurricular activities, such as community service activities;

5) to reinforce moral education;

6) to encourage a more cosmopolitan outlook; and

7) to improve the quality of teaching staff by revising training and hiring programs.

The Bill for the establishment of *Rinkyōshin* became law on 7 August 1984, and it was finally established on 21 August.[6] With the establishment of the Ad-Hoc council, the CCE was suspended for three years.

As Schoppa pointed out, crucial to the council's early deliberation process on education reform was the introduction of the idea of liberalization, one of the issues most espoused by Nakasone, into the existing system. The underlying ideas of proposals by the GDCE and the KGSGI were indeed further developed and deliberately woven together by the council.

Central to the debate on liberalization of the education system was the battle over the balance between equality and freedom of choice. Koyama Kenichi believed that characteristics such as liberalization and vitality were crucial to bettering Japan's educational system. However, the MOE dominated, which in turn led to classic uniform ways of teaching being held in high regard. Koyama strove to introduce a more competitive spirit to the philosophy of teaching, arguing:

> Liberalization of education means a reexamination of the bureaucracy's policies of authorization, regulation, and aid, to take decisive action to introduce private-sector vitality into the sphere of education. For instance, it also includes the point of reforming Article IV and VI of the FLE.[7]

As a definite plan, he proposed that more attention be given to privately funded schools (i.e., *juku*: cram schools) in order to bring compulsory education up to a higher standard, a level in which other forms of education are officially acknowledged.[8] In this regard, the council emphasized the value of freedom, particularly of parental choice in education, as a means of achieving equality of educational opportunity, stressing competition between public and private sectors. Indeed, the whole point of the liberalization was that parents would seek to enroll their children in the better schools, and this would stimulate schools to compete (especially in the public sector), by offering new courses, new methods, and new forms of teaching. It would also ensure greater investment of effort by teachers in order to attract more parents. The result would be equal access to high quality compulsory schools. Koyama believed that this would form an incentive to keep the state schools lively, entrepreneurial, and attractive. However, liberalization is a term that focuses on skills/characteristics and abilities that are seen as inferior in terms of developmental quality by the educational system. In this way, the economy could respond to the demands and changes that were already occurring and those that were expected to occur in the future.[9] Thus, some of the AHCE members assumed that the market economy system would not only serve the interests of the free individual, but would also advance Japan's economic situation in the world.

However, Schoppa argued that the term *jiyūka* was largely stymied, mainly by older members of the MOE. One of the problems lay in the difference of goals among Nakasone and the education *zoku* (cliques of politicians with similar interests) and the MOE.[10] Nakasone hoped that the council would put forward proposals that would lead to a complete reform of the system, whereas some of the MOE and some within the LDP wanted the basic system to be maintained, with changes being made in a few areas only. The following reasons were given for the initial stance of opposition to liberalization: guaranteeing equal opportunity rights, maintaining and improving education standards that emphasized whole-person education, maintaining the nature of education, and guaranteeing neutrality and respecting the role of the government—all of which would be much more difficult for the MOE to ensure if liberalization took place. In the 1970s and the 1980s, Nakasone and his followers strongly supported liberalization. However, many in the LDP education *zoku* and the MOE were not convinced that the increased freedom would supply any kind of resolution to the problem of juvenile delinquency that seemed to be erupting throughout the nation. They criticized the council for its advocacy of liberalization at the compulsory level.

Moreover, those opposed to liberalization tended to consider this term abstract with fallacious ill-defined guidelines and inane aphorisms that could not possibly spark any kind of debate, let alone serious change. Supply-side competition, deregulation, and consumers' freedom of choice were a few of the economic-inspired notions that the JTU (*Nikkyōso*) strongly contested. However, these same ideas were exactly what the council was encouraging.

It is worth noting that in 1989 during the period covered by this chapter, the JTU broke into two organizations, one being the new JTU and the other the All Japan Teachers' Union (*Zenkyō*). Since 1989, the new JTU promoted the idea of compromise by both sides or *ayumiyori* (walking together) and gradually became supportive of the MOE's policies. According to Aspinall, this schism marked the end of an era for one of the largest unions in post-war Japan. The year of 1989 also marked the end of other eras. As Aspinall described:

> It was the year when the Berlin wall came down, heralding the end of the Cold War and the international ideological cleavage between capitalism and communism. It was also the year when the Liberal Democratic Party (LDP) lost control of the Upper House of the Japanese Diet for the first time since the party's formation. Such ideological and electoral watersheds have led observers of Japanese politics to talk about the end of the 1955 system.[11]

The 1995 system based its stability on the survival of two major camps: the conservative side, led by the LDP, and the progressive side, led by the JSP. The JTU, a strong supporter of what the JSP was attempting to accomplish within the educational system, witnessed a decline in the 1980s, bringing to an end the forlorn antagonism that existed, and hence, diminishing all hope of educational reform.[12] The JTU's compromising combined with the creation of the JSP and the LDP coalition government made any discussion about the "two camp" model redundant. The formation of a coalition government meant that the power teachers hold had been severely weakened and the future direction of the education system lay in the hands of the MOE and its allies. Ultimately, these obstructions not only from the MOE and some members of the AHCE, but also from the JTU did not deter Nakasone from putting his personal weight behind calls for introducing the liberalization principle into the school system.

Kosei Jūshi: Individuality and Freedom of Choice

As seen above, the discussion of liberalization within the council amid the uncertainty surrounding its meaning meant that more acceptable terms that still contained the original ideologies were sought. This process began during the debates of the council when liberalization was strongly linked with individuality, to the extent that some felt that the terms were being confused by the Council.[13]

By the time the council finally published its First Report Concerning Education Reform in June 1985, the supporters of liberalization in the AHEC had agreed to reduce its emphasis on *jiyūka* and accept a new phrase to describe the council's guiding philosophy: the goal of education for the twenty-first century was to have "an emphasis on individuality (*kosei jūshi*)." For instance the First Report said that "the 'Principle of Putting Emphasis on Individuality' is the fundamental principle" implicated in the future reform proposals.[14]

Within the Council's early discourse, complaints about existing education were made, and they took two main forms. In a world economy that was constantly changing with new and innovative ideas being the key to success, the Japanese education system did not seem to be promoting enough creativity. Other issues such as school violence (*kōnai bōryoku*), bullying, school refusal, and classroom breakdown (*ga'kkyū hōkai*) were also seen as contributing to the downfall within the educational system. There were various ideas on why these problems existed, but one was that uniform education was too strict and rigid and that a more relaxed, freeing environment needed to be implemented in order to encourage creative forward-thinking. The main emphasis in Japanese classrooms seemed to be on entrance exams alone. This only stifled students' unique abilities, which in turn led to issues of violence as stated earlier on.

Against this background, the council's Second Report, published in April 1986, developed the concept of individuality and contained very significant educational ideas that foreshadowed the trend in educational thought over the next decade. The Second Report insisted that:

> Standing on deep self-examination about the current educational issues, our nation's education recognizes the meaning of "completion of individuality" as a main purpose of education and must emphasize the importance of respect for the individual, individuality, freedom, independence, and self-responsibility.[15]

The council saw this new concept of individuality reform as the rejection of standardization, inflexibility, and ethnocentrism in the education system and it linked the concept to the idea that every student had to be given more choice through the schools' becoming more differentiated. In fact, Nakasone and some members of the Council thought that there was too much equality and not enough personality and individuality in the current education system. There was no doubt that the promotion of individuality and diversity were prescriptions with a very strong appeal for parents who had schoolchildren at the time.

One issue that was central to the individuality debate was the reform of the 6-3-3 system. Under this new concept of individuality, the Council made several recommendations under the heading "Diversification of Opportunities and Increase in Educational Routes" in the First Report, with a view to ending the existing standardized system of education. The three proposals enunciated in the First Report might be condensed into three categories:[16]

1) Liberalizing and Giving More Flexibility to the Qualifications for University Entrance: Based on the general perception that the opportunity for higher education should be as diverse and broad as possible, the government should consider, as soon as possible, concrete measures for granting university entrance qualifications to students who have completed an upper secondary course lasting three years or more at special training schools, as well as to other competent people.

2) Six-Year Secondary Schools in the Public Sector: Local governments, non-profit corporations entitled to set up formal schools, and other appropriate bodies should be allowed to establish 6-year secondary schools at their discretion. A 6-year secondary school should be a new type of school designed to contribute to the continuous and progressive development of the personality of students by combining the existing lower secondary and upper secondary education, and thus providing a consistent education suitable for adolescents.

Through this program it was expected that more educational freedom would result in a student having the opportunity to develop his or her own individual talents. Testing had always been the main focus of the Japanese educational system, but by allowing more independence, along with a lack of restrictions, educational levels were expected to rise. Aforementioned texts show that there was a split over how the educational system ought to be run. As we shall see later in this chapter, progressive educationists saw the 6-year secondary education programs that were implemented as a covert attack on egalitarian post-war pedagogy.

3) "Credit-System" Upper Secondary Schools: With a view to enabling students to have easier access to an upper secondary school education in accordance with their aspirations, schooling career, and living circumstances, a

new type of upper secondary school called a "credit-system" upper secondary school should be established that will recognize the acquisition of credits for each subject, as well as grant qualification for graduation from an upper secondary school course on the basis of the total number of credits each student acquires in various subjects.

In short, the concept was that students would be able to obtain more individuality when the school system was diversified with more choices. The AHEC reached a conclusion that as there was lack of individuality in the people, the apparent lack of creativity and abilities to judge and analyze had to be a result of the present 6-3-3-4 school system, and so the structure of the education system and contents of curriculums had to be improved. In other words, the Council attempted to apply its belief in the principle of market economy to education with the necessity for providing various types of secondary education, while endorsing them as measures for letting talented students break out of the rigid school-year structure and pursue their studies at a faster pace. The same access to the different types of secondary schools according to difference in ability and aptitude was thus demanded for children in the name of equal opportunity. In this context, the term equality was predominantly taken to require differentiation, and the meaning of opportunity was largely understood in terms of free choice, whereas identical treatment of children on educational grounds was considered a sort of inequality. Other areas of reform that had been recommended as a way of emphasizing individuality included the introduction of a system of grade skipping (*tobikyū*) (rather than students remaining with the same class whatever their progress), as well as attempts to provide more elite education. While some commentators might be skeptical about these measures, they had nonetheless achieved the status of common sense among not only the council members, but also the general public at the time. For instance Peter Cave argued that:

> There are no doubt many ordinary Japanese who see no particular distinction between the implications of the government's various policies, and welcome increased freedom and choice in all areas to do with schooling.[17]

Thus, as to the concept of equality of educational opportunity, which was now joined to individuality and freedom of choice, the AHEC and the CCE (as will be seen in a later part of this chapter) were able to "construct a reform program with relatively broad appeal, despite the inevitable criticisms [they have] faced, and [have] also been able to keep [their] policy options open for the future."[18]

Conservative Proposal

The AHEC's introduction of the new concept of emphasizing individuality in education, however, would cause tension between the simultaneous respect of the right of *individuals* to choose and the promotion of the interest of a nation as a *collective*; between the right of individuals to have more choice and the sovereignty of the nation to avoid collective stigmatization. The shift towards more individuality in education might threaten the achievement of too many of the goals associated with collective national control of people and tradition, which maintained a constant tension between these two needs—that of neo-liberalism and that of neo-conservatives.[19]

To avoid such tension, the council espoused that the term individuality not only meant the individual, but included the individuality of the family, the school, the community, and the country, all of which are linked.[20] In fact, the emphasis on individuality went along with an increased emphasis on moral education. The council stressed the need for a strong state in order to guide people's behavior, to protect the superior personal, cultural, and intellectual elites whose inherited values and standards had great and beneficial influence on public order, and to prevent authority and law from being undermined. It drew attention particularly to some areas (i.e., education) in which the state was seen to have lost authority and standards were deemed to have declined, posing real threats to public order. Therefore, a new concept was now being developed so that individuality in education would not lead to selfishness, immaturity, and a reduction in national tradition, which had often been associated with harming group harmony. In this regard, the council's main emphasis was on the diversification of schools rather than on the development of the individual. The AHCE seemed to be trying simultaneously to aspire to both greater diversity and greater conformity.

In fact, one of the most fundamental aims of the council's envisaged educational reform program was to make the more sensitive issue of revising the FLE moot. Nakasone was also known as a polemicist for his revision of the Japanese Constitution, particularly Article 9, which declares that the nation renounces war and the threat or use of force as a means of settling international disputes. Nakasone expressly linked his assertive approach to building up Japan's military strength with the issue of revising the Constitution and FLE. For him, as Schoppa acutely pointed out, the FLE, the 6-3-3 system, and the Constitution's peace clause "are all symbols of Japan's emasculation after the war."[21] In order to avoid prolonging this situation, he made revision of the FLE central to his neo-conservative strategies. As Schoppa and Hayao pointed out, Nakasone failed to implement the major part of his education reform program while he was in office. However, in his recent study, Hood suggests that Nakasone's initiatives on education should, on the whole, be regarded as a success rather than as a failure because of their influence on the long-term direction of education reform in the 1990s.[22] In fact, following the AHEC, the CCE's report of 1996 and the MOE's report of 2001 on policy direction effectively authorized many of Nakasone's viewpoints about the improvement of Japanese education outlined above.[23] Thus, as will be discussed later, Nakasone's effort to revise the FLE continued to influence the main arguments of the Education Reform National Conference's (*Kyōiku kaikaku kokumin kaigi*: ERNC) educational platform in the new millennium.

The Central Council on Education during the 1990s[24]

Since the mid 1990s, education has emerged as a key issue in a series of administrative reforms in Japan. Although it has perhaps failed to arouse quite as much passion as the controversy surrounding financial deregulation, it was made one of the top items of the political agenda by the LDP. At the time of writing, social changes such as globalization, information-based societies, technological developments, and the low birth rate had all affected modifications in the educational system that seem to directly fall in line with the AHEC's own philosophy. If we compared educational reform during the 1990s with that of the 1980s, we would see that instead of genuine concern over how children learn, structural and economical growth are what drove pedagogical reform. New educational policies were highly impacted by big corporations who felt that schools were not giving students enough freedom to enhance their own intellectual strengths. As these same companies looked at their current employees, they realized that in areas of management and human resources something new needed to be done in order to keep up with the new wave of multi-national markets.

"Ikiru-chikara": Power to Live

Once again, individuality was to become the means to solve the problems of standardization and supposed lack of creativity in the education system. In the next stage, the key words expressing these ideologies became *yutori* ("time for creative and exploratory activity") and *ikiru-chikara* (a direct translation is "power to live") in the CCE's reports during the 1990s. Five reforms stood out: curriculum reform and the Integrated Course, the introduction of the 5-day school week, the legitimating of grade-skipping, the establishment of 6-year state secondary schools, and the relaxation of school catchment areas. These reforms during the 1990s had particular significance because they affected almost all Japanese schoolchildren. This section will explore the direction of equality of educational opportunity in the 1990s by examining three reports issued by the CCE in 1991 and 1997.

The CCE, headed by Arima Akito, had been quick to develop a distinctive reform agenda for education. The 15th and the 16th sessions of the CCE, which commenced in April 1995, issued two reports titled "Concerning the State of Japanese Education on the Brink of the 21st Century." These reports addressed many issues faced by Japanese education and highlighted the need for the promotion of reform policies in many areas. Subjects that the reports identified as needing to be dealt with promptly include those that directly affected the current education scene, such as escalation of entrance examination competition ("examination hell"), school refusal, dropping out, and physical and psychological bullying (ijime) in schools, as well as the great social changes resulting from a drastic demographic decrease in the number of children, in addition to the internationalization of Japan and the spread of information media. The following were the main topics for the 16th session of the CCE:[25]

1) improving procedures for selecting school entrants at upper secondary and university level to reduce examination competition; and

2) Establishing a diversified education system that was suited to each individual's abilities and aptitude.

Deliberation on these two topics was based on (1) the importance of decreasing the mental pressure placed on children, recovering human dignity, and valuing ikiru-chikara;[26] and (2) equality of educational opportunity for the nation's pupils corresponding to their different abilities and aptitudes. After an exchange of opinions about the above points, the CCE submitted its second report to the MOE in June 1997, in which it offered various definite recommendations. First, the report proposed a variety of reforms relating to upper secondary and university entrance selection procedures, including promoting the diversification of selection criteria and the provision of multiple opportunities to take the entrance examination for national and local public universities. Improvements to career guidance in lower secondary schools were also recommended in order to reduce the excessive emphasis on a standard score (hensachi). Secondly, the report recommended special educational measures that would allow gifted upper secondary school students contact with university level educational research in special fields such as mathematics and physics. Thirdly, it recommended a new 6-6-year school system (6-year elementary school, and 6-year secondary school) at a small number of experimental schools, aiming at diversification of the state secondary education system.

It seemed that the same degree of emphasis was given to each of the three recommendations. Yet the CCE's major concern tended to concentrate upon the third recommendation, establishing a 6-year secondary school system. Indeed, the CCE's proposals concerning this issue provided a new definition of equality of opportunity, but there was also a risk that they could destroy the 6-3-3-4 system.

Equal Opportunity for the More Prestigious High School

Before examining the trend of the concept of equal opportunity during the 1990s, it is first necessary to clarify the concepts of equal opportunity in education to which the CCE had been pledged and to examine how these concepts had been discussed from the 1980s.

The battleground in the debate over the issue of equal opportunity after the period of educational expansion during the 1960s and the 1970s had gradually shifted (see chapter 4). The older form of the debate was essentially about inequality of chances for entry into upper secondary schools or universities. In fact, the numbers of students going to upper secondary school and university were, respectively, only about 50 percent and 6 percent at the end of the 1950s. Entering upper secondary school itself meant that the student had a relatively high academic background at the time. This older form of inequality faded with the quantitative expansion of the number of upper secondary schools and higher institutions.

Instead, signs of a growing new form of inequality in education emerged gradually from the late 1970s onwards. This new inequality arose among upper secondary students due to the more prestigious and highly ranked private schools becoming more and more dominant in terms of their pupils' success in the examinations for admission to the most prestigious universities, such as Tokyo University or Kyoto University. These private schools (and a few national schools) mostly followed the 6-year secondary education system. These schools charge considerable fees. In fact some research findings reveal that more than 10 million yen (approximately £40,000 at the time of writing) in annual income was needed to send one child to a 6-year private school and, in addition, cover the fees of *juku* and *yobikō*, which provided a better chance of entering a prestigious university.[27] Parents who could afford to send their children to more expensive institutions greatly improved those children's educational chances.

Against, this backdrop, criticizing a situation where an increasingly large proportion of entrants to Japan's most prestigious universities come from such a 6-year private school background, the 1991 report of the CCE stated that:

> It is not easy for children who do not live within the large cities and are not born in a family with above average income to access 6-year private secondary schools. It is against the principle of equality of opportunity in education that such schools, to which able [but poor] children cannot gain access, have existed for a long time.[28]

In reality, however, because of the ranking of upper secondary schools and then universities, students and their parents set their sights on as prestigious an upper secondary education as possible and, therefore, they would rather go to one of the few 6-year private schools than into a 3-3-year (3 years junior high school followed by 3 years high school) state secondary education system, not only in order to enter high-ranking universities, but also to avoid the entrance examination at age fifteen. The CCE reports in the 1990s condemned this situation for inducing many children to compete with others too early in life and for being the chief source of the problems (bullying, and examination hell, etc.) that were perceived as endemic in the Japanese education system. Therefore, the report of the 16th session of the CCE proposed the introduction of a 6-year state secondary school, with the aim of expanding student choices in the education system. The report attempted to establish this new school system on market principles, such as liberalization, flexibility, and diversification of the education system, all of which were espoused by the AHCE during the 1980s as discussed in the first part of this chapter. Equality of opportunity was again referred to in all the arguments for these principles, in which the CCE justified its proposal to introduce the new type of secondary school. In the foreword to the second report of the 16th session the CCE wrote:

> Since World War II Japan has experienced a dramatic spread and development of education based on the principle of equality of educational opportunity for all and has at the same time succeeded in maintaining its high standards and improving its quality. . . . However, since we have placed too much value not only on formal equality, but also on equality of outcome in education, it is true that our school system is uniform and inflexible. . . . We have not considered education which is suited to each individual's abilities and aptitudes. . . . As to the present education [6-3-3-4] system, *it is extremely important for us to promote diversification, liberalization, and flexibilization [(flexibility)] of the system and to expand more children's and parents' choices in order to provide each child with an education according to their different abilities and aptitudes.*[29]

Analysis of the deliberation of this proposal showed that the CCE's advocacy of the six-year state secondary school seemed to have stemmed from two major concerns: (1) the established 6-3-3-4 system was seen as failing to foster national talent at state schools and to compete with its counterpart at the secondary level, the private six-year secondary school; and (2) current educational issues such as bullying and school violence, which the CCE believed could be resolved by introducing market competition into the education system in order to force each school to improve its functioning and environment.

Thus, it is important to note that the CCE's proposal for introducing a 6-year state secondary education system must be seen as essentially continuous with the AHCE's proposals for reform in the 1980s, since the CCE viewed a diversified state school system as crucial in the larger process of the introduction of the market principle into the education system. Moreover, it is noteworthy that the gloss on equality insisted on for most of the post-war period by the conservatives—Nōryokushugi (diversification by ability)—was revived as one of the most important yardsticks in evaluating equality in education. In short, the CCE's proposal for this new type of school was an attempt to put into effect the principle of Nōryokushugi through diversification of the state secondary school system, an aim which had been pursued by the conservatives, the AHCE, and the CCE's precursors.

Debate over Introducing a 6-Year State Secondary Education System

The opposed points of view on the 6-year state secondary school were well represented by the arguments of two well-known Japanese educationalists, Yamazumi Masami, the president of Tokyo Metropolitan University, and Fujita Hidenori, former professor of sociology of education at Tokyo University.[30]

Yamazumi, a strong proponent of the 6-year state secondary school system, emphasized the necessity of fostering a national elite of *shinshi* (gentlemen). His view was largely supported by the LDP and business world. Against the background of scandals resulting in the arrests of high-ranking bureaucrats in the 1990s, Yamazumi expressed his desire for the development of a systematic and proper education to produce an elite in a continuous 6-year process at secondary level and to improve the moral character of bureaucrats. Identifying the urgent need to produce a national elite (although this is not clearly expressed in the report of the 16th session of the CCE), Yamazumi and other proponents of the 6-year state secondary schools claimed the following main advantages for them:

1) They would eliminate the severe examination hell to which 15-year-olds are subjected and secure *yutori* for all children;

2) they would minimize curriculum overlap between lower secondary school and upper secondary school;

3) they would enable systematic and long-term educational guidance to be conducted for each student according to their different abilities and aptitudes; and

4) they would encourage beneficial social integration and interchange between students of different ages (from 12 to 18 years) in the same school (for instance, clubs and other student activities would not be interrupted by preparation for entrance examinations).

In addition to the above, the proponents of 6-year schools insisted that the introduction of the new system was aimed at expanding educational opportunities and enabling parents to make their own decision on the right and desirable school for their child. As already pointed out, this approach was in keeping with the market idea of giving a greater power of choice to consumers—in this case, the parents. From the 1980s onwards, parental choice had become a central plank of conservative education policy, not necessarily only for educational reasons, but also because the conservatives had become increasingly captivated by the market principle. The reports of the CCE in the 1990s strengthened this trend by proposing the creation of a new state secondary school system based on competition not only between private schools and national 6-year secondary schools, but also between state schools. This was regarded as the main tool to restore high standards in state secondary schools. Their assertion was based on the assumption that state secondary schools would be self-correcting and self-renewing institutions, produce a national elite effectively, and succeed in competition with the private 6-year schools. Thus, under the principle of parents' freedom of choice, the introduction of the new school was reaffirmed as an important measure to enable state schools to recover from their alleged discouraging state and to encourage local effort to improve secondary schools in each area.

On the other hand, Fujita, a fierce opponent of the CCE's current educational reform, was skeptical about the advantages of the new secondary school, and defended the present 6-3-3-4 system. Asserting that "the CCE's proposal of the 6-year state secondary school would destroy the equality it promises," Fujita insisted:

> It is nothing but a deception that the CCE wants to introduce the 6-year secondary school for the sake of mitigating the examination hell and ensuring *yutori* for children. . . . The members of the CCE, educationists, and the proponents of the reform only consider the advantages for students within large cities. If the number of 6-year state secondary schools increases at the provincial level, the problem of examination hell which affects Tokyo will inevitably spread to the provinces. . . . Overall, the proposal just induces the state secondary schools to participate in the examination race along with the private secondary schools.[31]

Fujita came out against the introduction of the proposed secondary system for the following reasons:

1) entrance to the 6-year secondary school would inevitably come to be based more on academic ability than on an assessment of all-round character, experience, and motivation and would consequently lead to an acceleration of competition at the primary school level;

2) the 6-year secondary school would inevitably be generally recognized as an elite school and the curricula in the school would become examination-oriented;

3) transfer at 15 years from the present 3-year lower secondary school to the 6-year school would be difficult due to problems of curriculum, administration, and capacity;

4) transport arrangements would be complicated because the new school would recruit its pupils from a wide area with various school districts; and

5) there were great physical and mental disadvantages rather than advantages, brought about by the close association of children in a 6-year secondary school who differed in age, physical development, and intellectual ability, that were recognized in several volumes of psychological and sociological research findings.

In particular, Fujita asserts that the introduction of this new secondary system would run entirely counter to the effort to reduce the examination hell; rather, it would mean much earlier selection, as in the pre-war education system. He pointed out that, despite their use of the slogan *"jūgo no haru o nakasuna!"* (Don't make children cry in the spring at age 15), the proponents of the 6-year school could ensure *yutori* (free time or freedom from the pressures of the selection examination) only to the handful of pupils who were in the 6-year school track. Thus, Fujita concluded that there was no valid educational reason for introducing such a system unless the members of the CCE took proper measures to meet the afore mentioned objections.

A Critical Moment for Post-war Japanese Education

In addition to the predictable side-effects spelled out by Fujita, there was fairly general agreement among Japanese progressive educationists[32] that the CCE's proposal of a new type of state secondary school would be seriously destructive of the democratic elements in post-war Japan's education for the following reasons: (1) it would cause the present 6-3-3-4 system to collapse; (2) it would open the possibility of freedom of choice at the compulsory level; and (3) it would crystallize social class distinctions and differences within state secondary education at an early stage.

(1) The Potential Collapse of the 6-3-3-4 System

First, the introduction of the 6-year state secondary school constitutes a blueprint for ending the existing 6-3-3-4 system of education. The CCE's proposal diversified the existing secondary education system into two different tiers: on the one hand, the 3-3 year lower and upper secondary schools, with entrance examinations for entry to upper secondary; and on the other hand, the 6-year schools which would conduct an entrance examination at age 12, with each school recruiting pupils from a wide range of school districts.

What the opponents of the proposal most feared was the emergence of a disparity in social esteem between the present 3-3 year secondary schools and the new 6-year schools. It seemed to them impossible to ensure the validity of the logic of the separate but equal ideology which the CCE's report strongly emphasized. After the example of the Gokase 6-year secondary school in Miyazaki, which was established in 1994 as an experiment, there was no doubt that the new 6-year secondary school would be given preferential treatment, that was to say, higher funding, a higher level of investment in facilities, and better qualified teachers, and would consequently gain a better reputation than the state schools.[33] Since the 6-year schools would be expected to be elite schools, as Fujita suggested, it was evident that so long as children were segregated into the present

3-3 system, most of the nation's children would continue to go on to 3-3 system schools and would suffer from a stigma stemming from the higher academic status of the 6-year school.

Moreover, the disparity between state secondary schools would intensify the severe competition at the primary education level, which had already been identified among those entering 6- year national and private schools. This would be inevitable unless the CCE could devise non-competitive selection procedures for entry to the new secondary school. Thus, as Fujita indicated, "the relationship between the present 3-3 year system and the new 6-year system in secondary school will not be parallel but vertical or hierarchical" and this would reduce the democratic character of the 6-3-3-4 system.

(2) Freedom of Choice at the Compulsory Education Level

Secondly, the creation of the new 6-year school system would open up for parents the possibility of choice between schools at the compulsory education level. This would be an epoch-making moment in the history of Japanese education. Under the School Education Law, parents at the time were not allowed to choose among secondary schools, except for the few national secondary schools, which accounted for a tiny minority of children. Which elementary schoolchildren went to which secondary school was prescribed by the law. It, therefore, seemed necessary to amend the relevant provision if choice were to be given only to the small number of entrants of the new state school at the compulsory education level and not to the majority, i.e., children going on to the 3-year school under the existing law.

Thus a new issue of inequality of educational opportunity would emerge between children in the different tracks in the same state secondary system. It would be surprising if the majority of pupils excluded from the 6-year school track and their parents did not complain about not having the same right to choose a school outside their school zone as the fortunate minority had, in spite of the fact that they were in the same compulsory state secondary system. Next, they would insist on the same right to choose within the 3 year state system beyond their school districts. This would lead all the way down the road to a market system in education, offering the parents (customers) a choice between compulsory secondary schools as commodities. There were two possible types of request: most requests, coming from the entire social class spectrum, would arise from the wish to avoid schools in areas of economic and social deprivation and enter schools that had fewer socio-economic problems. Moves to non-adjacent schools would involve travel over considerable distances for children from families where the parents were able to finance the transportation costs to schools in middle class areas and areas where a high proportion of parents had been through higher education.

Moreover, equal opportunity for upper secondary education would also emerge as a new issue in education. That is to say, the pupils on the 3-year school track would have to take an entrance examination in order to advance to the upper secondary school at the age of 15, while the pupils on the 6-year track did not have to do so. As the number of the 6-year schools increased, the new system would undoubtedly seriously threaten the principle of equality of opportunity and students' ability to enter the upper secondary school of their choice. Thus, the introduction of the 6-year school would not only create discontent with the 3-year system among parents and students, but also make the relevant education laws gradually lose their legal ground to regulate freedom of choice at the compulsory education level.

(3) Expanding Social Class Inequalities in Educational Opportunity in the State Secondary Education System

Finally, a more powerful criticism voiced by those opposing the introduction of 6-year schools concerned the question of whether or not this proposal promoted equality of opportunity for different social strata. Indeed, they were anxious about the inevitable emergence of a definite correlation between family background and success in gaining entry to the 6-year school.

Since it is difficult for young students to make an important decision at the age of 12, the choice of whether they went to the 3-year school or the new 6-year school was highly dependent on their parent's opinions and decisions. In fact, a growing body of sociological and pedagogical research findings revealed that differences in scholastic achievement and consequent advancement of children could be explained by differences in the degree of motivational, linguistic, and other cultural continuities/discontinuities between family and school, or institutionally by teacher's biased treatment of and attitudes towards children of different social classes.[34] For instance, some sociological findings claimed that the proportion of Japanese pupils attending prestigious higher institutions in education varied according to the father's occupation, academic background, and income, and that this had remained unchanged since the war, despite the general increase in the percentage of children in higher education regardless of social origin.[35]

Therefore, as Fujita predicted, the 6-year state secondary school might promote stratification of the state secondary education system along the lines of social class, a situation that already existed in the prestigious 6-year national and private schools. Even if the level of children's academic performance were the same at the primary education level, the higher the parents' occupation, academic background, and income, the more likely the child was to be given the opportunity to go to the newly established 6-year secondary school. It was clear that the opportunity to choose a secondary school at an early stage in life would not aid children from the lower social classes whom the provisions of the FLE was purportedly intended to help. Thus, the new secondary school would challenge the principle of equality of opportunity in the existing education system, and family background would still remain a critical factor determining pupil's eligibility for such a school, without any remedial treatment for children who were able, but had a poor family background.

Revising the Fundamental Law of Education[36]

Japan's educational reform in the new millennium began in the context of a total examination of post-war education (sengo kyōiku no sōtenken). Former Prime Minister Obuchi Keizō held the view that the existing education system was imposed by the American Occupation authorities, and wanted drastic changes through the revision of the 1947 Fundamental Law of Education (FLE) or Kyōiku kihonhō, which defined the basic right of the people to receive education in accordance with the spirit of the new Constitution (see Chapter 2 of this study).[37] On numerous occasions, politicians of the LDP, including Obuchi, had criticized the FLE for its failure to champion traditional Japanese values. Obuchi wanted educational reform based on an inquiry by a private advisory body (similar to the AHCE in the 1980s), rather than relying on the CCE which operated within limits imposed by the Ministry of Education, Culture, Sports, and Technology (MOE).[38] In setting up such a private body, Obuchi hoped that the inquiry would be more independent of the CCE and that the MOE would bring about the same kind of large-scale proposals for changes that he had seen in the AHCE's previous attempts in the 1980s.

The Education Reform National Conference (ERNC) or Kyōiku kaikaku kokumin kaigi, set up in March 2000 to meet the needs of Obuchi's education reform plan, was quick to develop a distinctive reform agenda. The ERNC's membership was dominated by representatives of the business sector, the bureaucracy, and Obuchi's own intellectuals, and included very few progressive educationalists. Ezaki Reona, the chairman of the panel, was a Nobel Prize winner for physics in 1973, which demonstrated the link between the business sector and the state education system. On 27 March 2000, the panel began its deliberations, asserting the need for reform policies in many areas of Japanese education. Issues directly affecting the contemporary educational scene, such as an increase in the number of dropouts or those refusing to attend school (tōkō kyohi), and bullying in schools, were identified by the panel as requiring immediate consideration.[39] However, the panel was more concerned about the revision of the FLE and proposed to enact a new law. As discussed later in this section, the ERNC's proposal for a new law could threaten the democratic ideals of post-war Japanese education.

Gist of the ERNC's Proposals for Education Reform

When Prime Minister Mori Yoshirō assumed power after Obuchi's sudden death in May 2000, he announced his intention to proceed with Obuchi's education reform by cooperating with the new panel. The running themes of the ERNC's discussion were cultivation of patriotism, respect for Japanese history and traditional culture, and international coexistence. After one year of deliberation, the panel released its final report on 22 December 2000 and then disbanded. Its core recommendations were:[40]

1) revision of the FLE;

2) re-examination of history textbooks and introduction of "new perspectives" into Japanese history;

3) introduction of "volunteer activities" as national service for all students from elementary to high school;

4) an increased emphasis on moral education;[41]

5) reform of the 6-3-3-4 system and establishment of a diversified education system which was suited to each individual's abilities; and

6) implementation of "special educational measures" that would allow gifted upper secondary school students to experience university-level education research in a scientific field.

Some feared that the first four recommendations, if implemented, would result in neo-nationalist initiatives, aimed at strengthening the sense of belonging to the nation-state. The last two, however, were designed more as tools to maintain Japan's superiority in the global economy by exploring the ways in which creative elites could more readily be identified and nurtured at a younger age. It seems that the same degree of emphasis was given to each of the six recommendations. Yet, the ERNC's concern tended to concentrate upon the first recommendation, revision of the FLE. While the panel's interim report submitted in September 2000 only called for the necessity of a national debate on the FLE, the final report went one step further and called for a revision of the law.

Debates on the Issue of the Revision of the FLE

There is no doubt that the ERNC's proposal to revise the FLE was an attempt to reorganize the post-war educational institutions, an aim that had been pursued by previous generations in the conservative camp. On the other hand, the conservatives' intense antagonism towards the democratic principles of the FLE was matched by the degree to which the JTU developed support for them (see chapters 2–4). Their confrontation over this issue continues to the present day.

The opposing points of view on the issue of revision of the FLE were well represented by the arguments of Machimura Nobutaka, a former LDP minister of education and a significant figure in the ERNC, and Sakakibara Takekazu, chairperson of the JTU. Against the background of the suicide of a high school principal in Hiroshima,[42] Machimura, a proponent of FLE revision, emphasized the necessity of fostering a "Japanese ethnic culture and identity" as follows:

> If we review our post-war education, we cannot avoid recognizing that the system grounded in the ideals embodied in the FLE is deficient in a number of important areas which are needed to successfully preserve Japan's long traditions and which are appropriate to Japan's spiritual uniqueness. . . . These deficiencies directly lead to the problems in today's education issues.[43]

Analysis of the deliberation on the ERNC's comments suggests that its advocacy of FLE revision stemmed from two major concerns: (1) existing educational issues such as bullying and school violence, which the panel believed could be resolved by creating new legislation and by introducing volunteer activities designed to introduce systematic moral and patriotic education into the school curriculum in order to improve pupils' sense of ethics; and (2) the belief that the established 6-3-3-4 system was failing to foster national talent at state schools because Article 3 of the FLE placed too much emphasis on formal equality in education.[44] As far as (2) was concerned, the ERNC recommended a new "4-4-4" or "6-6" school system at a small number of experimental schools, aiming at diversification of the state secondary education system. Table 5.1 lists the relevant features of the pre-1945 Imperial Rescript, the FLE, and the ERNC's proposed legislation, and identifies the clear similarities and differences among the three.

It is noteworthy that the inculcation of tradition and Japanese ethnic identity emphasized for most of the post-war period by the conservatives was re-evaluated as one of the most important yardsticks for educational reform in the twenty-first century. Thus, ERNC's proposal to revise the FLE was an attempt to move away from the democratic principle in the post-war education system back towards nationalistic elements in the pre-war Imperial Rescript system.

On the other hand, Sakakibara, an opponent of educational reform as convinced by the ERNC, was skeptical about the revision of the FLE. Asserting that "there might be some political conspiracies behind the panel's proposal for revising the FLE," Sakakibara stated that:

> Ongoing education reforms conducted by the politicians and scholars who have critical views of post-war democratic education . . . would foster an exclusive

Table 5.1. Comparison of the Characteristics of the Imperial Rescript, the FLE, and the ERNC's Proposed Legislation[45]

	Imperial Rescript	The FLE	The ERNC's PL
Legal Subject	Emperor	Whole People	State
Principle	Imperialism	Democracy	Neo-Nationalism
Ethos	Ultra-Nationalism Militarism	Pacifism Egalitarianism	Neo-Conservatism Neo-Liberalism
Aims	—preserving national polity	—a more equal, more homogeneous society	—preserving the high standard of education
	—increasing loyalty to Emperor	—reduction of social inequality	—fostering of elites for state instrumentalism
	—inculcating national morality	—development of the child's qualities as a citizen	—re-inculcation of Japanese culture and traditional values
Structure of System	—class-based, multi-track system	—6-3-3-4 system, based on U.S. model	—diversified system, based on merit
School Ethos	—a hierarchy of merit	—egalitarian	—a hierarchy of merit
	—separation between boys and girls schools	—co-operative, pluralistic, permissive	—competitive
	—fostering people as servants of the emperor	—standing against the demands of the occupational structure	—geared to more efficiently meet society's need for trained manpower
Curriculum	—imperial subjects	—common curriculum	—highly varied
	—moral training-centered	—delayed specialization	—early specialization
Consciously Opposed to	Western thought	Imperial Rescript	The FLE

Sources: Marshall, *Learning to be Modern*, 51–142; Schoppa *Education Reform in Japan*, 1–52; and Monbushō *The Education Reform Plan for the 21st Century, the Rainbow Plan, the Seven Priorities Strategies.*

ethnocentrism and "Liberal Schools of History" which seek to establish the spiritual foundations of the Japanese State in the minds of the people. . . . These policies would contribute to creating an atmosphere in which the Japanese people affirm war as a justifiable tool of self-defense.[46]

Sakakibara and other critics came out against the LDP's proposed education reforms for various reasons. In their view, the ERNC's proposed FLE would:

1) allow the introduction of volunteer activities and moral education to encourage loyalty to the state;

2) allow the state to compile de facto Liberal School of History[47] textbooks in order to construct a prejudiced Japanese national identity;

3) support the view that the national school system should function almost exclusively for producing and differentiating human resources to meet changes in the industrial structure;

4) privatize higher education with the aim of making higher education open, and directly connected, to private companies;

5) increase the MOE's control over school administration and teachers;

6) release the state from its due responsibility for bearing the cost of educating its people, by conducting arbitrary priority-based distribution of budgets and increasing the education costs borne by individuals.[48]

In particular, they asserted that the ERNC's assumed construct of Japanese national identity and traditional culture, which was presented as comprising primordial features of the ethnic Japanese, remained problematic. They insisted that such a construct was accepted neither by many Japanese people, nor by the people of East and South East Asia who were reminded of Japanese ethnocentric ideology propagated during World War II.

In addition, another powerful criticism voiced by those opposing the revision of the FLE concerned the question of whether or not the ERNC's proposal promoted equality of opportunity for different social strata. Indeed, critics were worried that the panel's measures of diversifying the school system to address freedom of choice or individual differences had been directed principally towards high achievers or students with special talents, with little reference made to children with other special needs (e.g., low-income, disability, minority status). Furthermore, critics insisted that the introduction of a new diversified school system (i.e., a 6-year state secondary system) would run entirely counter to the effort to reduce examination hell: rather, it would mean much earlier selection, as in the pre-1945 education system. They argued that entrance to the 6-year secondary school would inevitably come to be based more on academic ability than on an assessment of all-round character, experience, and motivation, and would consequently lead to an acceleration of competition at the primary school level. Thus, opponents concluded that there were no valid reasons why revision of the FLE should deal with the educational issues unless the members of the panel first took proper measures to meet the above objections.

Political Parties' Responses to the ERNC's Final Deliberation

Debate on the ERNC's final report and proposed FLE revision had recently been heated, with a clear divide between the ruling coalition and the opposition parties as illustrated in Table 5.2.

Officials of the coalition partners—the LDP, New Kōmeitō and Hoshutō (New Conservative Party)—basically agreed with the recommendations of the final report. However, while the LDP and Hoshutō, wanting to revise the FLE and also introduce one year of "voluntary" service based on the panel's recommendations, consequently submitted a bill at the Diet session in the summer of 2001, New Kōmeitō (backed by the lay Buddhist organization *Sōka Gakkai*) was less than enthusiastic about these two aspects. Shinzaki Takenori, the party leader, made a turnabout. Mori's nationalistic rhetoric about Japan being a divine nation (*kami no kuni*) convinced Shinzaki that the LDP members would reform even the basic precept of religious neutrality in the post-war education system. At the same time, some members of New Kōmeitō had expressed anxiety that other religious groups were returning to the LDP fold because of the hugely popular Prime Minister Koizumi Junichirō. Thus, although New Kōmeitō was initially willing to support the panel's report, it too demanded certain concessions.

The opposition parties, especially Shamintō (Social Democratic Party) and Kyōsantō (Japanese Communist Party) rejected any change in policies through review of the law by the coalition cabinet and strongly criticized the final report for its potential to broach the even more sensitive issue of constitutional revision. If the ERNC was meant as an attempt to achieve such a reform, the two

Table 5.2. Political Points of View Concerning the ERNC's Education Reform

	Revision of the FLE	Compulsory Youth Service
LDP	○	○
New Kōmeitō	—	△
New Conservative Party (Hoshutō)	○	○
Democratic Party (Minshutō)	△	△
Liberal Party (Jiyūtō)	○	○
JCP (Kyōsantō)	×	×
Social Democratic Party (Shamintō)	×	×

○ agree   × disagree   △ undecided/other

Source: Asahi Shinbun, 23 December 2000.

parties would stand ready to obstruct Diet proceedings. However, another opposition party, the Liberal Party (Jiyūtō) had signaled a positive attitude toward the final report. Fuji Hirohisa, a chief cabinet secretary of the party, commented that the FLE should be revised to make it more adequately account for the importance of tradition, culture, and education at home. Much of the Jiyūtō's attitude toward the final report can be summed up in party leader Ozawa Ichiro's evident desire to turn Japan into a *futsū no kuni* (normal nation)—one that had a truly independent military and a "self-made constitution."

Finally, the Democratic Party of Japan (Minshutō: JDP), the main opposition party, was caught in the difficult position of not wanting to be criticized along with the Social Democratic Party and the Japanese Communist Party for opposing the proposals of the final report, but not wanting to take any responsibility for approving all of them, either. In fact, the party had still not decided on whether it would call for a revision of the FLE or not. The major dilemma facing the JDP was mostly the result of political considerations inside the party. JDP leader Hatoyama Yukio and some other members had not outwardly opposed the panel's proposals and wanted to assume joint responsibility for a revision of the law. On the other hand, the few former socialists within the party were already clamoring for it. The latter wanted to use the report for a confrontation with the ruling coalition. In this situation, rather than opposing the report outright, Minshutō had come out in favor of other activities that did not support the law's revision, but rather stressed the importance of life-long learning and the educational environment. Thus, the issue of revising the FLE had been a dilemma for Minshutō, with divided internal party opinion making it difficult to lay out an unambiguous position.

Koizumi's Attitude to the Current Education Reform

To conclude this chapter, it is certainly tempting to observe Koizumi's attitude to the ERNC's final proposals as illustrative of the existing educational debate over the FLE.

Following the LDP's landslide victory in the Upper House election on 26 April 2001, Koizumi Junichirō was appointed as prime minister. Soon after, the Koizumi administration poised itself to embark on a series of structural reforms (*kōzō kaikaku*). Koizumi's pledge to restore fiscal discipline by slashing traditional public works spending and reallocating limited budget resources formed the cornerstone of his "reform with no sacred cows" (*seiiki naki kaikaku*) agenda. He intended to overhaul the bureaucracy and reform the legal system. According to public opinion surveys conducted by newspapers, Japanese people were pleased that the Koizumi cabinet was determined to execute the structural reforms. Consequently, in its early days the cabinet's support ratio hovered around 80 percent, an all-time high.

As expected, education had come to the forefront of the political agenda. It might be said that the ethos of Koizumi's educational reform epitomized a combination of neo-liberal and neo-conservative ideologies, resembling those of Nakasone in the 1980s. An example of Koizumi's neo-liberal thinking was his stress on the need for a forum to discuss whether or not the running of national universities should be privatized to improve their structure. His neo-conservative leanings were evident in his consent to take over the ERNC's idea of education reform. This latter point clearly showed that the basic stance of the Koizumi cabinet was in line with that of the former Mori Cabinet. For instance, at the first meeting of the new cabinet on 26 April 2001, Koizumi stated:

> This cabinet is striving to create education reform that cultivates awareness and pride in Japan's traditions and culture, as well as an appreciation of the meaning of being Japanese. On the other hand, such reform also should facilitate deeper understanding of international society. Both education and judicial system reform remain priorities for this cabinet. I am committed to addressing these issues, and I implore you to make every effort to enable the expeditious passing into law of the legislation currently being submitted to the Diet.[49]

Koizumi went on to clarify his general stance on the revision of the FLE in a speech to the 151st session of the Diet on 7 May 2001:

> Educational reform is necessary in order to engender in youth both pride and self-awareness as Japanese, as well as to help develop skills critical for rebuilding Japan. My goal is to promote a national debate on how to proceed with a review of the Fundamental Law of Education.[50]

As is clear from the above two statements, there is no doubt that Koizumi wanted to amend the FLE. As mentioned in previous sections, the issue of revising the FLE had always been closely related to what national traditions and culture were thought necessary to be fostered in future citizens through the education system, so that Japan would be capable of responding to the demands and changes that were already occurring and expected in the future. Indeed, what was essentially the AHCE's neo-conservative agenda of nationalism was being echoed fifteen years later by Koizumi.

An important point to note here is that Koizumi's "reform with no sacred cows" was also concerned with the total reform of the post-war education system in general and the revision of the FLE in particular, and that these would attempt to symbolically break the taboo against sacrosanct post-war institutions, thereby paving the way for a revision of the Constitution's peace clause. Like Nakasone, at the first meeting of the new cabinet, Koizumi also professed his intention to revise Article 9 of the Constitution in order to recognize the Self-Defense Forces as armed forces. Moreover, the terrorist attacks on the United States on

11 September 2001 accelerated this trend. In order to be capable of responding to future terrorist threats, Koizumi had increasingly recited the necessity of revising or at least reinterpreting Japan's limited role in international peacekeeping efforts under the Constitution. Indeed, many inside and outside Japan started to believe that for the nation to be a more responsible actor in the international community, it had to "show the flag" rather than just send money from a safe distance, as in the case of the Gulf War and, for example, play a more active part in international peacekeeping operations such as providing rear-echelon logistical support to U.S. troops or a multinational force in the event of retaliation.

Against this backdrop, the debate over revising the FLE since the 1990s had entered a new phase. The older form of the debate was essentially about the FLE's deficiencies in fostering Japanese traditional morality and faithfulness to the state and in helping to solve serious educational problems such as bullying in schools. Instead, a new public sentiment was emerging which held that the inexorable trend towards Japan undertaking international duties against terrorism made the nation's diplomatic interests and the revision of the FLE more and more inseparable. Furthermore, these signs of a new perspective could enable Koizumi to use the arguments for revising the FLE as a strategic maneuver to facilitate changing the interpretation of Article 9 of the Constitution, so that a retaliatory operation could be brought within the definition of an emergency outside an area surrounding Japan.[51] Thus, the Koizumi cabinet's administrative reform hoped for a prompt solution to these problems and was starting to draw up its own education reform plans for 2002 with a view to dismantling pacifism in the FLE.

The legislation to revise the FLE was finally passed on 22 December 2006. The revised FLE changed the nation's post-war education system. Academics warned of the possible negative effects of the revised law on education, especially because of the influence it gave to the central government.[52] The revision also opened up possibilities of stifling efforts by teachers to improve education, molding children according to state values, and intensifying competition in education. The Education Ministry failed to form a consensus and familiarize the public with the reasons for the legislation. Changing the Fundamental Law of Education without public consensus damaged education and the way students were taught, creating the danger that education would become just a mechanism to inculcate the will of the state and produce children who lack autonomous judgment and critical minds.

Conclusion

The policy of educational expansion, which in the 1960s and 1970s was regarded as an investment in human capital and therefore as a contribution to economic growth, came to an end with the emergence of the AHEC in the 1980s, which was particularly due to the impact from the advocacy of neo-liberalism. This new view expressed, on the macro level, disappointment with the failure of the collective approach to social problems and called for a radical change of the old economic and educational policy and order. Subsequently, the new ideas became the basis of fundamental changes of educational values which inevitably affected the existing 6-3-3-4 school system. The Nakasone administration fostered the neo-liberal and the neo-conservative policy of coexistence of liberalization and centralization under the same umbrella. Liberalization or individualization based on market forces was a means of creating diversity and differentiation between schools, while centralization measures were used by the successive LDP governments and the CCE to ensure that this liberalization developed in the right direction.

The liberalization process first advocated by the AHEC developed gradually by the CCE reports during the 1990s in two main phases: first by individualization and secondly by diversification. This process was based on market rules and the assumption that better quality would be achieved through freedom of choice, autonomy, and entrepreneurship, and that state schools should not expect to rely any longer solely on government initiatives, but also on their self-correcting and self-responsibility. Increased freedom in the curriculum, the 5-day school week, 6-year state secondary schools, grade-skipping, and relaxation of the school catchment area were justified under the slogan *kosei jūshi* (individuality).

For tracing the shift in the major concepts of equality in education, the concept of individuality would contain significant elements: on the one hand, the repudiation of the popular logic of providing equal opportunities of receiving education according to children's ability, and on the other, the reinterpretation of the meaning of equal opportunity. This was accomplished by proposing the new concept of opportunities for individualization of each child, which used the term "equality of free choice."

The CCE's series of reports in the 1990s would conclude an era of almost four decades of attempts by conservatives to create an elite track in the present 6-3-3-4 system by introducing the 6-year state secondary school system as a step towards a new order in which state school standards could be restored. Yet, as analyzed in this chapter, this proposal of the CCE raised the question of whether real equal opportunity in education would be achieved or not. In fact, the 6-year state secondary school would be unlikely to bring about the extended freedom of choice, which the CCE desired to achieve, and would merely further promote social inequalities in educational opportunities which were already entrenched in the existing education system.

Together with the issue of reforming the state school system, the dispute over revision of the FLE illustrated the struggle between the conservatives and progressives in post-war Japanese education. The ERNC's series of deliberations were also an attempt to conclude an era of more than five decades of demands by conservatives to remove those parts of Occupation reforms that were considered too foreign to suit the traditionalist image of what Japanese education should be. However, the most serious dimension of the revision of the FLE by the ERNC and Koizumi government was their clear identification of pacifism in Article 9 of the Constitution as their ideological enemy.

Notes

1. Rinkyōshin engaged in three years of conducting concentrated deliberations from a broad perspective up to August 1987, during which four successive reports were submitted to Nakasone. Useful accounts include the studies of Schoppa, *Education Reform in Japan*; Hayao, *The Japanese Prime Minister and Public Policy*; Marshall, *Learning to be Modern*; Fujita et al., *Kyōiku to Shijyō* (Kyōikugaku nenpō); and Hood, *Japanese Education Reform: Nakasone's Legacy*.
2. See Goodman, *Who's Looking at Whom?*; and Schoppa, *Education Reform in Japan*, 223–50.
3. Quoted in Namimoto, *Gendai Kyōiku Seisaku no Tennkai to Doukou*, 163.
4. The 1984 proposals by the KGSGI are reprinted in Beauchamp and Vardaman, *Japanese Education since 1945*, 280–84.
5. Quoted in Beauchamp and Vardaman, *Japanese Education since 1945*, 270.
6. The full membership of the AHEC is given in Schoppa, *Education Reform in Japan*, 220–23.
7. Koyama Kenichi, *Kyōiku Kaikaku no Kihon Hōkō Ni Tsuite no Teian* (cited in Yamazaki Masato, *Jimointō to Kyōiku Seisaku*, 176).
8. Schoppa, *Education Reform in Japan*, 234–35.
9. Hood, *Japanese Education Reform: Nakasone's Legacy*, 105.
10. For further details of *zoku*, see Park, *Bureaucrats and Minister in Contemporary Japanese Government*, 34–39; Schoppa, *Education Reform in Japan*, 225–32; and Hood, *Japanese Education Reform: Nakasone's Legacy*, 24–25.
11. Aspinall, *Unions and the Politics of Education in Japan*, 1.
12. See ibid., 57–89.
13. Hood, *Japanese Education Reform: Nakasone's Legacy*, 105–07.
14. Rinji Kyōiku Shingikai (Ad-Hoc Council on Education), *Kyōiku Kaikaku ni Kansuru Daiichiji Tōshin*, 2. An English translation of a summary of the First Report is available in Beauchamp and Vardaman, *Japanese Education since 1945*, 297–303.
15. Rinji Kyōiku Shingikai (Ad-Hoc Council on Education), *Kyōiku Kaikaku ni Kansuru Dainiji Tōshin*, 2.
16. Rinji Kyōiku Shingikai (Ad-Hoc Council on Education), *Kyōiku Kaikaku ni Kansuru Daiichiji Tōshin*, 4–5. An English translation is available in Beauchamp and Vardaman, *Japanese Education since 1945*, 297–303.
17. Cave, "Educational Reform in Japan in the 1990s," 184.
18. Ibid. On this subject, also see Cave, "Japanese Educational Reform: Development and Prospects at Primary and Secondary Level."
19. See, for example, Lincicome, *Principles, Praxis, and the Politics of Educational Reform in Meiji Japan*; Roesgaard, *Moving Mountains*; and Hood, *Japanese Education Reform: Nakasone's Legacy*, 49–58.
20. Rinji Kyōiku Shingikai (Ad-Hoc Council on Education), *Kyōiku Kaikaku ni Kansuru Dainiji Tōshin*, 1–3.
21. Schoppa, *Education Reform in Japan*, 56.
22. See Hood, *Japanese Education Reform: Nakasone's Legacy*.

23. Chūō Kyōiku Shingikai (Central Council on Education), "Chūō Kyōiku Shingikai Dainiji Tōshin"; and Monbushō), *The Education Reform Plan for the 21ˢᵗ Century*.

24. Most of the materials, arguments and discussions treated in this section are derived from the following article written by the author: Okada, "Secondary Education Reform and the Concept of Equality of Opportunity in Japan."

25. Chūō Kyōiku Shingikai (Central Council on Education), *21 Seiki o Tenbō Shita Waga Kuni no Kyōiku no Arikat ni Tsuite*, 8; see also Monbushō, *Chūō Kyōiku Shingikai Dai'Niji Tōshin*, *Monbujihō*, no. 1451.

26. *Ikiru chikara* is a very broad concept including all that will be needed to live successfully in twenty-first century society—including qualities of character as well as intellectual abilities and skills. For further analysis of proposals of the 15ᵗʰ session of the CCE, see Kamei et al., *Chūkyōshin Tōshin Kara Yomu 21 Seiki no Kyōiku*.

27. For example, see Tokyo Daigaku Kōhō Iinkai, *Gakunai Kōhō*.

28. Chūō Kyōiku Shingikai (Central Council on Education), *Reform of Various Education Systems to Make Them Relevant to a New Age*, 5.

29. Chūō Kyōiku Shingikai, *21 Seiki o Tenbō Shita Waga Kuni no Kyōiku no Arikat ni Tsuite*, 57–68 (emphasis added).

30. See *Asahi shinbun Weekly AERA*, 6–11; and *Nihon Kyōiku Shinbun*, 1.

31. *Asahi shinbun Weekly AERA*, 9.

32. For example, Fujita, *Kyōiku Kaikaku*; Kurosaki et al., *Kyōiku Shi-zō no Saikouchiku*; and Horio, *Gendai Shakai to Kyōiku*.

33. Gokase School was established in Miyazaki prefecture as the first 6-year state secondary boarding school in Japan. The Ministry of Education permitted this school to be set up as an experimental school, with selection not by written examination, but by the recommendation of primary school principals, interviewing, student discussions, and newspaper-making. After these procedures, successive applicants were selected by open drawing of lots. Gokase School was very popular; in the first year, 1994, for one grade, the number of pupils recruited was 40, from 423 applicants, and in the third year, 1996, 40 from 365. The total number of students was 162 (ratio of boys and girls is 6:4) and the number of teachers was 33 in June 1995. See *Asahi shinbun*, 5 June 1995; and *Ashahi shinbun Weekly AERA*, 3 February 1997.

34. On this subject, see Floud et al., *Social Class and Educational Opportunity*; Jackson and Marsden, *Education and the Working Class*; Coleman, et al., *Equality of Educational Opportunity*; Moriguchi, "Shin'Gaku no Kitei Sho'inshi ni Kansuru Ichikenkyu"; Jencks et al., *Inequality: A Reassessment of the Effect of Family and Schooling in America*; Nakano, "Kaisō to Gengo"; Ushiogi, "Shinro Ke'ttei Katei no Pasu Kaiseki"; Bernstein, *Class Codes and Control*; Bourdieu and Passeron, *Reproduction in Education, Society and Culture*; Halsey et al., *Origins and Destinations*; Kikuchi, *Kyōiku to Shakai Idō, Gendai Nihon no Kaisō Kōzō*; Miyajima and Fujita, "Bunka no Kōzō to Saiseisan ni Kansuru Ji'ssyōteki Kenkyu", 32; and Ishida, *Social Mobility in Contemporary Japan*.

35. See Ehara, *Gendai Kōtō Kyōiku no Kōzō*; Imada, *Shakai Kaisō to Seiji*; Ishida, *Social Mobility in Contemporary Japan*; and Kosaka, *Social Stratification in Contemporary Japan*.

36. Most of the materials, arguments and discussions treated in this section are derived from the following article written by the author: Okada, "Education of whom, for whom, by whom?."

37. *Mainichi shinbun*, 9 September 1999.

38. Monbushō changed its name to the present form (Monbukagakushō) in January 2001.

39. *Asahi shinbun* 25 March 2000; and *Asahi Shinbun* 28 March 2000.

40. *Asahi shinbun* 18 February 2000; *Asahi shinbun* 28 March 2000; and *Asahi shinbun* 23 December 2000.

41. On this point, see Yoneyama, "Japanese 'Education Reform.'"

42. On 28 February 1999, perhaps due to the stress of being caught in the middle of a conflict between the prefectural board of education and the prefectural teachers unions along with

the local chapter of the *Buraku* Liberation League, the principal of Sera High School in Hiroshima prefecture committed suicide. His death brought public attention to the dispute over whether or not to fly the *Hinomaru* flag and sing the *Kimigayo* national anthem at the upcoming school graduation ceremonies. The Hiroshima Prefecture of Education, in line with the Ministry of Education's policies, was trying to enforce respect for these national symbols at school entrance ceremonies, but the unions and the Liberation League had already won the support of the teachers and were opposed to this policy. On this theme, see Aspinall and Cave, "Lowering the Flag: Democracy, Authority and Rights at Tokorozawa High School."

43. *Asahi Shinbun*, 25 March 2000.
44. Jiyūminshutō (Liberal Democratic Party), *Ge'kkan Jiyūminshutō*, 103–09.
45. Marshall, *Learning to be Modern*, 51–142; Schoppa, *Education Reform in Japan*, 1–52; and Monbushō, *The Education Reform Plan for the 21ˢᵗ Century, the Rainbow Plan, the Seven Priorities Strategies*.
46. *Asahi Shinbun*, 14 April 2000.
47. The Liberal School of History was founded in 1995 by Professor Fujioka Nobukatsu of the Faculty of Education. Other prominent members are Nishio Kanji, Takahashi Shirō, Sakamoto Takako, novelist Hayashi Mariko, and *manga* writer Kobayashi Yoshinori. This school believes that Japan's post-war history textbooks portray Japan in an unduly unfavorable way, and that history textbooks should instill pride in one's country and its achievements. Liberal School members have campaigned for the removal of references to "comfort women" from school textbooks, and have even questioned the factuality of the Nanking Massacre. They have produced a number of books detailing their views on Japanese history, culminating in the production of a junior high history book in 2001 and 2005—although the textbook was chosen for use at very few schools. Several groups of conservative Diet members support the Liberal School. For more details, see Kersten, "Liberal School of History."
48. See Hirahara, *Kyōiku to Kyōiku Kihonhō*; and Kawai and Muroi, *Kyōiku Kihonhō Rekishi to Kenkyu*.
49. *Asahi Shinbun*, 27 April 2001.
50. *Asahi Shinbun*, 7 May 2001.
51. Existing interpretations of Article 9 only permit the SDF to respond to threats to Japan's security within Japan's territorial waters. It is now argued that the SDF should be allowed to respond to threats against Japan and its citizens wherever they occur in the world.
52. See in particular Namimoto and Mikami, *"Kaisei" Kyōiku Kihonhō o Kangaeru*; and Sasaki, *"Kaisei" Kyōiku Kihonhō*.

6

EDUCATIONAL REFORM AND EQUALITY OF OPPORTUNITY IN CONTEMPORARY JAPAN

Throughout previous chapters, this study has examined the historical formation of the concept of equality of opportunity, which has been applied to the educational policy in Japan, particularly from the end of World War II to the new millennium. This book is therefore an analysis, not of the history of educational expansion in its entirely, but of those significant educational policies that relate to the different interpretations that have been given to the term "equality of opportunity."

Recently, as is seen later in this chapter, there had been concerns that equality of educational opportunity has been lost and that this is leading to the stratification of Japanese society through the widening of income differentials, in a "gap society" (*kakusa shakai*). In such a disparity society, secure full-time jobs are increasingly becoming limited to those who graduate from prestigious universities, and entry into those institutions is becoming connected more clearly with family income and investments. Parental attitudes towards their children taking extra lessons after school, going to cram schools (*juku*), getting into university, and getting into a relatively highly-ranked university have influenced educational costs.

The CCE's education reforms since the 1990s, created to give students more free time to explore their own interests (so-called *yutori kyōiku*) (see chapter 5), worked to accelerate these gaps. Because educational success was visibly related to family background, the reforms led to the development of children who could no longer see the point of working hard in school, who then dropped out of the system altogether or became disruptive within it. These children became unemployed or only engaged in casual work, further enforcing the disparity cycle.[1]

The purpose of this chapter is to expand on the previous chapters and the existing literature on educational policies in contemporary Japan by examining

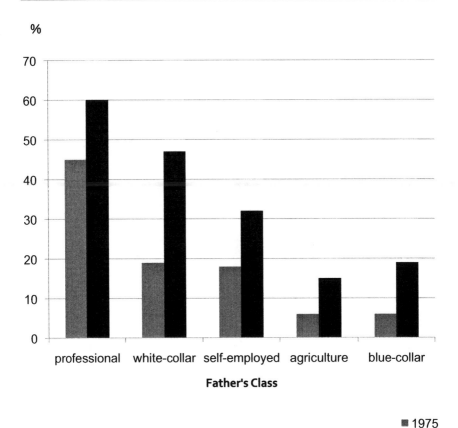

Figure 6.1. Fathers' Occupations and Percentages of Students
Who Advance to Higher Education
Source: *Shūkan tōyō keizai*, 17 May 2008, 38.

how the current educational reform efforts have affected equality of educational opportunity among children from different family backgrounds. It also examines new disputes concerning equality of educational opportunity and analyzes criticisms of educational inequalities.

Gakurekishugi (Degreeocracy) and the Japanese Sense of Equality of Educational Opportunity

Before examining disputes concerning equality of educational opportunity, it is worth pausing here to recapitulate and clarify the phenomenon of "degreeocracy" (or educational credentialism) because it has strongly affected the Japanese general public's sense of equality of educational opportunity.[2]

In analyzing issues of educational opportunity in Japan, we come across a very specific term: *gakureki-shakai* or "degreeocracy." It is a widely held belief in Japan that in no other industrial nation is career determined by academic background alone. Japanese parents urge their children to climb as high up the educational ladder as possible, believing that they will never obtain a satisfactory occupational position without graduating from prestigious higher institutions. This section re-examines such popular conceptions of degreeocracy in Japan and throws light on the social class inequality of educational opportunity issues.

What is the Meaning of Degreeocracy?

In the course of the 1960s and 1970s, degreeocracy in Japanese society came to be a theoretically and empirically significant subject. A number of definitions or explanations of degreeocracy have been developed by both Japanese and foreign scholars.[3] For instance, in research conducted by the OECD in 1971 about the Japanese educational system, Galtung explained the characteristics of degreeocracy as follows:

> It [degreeocracy] is essentially an ascriptive system in the sense that once one is allocated to a group it is very difficult to change one's social class. It is like being born into a class, only that in a *degreeocracy social birth takes place later than biological birth*. More precisely, it takes place at the time of the various entrance examinations, and like all births it has pains. . . . Biological birth is dramatic and the social birth of fully conscious individuals even more so. . . . [T]he entrance examination is to be born again, and once it has happened one's future life is as predetermined as in any Model I society [conservative society in which one's social status is determined by birth, as in a caste system]—only more effectively so because the society is more rational, more technically adequate.[4]

According to Galtung, therefore, the impact of educational credentials on socio-economic achievement was greater in Japan than in many other societies. He argued that the Japanese education system sorted out children as they moved up the school ladder and, based on their academic abilities, allocated them suitable positions in the social hierarchy.

The convergence debate gained another twist with Dore's formulation of the diploma disease hypothesis.[5] According to his argument, the late-developing countries in modernization ("late starters" in Dore's terms) have tended to place great importance on the selection system since their industrialization periods and have become used to regarding the function of education as a meritocratic mechanism for catching up with developed nations and responding to the urgent need to create a national elite. Dore's thesis of the late development effect (in which academic qualifications are more significant for getting jobs, qualification inflation is faster, and there is a stronger tendency for schooling to become examination-oriented) clearly described Japanese trends. These trends accelerated especially after the 1960s, a period characterized by a significant expansion in education, during which the concept of "qualification escalation" gained currency. By the 1990s, nearly 96 percent of all Japanese children went on to upper secondary school, and no less than 50 percent of all 18-year-olds were in higher institutions, mainly universities and junior colleges. We can therefore see that Dore's late development thesis had become particularly pronounced.

The Core of the Postulate of Degreeocracy

If one attempts to summarize the generally accepted core of assumptions about degreeocracy proposed by previous research, two elements come to the fore. On the one hand, educational opportunities are open to all the members of society, and individuals who are talented and work hard will achieve higher levels of education via standardized examination. On the other hand, the children's prospects of finding eventual positions in the society should not vary in any systematic and significant manner with respect to their arbitrary native characteristics.

According to Amano, a series of post-war social changes, together with the educational reforms, amounted to a process of producing a credential society in Japan.[6] The giant *Zaibatsu* (conglomerates) were broken up into large corporations and followed their own independent growth patterns. Dore appropriately described this as "the typical late developer's large corporation-centered growth pattern."[7] At the time, the practice of yearly mass recruitment of new graduates had become established. In addition, land reform abolished the landlord system and created millions of new owner-farmer families. This fundamental reform provided the basis for a rapid increase in the supply of aspirants to participate in higher levels of education—middle school, upper secondary school, and university. This, together with the narrowing of wage differentials between these categories, made it easier for corporations to hire graduates from this higher level. Furthermore, the convention was established for salary levels to be standardized across companies according to educational qualifications. This intensified the competition among companies to hire graduates from the best universities. The difference in the ability of students from different universities was very apparent, although their salary costs were the same. Finally, these processes of democratization produced a combined, mutual feedback effect and led to greater equality of income and greater homogeneity of education, living standards, and lifestyles. Consequently, opinion polls in 1987 showed that more than 80 percent of the population believed that they belonged to the middle class.[8] Thus, the degreeocracy has to be seen against the background of this noticeable post-war transformation of economic, social, and educational structures.

Degreeocracy has become a much-discussed issue throughout Japanese society especially since the 1960s, when Japan was in the middle of a period of high economic growth. Educational policy during the period was consciously designed to foster economic development (see chapter 4 of this study). The national emphasis on the "labor force approach" and the prevention of waste of talent accelerated the speed of the educational expansion that covered the whole range from preschool to university. As a result, the interests of *Zaikai* (business representatives) became extremely influential in shaping educational policies.

The conservative LDP government at the time, in partnership with the *Zaikai*, stressed the link between economic growth and the education system through a new concept of *Nōryokushugi* or the ability-first principle. In fact, the Economic Deliberation Council's 1963 report was the first clear declaration of the imperative to reorganize Japanese society on the basis of this ability first principle.[9] Thus, the meritocratic principle was demanded and justified by the government in the name of equal opportunity. Schools were expected to not only teach the basic skills more efficiently, but to also secure the talents and capacities required to successfully realize the aim of high economic growth. It can be said that the espousal of *Nōryokushugi* by the government and the industrial circles had the effect of accelerating the transition to a degreeocracy society.

The Issues of Degreeocracy

Together with the issues raised by Dore's hypothesis, since the early 1970s, degreeocracy has been seen as the most important problem with which educational sociologists in particular have had to deal.[10] In summing up the debate on degreeocracy, we might raise three issues.

First, degreeocracy was criticized because it produced extremely fierce competition in examinations. By relying on academic background to determine occupational role and therefore income, social status, and even political power, Japanese society had produced a system of *shiken jigoku* or "examination hell."[11] In Japan, as much as, if not more than, in other industrial societies, institutions of higher education, especially universities, were ranked in terms of prestige and reputation in such a way that a degree from a top-ranking university (e.g., Tokyo and Kyoto Universities) was regarded as an essential qualification for higher positions in the occupational hierarchy. As life-time employers, Japan's large corporations were believed to promote employees on the basis of the university they graduated from.[12] It was stressed that the employers gave much more weight to general intellectual ability than to any specific area of already acquired skills. Such a belief induced many entrance examination candidates to choose a prestigious school or university rather than a discipline in which they were interested or a department that had a good reputation. Indeed, as Amano pointed out: "Japan is not a 'what level' credentialing society so much as a 'what institution' credentialing society."[13]

Those who aspire to higher education were intensely competitive in preparing for the entrance examinations of prestigious universities. This severe examination hell, criticized by educational sociologists, had been seen as the chief source of problems such as refusal to attend school, dropping out, and bullying that are endemic in the existing Japanese education system.

Secondly, degreeocracy was condemned on the grounds that it did not reflect children's real ability or aptitude.[14] In the degreeocratic society, since the result of the entrance examination determined the pupil's social birth, as Galtung has pointed out, an elaborate system of criteria for assessing their ability was necessitated to avoid subjective evaluation. Consequently, these criteria tended to give high priority to the supposedly objective appraisal of students' capacity to memorize facts, numbers, and events and to solve mathematical and scientific equations. The cornerstone of the assessment system was the development of an objective achievement scoring system—*hensachi*, or the standard deviation score—which served to rank both individuals on the one hand, by the average scores of those entering, and upper secondary schools and universities on the other. Many Japanese teachers criticized this framework for attaching little importance to children's real intelligence or aptitude for study, and instead placing great emphasis simply on the skillful control of material in the entrance examination. Furthermore, the system was also accused of being the main cause of stifling the development of individual creativity, original problem formulation, and critical analysis in the area of social issues and political debate.[15] Thus, a selection system based on a standardized entrance examination was considered dubious with regard to meritocratic selection, since it was subject to a certain degree of chance, which meant that the best students were not necessarily those selected.

The third issue was that degreeocracy tended to lead to the formulation of *gakubatsu* or school cliques. *Gakubatsu* denoted the group consciousness deriving mainly from a common university background. Graduates of the same university shared an in-group feeling, a ready familiarity. If one's school was among the higher ranks, one's school contemporaries were also likely to be successfully climbing the ladders of other institutions, so that they were able to render mutual services when needed. However, the function of *gakubatsu* was severely condemned by some educational sociologists because the network of the *gakubatsu* offered unreasonable advantages inside and outside one's place of work.[16] Japanese educational sociologists suggested that once recruited into any corporation, the subsequent competition for promotion should be meritocratic and not dependent on the university from which one graduated.

In short, criticism of degreeocracy was founded on the proposition not only that it made examination hell fierce, but also that it did not reflect pupils' real capability to do well-paid jobs. Even if one graduated from a prestigious university, the graduation alone was not conceived of as something that would show one's real ability in business. Yet, graduates of prestigious universities were granted privileged positions through *gakubatsu* even though their ability was not right for the position. Criticism was thus focused on the irrationality and unjustness of degreeocracy. However, despite the fact that not only Japanese but also non-Japanese scholars have criticized degreeocracy and its effects, these debates risked overlooking the social class inequalities in the selection process.

"Unequal Competition from the Start"

Since the mid 1990s in Japan, there has been extensive coverage in both the mass media and academic books and articles describing how low birth rate results in parents' excessive willingness to invest in their children's education, paving the way for extra instruction at cram schools outside formal schooling.[17] In 2000, the fertility rate was only 1.35. The proportion of children under 15 in the total population had reached a historic low of less than 15 percent. Some observers have gone so far as to proclaim that this demographic shift would mean the end of Japan's examination hell or *shiken jigoku*. The so-called "2009 Crisis" was so named because it was thought that year would be the first when there would no longer be any competition to get into university since the places available at higher education institutions would equal the number of potential applicants.[18] However, this did not mean, as some have intimated, that the competition to get into higher education would disappear.

Instead some educationalists and sociologists have suggested that examination hell would continue in an altered form and would be coupled with unequal competition from the start of children's lives (*hajime kara fukōhei na kyōsō*). Most troubling to many critics were the emerging fixed inequalities in educational opportunities among the different social strata through all stages of schooling. Famous private middle schools, offering guaranteed access to a prestigious private high school and a high probability of getting into a top university, had been attracting increasing numbers of students. Students who began this process early commenced their preparations in elementary school. Indeed, richer parents had always been able to supplement their children's education with costly extra tuition and, to an extent, the education system therefore reproduced the class profile of Japanese people.

An editorial in the *Asahi Shinbun* on 21 May 2006 under the headline "Educational Opportunity Depends on Parents' Income" reported this tendency in the following terms: "21 million yen about $200,000 dollars (US) per child was needed to send them to a private kindergarten, middle school, high school, and university." According to the article, a 2005 survey of household expenses conducted by the Ministry of Internal Affairs found that average annual income of a working household was only 5,680,000 yen, an amount that had been decreasing in recent years. The survey concluded, "It is extremely difficult for an average family to send two children to private middle schools." Likewise the survey concerning an educational expenses conducted by the Ministry of Education, Culture, Sports, Science, and Technology (MEXT) in 2004 reported that "the educational expenses for the private middle schools (i.e., tuition fees) have never stopped increasing. It costs about 960,000 yen per child per year. The expenses for preparatory cram schools have been increasing in general." The AIU Insurance Company calculated that educational expenses cost 20,630,000 yen for liberal arts graduates (i.e., humanities and social sciences) and 21,790,000 yen for natural science graduates, assuming that the child went to private schools from kindergarten to university (excluding elementary school).

The Asahi article cited above quotes the critical comments of Mimizuka Hiroaki, a professor at Ochanomizu University, concerning "unequal competition from the start," as he expressed apprehension about generating inequalities of educational opportunities according to earning differentials of families:

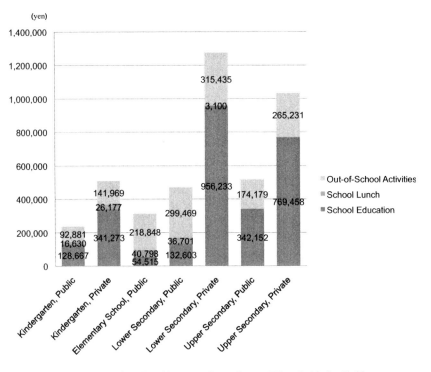

Figure 6.2. Details in Total Learning Expenditure of Households for Children
Source: Ministry of Education, Culture, Sports, Science & Technology,
Survey Times of Household Expenditure per Student.

Nowadays, the difference between each family's economic situation and culture is greatly influencing children's academic ability. It is an unfair competition from the start. Data from a survey of elementary school children aged 12 years in a suburban city of Tokyo with a population of 250,000 showed that 14 percent go to cram schools. 22 percent of the children who attend cram schools scored over 90 points (scale of 100) on a standard mathematical exam. On the other hand, in the case of children who do not go to cram school, only 1 percent scored over 90 points on the same exam. The difference of academic ability between children who go to cram school and those who do not has been expanding even in the provinces, for example in the cities with the seat of the prefectural government where private junior high and high schools and prestigious cram schools are often found.[19]

In fact, the Gini co-efficient (a measure of income inequality ranging from 0, representing perfect equality, to 1, representing perfect inequality) of Japan is on the increase according to various surveys. A study released in 2005 by the OECD ("Income Distribution and Poverty in OECD Countries," covering the period from the second half of the 1990s) found Japan to have a slightly higher level of inequality than average among the industrial nations (with a Gini co-efficient of 0.314, as measured against the OECD average of 0.307).

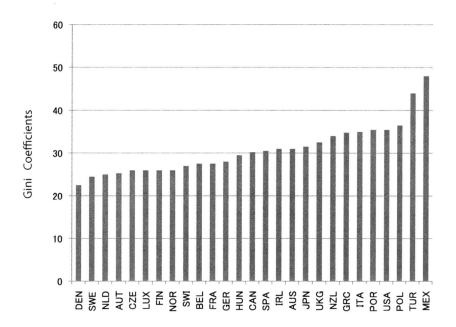

Figure 6.3. Gini Co-efficients of Income Concentration in 27 OECD Countries, Most Recent Year
Source: Forster and d'Ercole, "Income Distribution and Poverty in
OECD Countries in the Second Half of the 1990s," 11.

The number of children and students who received financial aid for stationery and school lunches in public elementary and junior high school reached 1,340,000 in 2004 nationwide. This represented an increase of 40 percent over 4 years. The article remarked that "there are many children for whom choosing to go to private middle school and cram school is ruled out from day one because the annual income of their parents is low."

Many social scientists point out that under the LDP, education policies for the underprivileged were being counteracted by policies to provide more educational choice. This statement referred to the LDP government's policies which were aimed at protecting the educational interests of the least educationally advantaged and the most vulnerable to failure, on the one hand. On the other hand, there were policies for those already well placed in the market, aimed at broadening their educational options.

For instance, educational sociologists denounced the educational reform carried out by the Ministry of Education, including the revised Course of Study during the 1990s, on the basis of data about the number of hours children were studying outside of school.[20] According to academic research data, the MOE's relaxation of educational standards, the introduction of so-called *yutori kyōiku*, had diminished children's interest in learning.[21] Indeed, research found that the enfeeblement of the value of studying was especially pronounced in the lower social strata. The diffusion of the idea that competition based on examination (*shiken jigoku*) was a vice that had made it harder for those in the lower strata to maintain an interest in learning. Under the LDP government's educational policies, the widening gap between the upper and lower strata in terms of children's eagerness to learn and advance academically would cause Japan to turn into a fully-fledged "class society."[22]

Overlooking Social Class Issues in the Debate over Equal Opportunity in Education

Here, we return to one of the substantive concerns governing this study, which was to elucidate why class issues had not attracted attention from Japan's general public in the educational debate and how it was possible to maintain an ideology of meritocracy when it had become clear, as analyzed in the previous section, that wealthier families had better educational opportunities than less wealthy ones. As noted in the introduction to this book, Halsey's thesis argued that a key element of the debate over equality of opportunity concerned the inequality between different social groups in education. Terms such as class inequality or social group bias had been widely used in industrial western countries. In those countries, there was a growing volume of evidence that poverty in childhood adversely affects success in adulthood.[23]

Just as in other advanced nations such as the United States, Canada, and Germany, Japan's existing social policies had been challenged by child poverty.[24] Research confirmed that children from underprivileged families educationally failed to attain higher achievement in general because they faced greater challenges of poverty, had lower self-esteem, and were more often afflicted with inferior health. Within a widening environment of income inequality and increasing poverty risks, Japanese researchers had become increasingly concerned over the prospective transmission of poverty from parents to children.[25]

However, as discussed in chapter 4, the issue of children's social backgrounds did not attract much attention in the official debates on education, although some educational sociologists revealed the existence of social bias in both children's academic achievement and in the proportion of school-leavers entering higher education. The post-war Japanese government led by the LDP, as analyzed throughout previous chapters, had maintained a policy based on the meritocratic principle. Indeed, the issue of inequality between social groups faded from the educational debate for a long time, and instead there arose increasing concern about other issues such as examination hell or *ijime* (bullying).

In recent years, Kariya conducted studies directed at the issue of inequality between social groups.[26] He argued that the attention of the people was given to the inequalities brought about by the effects of degreeocracy as mentioned before, but the actual degree of educational inequalities based on various socially important initial preconditions, such as social origin or regional background in the process of selection, went mostly ignored.[27]

According to Kariya, the distinctive elements of the Japanese sense of degreeocracy, as discussed in the early section of this chapter, did not call into question the inequality that existed in the process of selection. He argued that there were three distinctive elements in the Japanese educational system which tended to lead to neglect of the social class disparities within the selection process.[28]

First, many teachers in the JTU, along with a broad spectrum of the Japanese public in general, were very suspicious of any reference to the relationship between poor learners and their environments—family, economic, and social. These teachers in the JTU, laboring under the principle that ability is not inherited from parents' social status, but acquired in the society, regarded mere reference to the relationship itself as a form of discrimination (see chapter 4 of this book). Kariya stated that it was taboo to mention and deal with the issue of class in the debate on equality of educational opportunity.

Second, some research maintained that Japanese people believed to a greater extent than their western counterparts that every child possessed the same innate ability, and they emphasized *doryoku* (effort) instead of ability as a primary factor determining academic performance. In other words, Japanese people were liable to attribute poor performance to lack of effort instead of ability.[29] Consequentially, losers more readily accepted culpability as well as the superiority and authority of others who were more successful in climbing the ladder. Concern over qualifications resulted in fragmented, individual self-blame by those who had failed to achieve their goals. Such an attitude further blinded them to the inherent structural inequalities to which they were subject.

Thirdly, with the increasing emphasis on qualifications, the Japanese tended to believe that opportunities for educational advancement were in general open to all members of Japanese society and that individuals who were talented and worked hard could achieve higher levels of education regardless of their social origin. Entrance exams were perceived as culturally neutral. Because of this, the critics of educational inequality began to point, not to social class inequalities in the process of selection, but to other phenomena connected to qualifications, such as *gakubatsu* (school cliques). *Gakubatsu* denotes the group consciousness derived mainly from a common university background. Graduates of the same university shared an in-group feeling, a ready familiarity. If a school were highly ranked, the graduates were likely to be successful in climbing the ladder in other institutions and were able to help each other when needed.

Kariya argued that this illustrated the common perception about qualifications prevailing among Japanese people since World War II. In other words, this sort of egalitarianism within a framework of qualifications was conceived most directly in terms of an open process with transparent hierarchies and criteria of success, which made it achievable. Therefore, the majority of the Japanese populace held that, despite social origin, everyone had the ability to compete for upward social mobility through standardized entrance examinations. Indeed, a widely held belief and trust in the transparency and openness of the selection process and criteria in Japan pervaded the public consciousness. Including measures for nationwide common curricula and textbooks, the elimination of the pre-war diversified system, and equal access for students to entrance examinations based on standard curricula, post-war educational reforms had, without doubt, been essential in shifting Japanese perceptions concerning equality of educational opportunity—a move away from education for a tiny national elite toward mass education. This fresh vision of education anchored in the reforms was hastening the evolution to a so-called Mass Education Society (*Taishū kyōiku shakai* in Kariya's terms) in which concern for qualifications dominated. Therefore, the Japanese awareness of educational inequalities was intrinsically coupled with the negative effects of the emphasis on the selection process itself (such as *ijime* and *gakubatsu*) and only faintly with class inequalities existing prior to the process of selection.

The Advent of *Kakusa Shakai* (the "Gap Society")

It is worth noting here that, despite the prevailing emphasis on qualifications in a society of degreeocracy as explained above, the issue of the inequality existing in the process of selection has gradually been raised in Japan, particularly since the economic recession of the 1990s. The significant concern here was that academic achievement was becoming polarized between two groups: children who came from wealthier families and those who did not. In other words, the differing home environments of students were leading to the creation of one stratum that studied and one that did not. When this was linked with the gap between the well off and the badly off, as critics warned, the result would presumably cause greater social inequality in the future.

The increasingly distinct divide between rich and poor was so vivid in the national consciousness that it was given a name: *kakusa shakai* (literally meaning "society of disparity" or "gap society"). Since 2000, the term *kakusa shakai* has turned up frequently in Japan. Certainly many Japanese had paid attention to disparities for a long time, for instance, those between regions and between industries. However, attention was now also focusing on the gap at an individual level. Actually, the Ministry of Internal Affairs had presented statistics indicating that household income differentials had been widening steadily since 1979, with a wider gap as student age went up. Moreover, a comparison of the figures for 1999 and 2004 suggested an increased disparity in the under-30 age group.[30] Economists suggested that this gap had been caused by a decline in the hiring of regular employees, leaving many young people unemployed or doing low-paid temporary work.

Chūō Kōron published a paperback in 2001 titled *Ronsō—Chūryū Hōkai* (*Debate—The Breakup of the Middle Class*) that gave an overview of issues such as the "breakup of the great middle (class)" and the emergence of an "unequal society" in Japan. A decade ago, about 90 percent of Japanese considered themselves middle-class.[31] The public's increasing awareness of a *kakusa shakai* was reflected in the Japanese media's obsession with who was going up and who was going down. In other words, the domestic debate was dominated by the idea of *kachigumi* and *makegumi* (the winning team and the losing team). For this account, Miura pointed out that the ongoing change in the consciousness of the Japanese would affect the pattern of parents' behavior in choosing schools for their children.[32]

Along with the major newspapers and magazines, sociologists and educationalists published numerous books and articles discussing *kakusa shakai* in Japan. Perhaps the earliest books were *Nihon no keizai kakusa* (Japan's economic disparities) published by Tachibanaki Toshiaki in 1998, and *Fubyōdō shakai Nihon* (Japan's Unequal Society) by Sato Toshiki, published in 2000.[33] Tachibanaki also analyzed the factors contributing to the polarization, such as the introduction of performance-oriented evaluation and the increase of non-regular employment.[34] He attributed the sense of widening disparity to earnings differentials among workers that had become larger with the introduction of merit-based pay, as well as to a rapidly aging society, which put a greater welfare burden on younger workers. He claimed that the degree of inequality in Japan had become greater than that in the United States and the United Kingdom.

From a different angle, the sociologist Yamada Masahiro, in his 2005 book *Kibo kakusa shakai* (*Society of Disparities in Expectations*), suggested that statistically verifiable data on quantitative income gaps did not necessarily directly match individuals' sense of living in poor social conditions, therefore pointing out considerable disparities between perception and objective reality. The declining academic ability of Japanese young people, according to Yamada, was a result of the growing perception that effort in the educational arena would not be rewarded. Yamada and others highlighted the fact that young people no longer dreamt of becoming salary workers because they knew that even if they studied hard, entered a famous university, and were hired by a major company, that company was at risk of going bankrupt. The need to acquire academic proficiency had traditionally been premised on the goal of becoming a white-collar worker after completing one's education. If the youth were unwilling or unable to follow this path, as Yamada argued, there was no need for them to study. Thus, the re-differentiation of Japanese society was sensed by younger Japanese youths as a loss of career chances and personal future options.

Many Japanese, as well as the mass media, interpreted the reforms under the Koizumi administration as the direct cause of *kakusa shakai*. Though the flexible regulation policies implemented throughout the period of the Koizumi administration contributed to the reactivation of the economy, many people thought that there were losers (*make-gumi*) because of Koizumi's policies, which focused on deregulation, privatization, spending cuts, and tax breaks for the rich. "I don't think it's bad that there are social disparities," Koizumi once said in the Japanese Parliament.[35] Japanese people were quick to recognize the widening of these disparities.

The Issues of Jobless Youth

The issues surrounding the inequality of job opportunities were exacerbated during the recession of the 1990s. In 2002, a survey showed that the number of jobless youths had reached 2,132,000 individuals nationwide.[36] The sociologist Genda Yuji, labor economists, and others were arguing that the rapid rise of the new phenomenon of so-called *furiitā* (youth who do not find employment as full-time permanent employees and work in non-permanent short-term and or part-time jobs after leaving school) and NEETs (an acronym for "Not in Education, Employment or Training" applied to youths who do not engage in any type of employment at all after leaving school) had been striking.[37] According to the Ministry of Health, Labor, and Welfare statistics, while the overall population of NEETs was approximately 400,000 in 1993, it reached 640,000 in 2003. As for the 30- to 34-year-old group, the number was around 90,000 in 1993, but doubled to 180,000 in 2003.[38]

The term NEET was first identified as a problem in Britain in relation to people between 16 and 18 years of age, and was adopted by the Japanese, who modified it to indicate people aged between 15 and 34, excluding married women. Concerning the problem of jobless youth, three problems stands out: (1) opportunities for full-time employment would continue to be limited among the *furiitā* and NEETs; (2) the appearance of new categories of jobless people in their late 20s and early 30s is likely to further exacerbate the declining birth rate, given the difficulties such people will have in supporting a family; and (3) the system of company recruitment of university (or college) graduates deprives others of employment opportunities.[39]

The Influence on Social Structure

Genda argued that there was a clear distinction between the characteristics of the unemployed, as represented in the labor force survey conducted by the government, and the NEETs.[40] The former were those who wished to work for earnings and actually searched for jobs (the so called job-seeker type), while the latter could be classified as non-seekers or discouraged who had no wish to work and therefore were not counted statistically as unemployed. Genda suggested that the NEET phenomenon would have serious effects on the social structure of present-day Japan. He suggested that jobless youths with higher education tended to become job seekers, while jobless persons with lower levels of education were more likely to give up their search for work entirely, become non-seekers and not be counted in government unemployment statistics.

Moreover, in addition to educational background, as Genda argued, a large decline in family income had a strong influence on the number of NEETs in Japan. A significant number of them came from economically disadvantaged families. Genda stated this as follows:[41]

> Granted, some NEETs do come from wealthy families; more that 20 percent of households with "non-seekers" earned more than 10 million yen/year in the 1990s. However, for households living with "discouraged" jobless youths, the proportion of such rich families fell from 23 percent in 1997 to 14 percent in 2002. As a result, in the 2000s, upper-income households have become less likely to generate the "discouraged" jobless youths, while lower-income households have become more likely to produce NEETs.

Genda suggested that in Japan, as in the UK, people's educational attainment and family income had a strong effect on whether they would become NEETs. Youths with lower levels of education and those from poor working class backgrounds were more likely to quit their jobs. He concluded that such a class structure, or social segmentation, evolved during the long recession, and the presence of so many NEETs in Japan today was one outcome of the changing social structure in Japan in the 1990s and 2000s.

Educational Policies of the Democratic Party of Japan

To conclude this chapter, a general view of the party in power (at the time of the writing this chapter) will be taken. The Democratic Party of Japan (DPJ, Minshutō) won a landslide victory in the 30 August elections of 2009 in the House of Representatives, and Yukio Hatoyama was elected Japan's new prime minister. Hatoyama underlined his resolve to challenge the ex-ruling LDP's structural reform drive and his adherence to the market principle in all aspects of social activities. Hatoyama proposed a general shift to an "economy for the people," placing greater emphasis on citizens' quality of life. Hatoyama's shift included providing adequate safety nets for employment and human resources development and adopting a consumer's perspective with regard to the economy instead of relying exclusively on economic rationalism and growth rates. Moreover, reform of the Diet, with the transformation of a bureaucrat-dominated government into one led by politicians as its core, was also noteworthy.

Hatoyama made his first keynote address to the Diet on 26 October. During the Diet session, he was urged to explain how he would put the DPJ's election pledges into practice. As far as the education issues were concerned, indicating a plan to review the policies of the LDP, he said as follows:

> Child-rearing and education are no longer simply personal concerns. We need to view them as investments in the future, whose cost is borne by all members of society in a mutually supportive manner. A humane society is rightly one where the entire society comes together to support its weaker members, including children and the elderly. Let us aim to build a country in which families do not have to give up having and rearing children for economic reasons, in which people do not have to give up their jobs for child-rearing or nursing care, and in which all those who harbor aspirations can receive high-quality education.[42]

In order to achieve these lofty aspirations while securing the requisite fiscal resources, he repeated many of the party manifesto promises, including the monthly child benefit, virtually tuition-free public high schools, and large-scale scholarship expansions.

At the top of the DPJ administration's policy priorities was the proposed child benefit. The DPJ's campaign manifesto of the August 2009 general election included a child benefit that would provide a monthly allowance of 26,000 yen for every child of middle school age (15 years of age or younger) in the nation.

Such an allowance required that 5.3 trillion yen be budgeted annually. In the initial year of the DPJ's pledged program, in which the allowances would be only 13,000 yen per child, the cost would reach 2.3 trillion yen with no income ceiling on households to receive the benefits. This outlay of funds was in addition to the existing child benefit system, where the national government, prefectural governments, and municipal governments funded a third of the 5,000 yen or 10,000 yen monthly allowances per child of primary school age or younger.

With no household income limit for the subsidy, the DPJ's envisioned plan provided families with an annual subsidy of 118,800 yen, which was equal to the standard cost of a child's annual tuition at a public high school. This sum would double for lower income families with annual income not in excess of 5 million yen. The DPJ's child allowance further granted matching amounts to families whose children were in attendance at more expensive private high schools. The DPJ envisioned this child subsidy program covering 3.6 million students at a cost of 450.1 billion yen for the fiscal year of 2010, meaning the government would be supplying the essential subsidy funding required by high school operators such as the prefectural boards of education.

Another initiative on the DPJ's agenda was a reduction in tax deductions for families with dependent high school students—children 16 to 22 years old. The DPJ proposed to employ the savings resulting from these cuts in financing the free high school education plan. (This tax benefit reduced the taxable income of eligible households by 630,000 yen per child, cutting the total tax burden on households with high school students by more than 200 billion yen. The benefit was greater for higher-income families subject to higher tax rates.) The initiative's pivotal innovation rested in radically reducing the tax deduction while equivalently endowing tuition subsidies and thereby efficiently contributing superior financial support to lower-income families. Though the economic burden on more prosperous families would increase somewhat, the DPJ believed this new innovation served to supply equal education prospects to children regardless of their parents' income.

Yet there were high school education expenses other than tuition that required addressing. These included entrance fees, costs for teaching materials, and expenses for school excursions, beyond those the subsidy covered. For such additional expenses many lower income families still needed financial aid. To address these monetary needs of low-income families struggling to meet the costs of educating their children, prefectural governments offered high school tuition reductions or exemptions. Whenever possible, the MEXT and local governments needed to cooperate to figure out effective methods of employing the savings from the new DPJ child subsidy to augment financial support for these more disadvantaged households.

However, critics pointed out that it would be difficult for the DPJ administration to implement its election promise concerning education in the coming fiscal year. Given the serious financial squeeze, a cut in the deduction was necessarily considered. For this reason, the Government Revitalization Unit was established as a new organization by the Hatoyama administration to work on eliminating from JFY 2010 (Japanese Fiscal Year 2010: April 2010–March 2011) wasteful or unnecessary budget requests, to total more than ¥95 trillion ($950 billion [U.S.]).

Moreover, media coverage of the DPJ administration's handling of the education issue brought to light problematic issues. First, though the Hatoyama administration proposed monetary assistance through its child subsidy program that allowed for free public high school tuition, the media's questioning exposed the lack of a plan or even an outline for attaining the DPJ's goal of expanding public assistance for children's welfare. Though the administration had committed to escalating measures to assist parents in child-rearing, they did not yet have a working model to attempt child care assistance, which should have been the central focus of its child policy. As a consequence, there were divided views within the government over whether central or local government had primary responsibility for administering child care services.

Second, although the Hatoyama administration stated its objective of a general shift to an "economy for the people" and "a major policy change" with its foundations in the child subsidy, Hatoyama's cabinet had thus far been unsuccessful in even producing the coordinator post in charge of resolving conflicting child policy views. With the DPJ government credibility at issue, more cabinet embarrassments and imbroglios were liable to ensue when child allowance deliberations commenced, unless this situation was rectified in advance of the Diet session.

Yet, any major policy shift was likely to induce divergent arguments. Lacking an effectual structure with which to implement new policy, no successfully efficient procedures could be fashioned. Unaided, the enhanced development of child subsidies would prove ineffectual against the increasingly severe shortage of day care centers. Moreover, the mitigation of issues such as child abuse and parental depression from child-rearing difficulties remained an impossibility, against which solely improving child allowances was ineffectual.

On 8 December 2009, Hatoyama's cabinet approved a policy package, which they depicted as offering emergency economic procedures to increase the Japanese people's sense of economic growth and personal security. Including measures to augment child care services, this package integrated the formation of a government panel to study procedures to assist the next generation of citizens. However, with the formation of such a government panel, the administration had to consider the urgent necessity of guaranteeing that the panel would effectively proceed to develop a general approach that included detailed methods to socialize child care tasks as well as engender scope for expansion of methods for potential future requirements.

Conclusion

As was discussed in this chapter, the ideology of *gakurekishugi*, or degreeocracy, widely affected Japanese society and resulted in the development of an examination culture across a considerable section of the Japanese school system. In such a society, it was believed that educational background played an extremely significant role concerning the distribution of occupations and careers. There was no doubt that post-war Japan had made enormous strides in providing expanded educational opportunities for its young people. The widespread popularity of these maxims of degreeocracy resulted from the belief that the post-war institutional changes brought about greater social equality and at the same time a stronger national economy. However, in recent years, this popular image of degreeocracy has given rise to enormous controversy regarding its existing conditions. There was a growing awareness among educational sociologists that: (1) opportunities for educational achievement were not open to all individuals, and (2) various social background characteristics did influence educational attainments. These findings of educational sociologists gave reason to question the assumptions about degreeocracy defined in previous literature, and the ideology of degreeocracy itself began to be more ambiguous and more open to debate.

Furthermore, for years after World War II many Japanese embraced the idea of a universal middle class, but the situation had changed substantially. Although Japan still tended to think of itself as one giant middle class, the wrenching economic and social shifts were splitting the nation into groups of haves and have-nots. There were even concerns that the equality of educational opportunity had been lost and that this was leading to the stratification of Japanese society through the widening of income disparities in a "disparity society" (*kakusa shakai*).

In fact, some research findings had begun to uncover evidence of a growing achievement gap between higher and lower socio-economic status children in Japan. Furthermore, there was some evidence that this gap could be attributable to non-economic reasons, such as different social status. Parental academic backgrounds and aspirations for their children were somewhat higher among those families of higher socio-economic status, who then used their cultural capital to pay for enrichment classes. Therefore, the CCE's educational reforms, which were implemented to give students more free time to explore their own interests, might actually have led to more students who could no longer see the point of working hard in school, becoming *furiitā* and NEETs. Since educational success was so visibly related to family background, more and more youths were dropping out of the system altogether or becoming disruptive within it.

The Democratic Party of Japan favored the entire society assisting in child care, which was not in line with the previous Liberal Democratic Party, which believed that child care was primarily the responsibility of each household. The basic approach of the Hatoyama administration should be considered fundamentally correct. Monthly child-rearing allowances and virtually tuition-free high schools, however, could never solve the problem of increasing inequality in educational opportunities among different social strata. Furthermore, it would be impossible to mitigate existing problems, such as child poverty, by simply improving the amount of child allowances.

Japan had reached a critical point, facing increases in both inequality of outcome and inequality of opportunity due to poverty. It had now become necessary to halt the worsening trend and revise the approach to the issue. It was urgent for the new government to ensure that the planned educational policies were effective, not only in their overall approach, but also in the specific measures taken to reduce educational inequalities and socialize child care.

Notes

1. See, for example, Genda, "The 'NEET' Problem in Japan."
2. Most of the materials, arguments, and discussions treated in this section are derived from the following article written by the author: Okada, "Japan as a Prototype of the 'Degreeocracy' Society?"
3. See in particular Shinbori, *Gakureki–Jitsuryoku Shugi o Kobamu Mono*; Dore, *The Diploma Disease*; and Ushiogi, *Gakureki Shakai no Tenkan*.
4. Galtung, "Social Structure, Education Structure and Life-long Education," 139 (emphasis in original).
5. Dore, *The Diploma Disease*.
6. Amano, *Education and Examination in Modern Japan*, 53.
7. Dore, *The Diploma Disease*, 125.
8. See Cabinet Office (Sōrifu), *The Mass Survey of Opinion of Citizen's Life*, 8.
9. Horio, *Educational Thought and Ideology in Modern Japan*, 343–48; and chapter 4 of this book.
10. Shimbori, *Gakubatsu*; Hashizume, *Gakureki Henjyū to Sono Kōzō*; Ushiogi, "Yureru Gakureki Shakai"; and Kariya, *Taishū Kyōiku Shakai no Yukue*.
11. On this subject, see Rohlen, "Conflict in Intuitional Environments: Politics in Education"; Kudomi, *Kyōsō no Kyōiku*; and Yashiro, *Gendai Nihon no Byouri Kaimei*.
12. Takeuchi, *Kyōsō to Kyōiku*.
13. Amano, "Education in a Modern Affluent Japan," 56.
14. Okada, *Equality of Opportunity in Post-war England and Japan*, 281–83.
15. Rohlen, *Japan's High Schools*.
16. Shimbori, *Gakubatsu*, 25.
17. For example, Shirahase, *Henkasuru Shakai no Fubyōdō*.
18. See Eades, Goodman, and Hada, *The "Big Bang" in Japanese Higher Education*.
19. *Asahi Shinbun*, 21 May 2006.
20. On this subject, see Okano and Tsuchiya, *Education in Contemporary Japan*; Kariya, *Kaisōka Nihon to Kyōiku Kiki*; and Phillips and Goodman, *Can the Japanese Change Their Education System?*
21. *Ronza*, January 2001.
22. Kariya, *Kaisōka Nihon to Kyōiku Kiki*.
23. For instance, Halsey et al., *Origins and Destinations*; and Jencks et al., *Inequality: A Reassessment of the Effect of Family and Schooling in America*.

24. Abe A., *Kodomo no Hinkon.*

25. Kikkawa, "Effect of Educational Expansion on Educational Inequality in Post-industrialized Societies: A Cross-cultural Comparison of Japan and the United States of America"; and Tachibanaki, *Nihon no Keizai Kakusa.*

26. Kariya, *Taishū Kyōiku Shakai no Yukue*; also see chapter 4 of this book.

27. Kariya, *Taishū Kyōiku Shakai no Yukue*, 144–52.

28. See ibid.

29. On this subject, see Lebra, *Japanese Patterns of Behavior*; Hayami and Hasegawa, "Gakugyō Seiseki no In'Gakichaku"; and Holloway et al., "Causal Attributions by Japanese and American Mothers and Children about Performance in Mathematics."

30. Ministry of Internal Affairs, http://www.stat.go.jp/data/zensho/2004/index.htm.

31. Cabinet Office (Sōrifu), *The Mass Survey of Opinion of Citizen's Life*, 8.

32. Miura, *Kayū-Shakai.*

33. Tachibanaki, *Nihon no Keizai Kakusa*; and Sato, T., *Fubyōdō shakai Nihon.*

34. Tachibanaki, *Nihon no Keizai Kakusa.*

35. *Asahi shinbun weekly AERA*, 7 May 2006, http://www.asahi.com/english/weekly/column/herald.html.

36. See *Social Science Japan*, no. 32 (September 2005).

37. See Genda and Kyokunuma, *NEET.*

38. Prime Minister Office, *Heisei 15 Nendo Kokumin Seikatsu Hakusho.*

39. Genda and Kyokumura, *NEET.*

40. Genda, "The 'NEET' Problem in Japan," 4.

41. Ibid.

42. Prime Minister Office, http://www.kantei.go.jp/foreign/hatoyama/statement/200910/26syosin_e.htm.

CONCLUSION

This book attempts to analyze equal opportunity in Japan's education system particularly in regards to the post-World War II era. This study looks at: the educational policies formed to create equal opportunity, as well as the various interpretations of how major political parties and teachers' unions feel about the current changes in the school system. Its goal is to analyze how these various arguments formed over time.

Examining the case of Japan has given us the opportunity to arrive at a fuller understanding of peculiarities in the process of the transformation of the concept. In its analysis, this study has focused on two fundamentally different versions of the concept—egalitarianism and meritocracy—and it has examined how equality of opportunity was understood when applied to educational policy in these two paradigms. Indeed, throughout this study we have seen interplay between egalitarianism and meritocracy which eventually caused a transformation in the concept of equality of opportunity over the period. The future remains uncertain, but the findings of this study suggest that this dialectical stress between egalitarianism and meritocracy will continue to plague policymakers not only in Japan but also in other industrialized countries. The struggle will continue to influence the distribution of life chances, the subsidies, and the inducements that shape the future of education.

In this final part, we return to the substantive themes underlying this study that were spelled out in the introduction. These substantive themes have not been dealt with in an ordered fashion nor concentrated in one chapter; it is therefore useful to attempt to bring together the findings from various chapters under a number of headings. The conclusions drawn can be divided into three categories:

1) Shifts in the Concept of Equality of Educational Opportunity: The Process in Japan

2) Verification: Applicability of the Analytic Model

3) Future Prospects

1) Shifts in the Concept of Equality of Educational Opportunity: The Process in Japan

During the early years of the twentieth century, equality of educational opportunity was not a burning issue in Japan (see chapter 1). After the 1870s, the state-provided elementary education for all was more or less accepted as socially just, and it was assumed that the education system was successfully supplying the nation with a stock of talent. In fact, this period witnessed the realization of equality of educational opportunity in terms of compulsory and free elementary schooling, while secondary and higher schooling was accessible only for those who had talent and could afford it. Yet, from the turn of the century, when the technological demands of the nations' economic prosperity pointed to the inadequacies of the education system in terms of the poor elementary education provided for everyone, in terms also of the lack of secondary and higher education facilities for all but the very few, and in terms of the completely inadequate provision for training and the association of certain kinds of education with the world of work, the notion of equal opportunity shifted to secondary schooling. However, this shift was not towards universal secondary schooling (middle school), but toward diminishing the differences among post-elementary schools and unifying their various types. Thus, the issue of equality in the pre-war period revolved around the argument that differences among such schools should be removed and that all students should be given compulsory secondary education. However, the advancement rate to secondary education was still only around twenty percent and the majority of its constituency was upper and middle class. A drastic change in the concept of equality of educational opportunity took place after World War II through the post-war educational reforms.

The Mid-1940s: The Initial Position of the Concept of Equality of Educational Opportunity

The general trend of the post-war reform period in Japan was originally to interpret the concept of equality of opportunity in an egalitarian way, emphasizing self-realization, rather than as a justification for differentiation between children. In this egalitarian view, the idea of social justice was much more important than considerations of national efficiency or the needs of the economy (see chapter 2).

The main goals of the American Occupation of Japan could be described as the democratization, demilitarization, and decentralization of Japanese society. These goals were clearly opposed to those which had been dominant in pre-war Japanese education, namely: the training of loyal subjects; a narrow nationalistic perspective; and a complex and hierarchical secondary education system comprising middle, vocational, higher elementary, and youth schools. The American Occupation recognized that reforming the pre-war education system was an indispensable element in achieving its aims, especially that of introducing the principle of equality of opportunity into social reforms. So, the USEM put forth some specific recommendations to achieve greater equality of educational opportunity. For instance, the single track 6-3-3-4 system was established to achieve the goal of equal opportunity. The separate tracking of boys and girls at the lower secondary school level was ended. The school-leaving age was raised from twelve to fifteen. The extension of the period of compulsory schooling from six years to nine years was well supported and soon put into practice by the Japanese, despite the severe financial and material conditions in the immediate post-war period.

The American ideal of equal opportunity was incorporated into Article 26 of the Constitution and Article III of the Fundamental Law of Education (FLE). These articles stipulated that all the people would have the right to an "equal" education "correspondent to their abilities" and would not be subject to educational discrimination on account of race, creed, sex, social status, economic position, or family origin. At first glance, these articles might be regarded as a logical balance between the two parallel premises—equality and meritocracy: their stipulation of "equal education" emphasized one premise (equality), yet they also stressed the other premise (meritocracy), upon which allocation of children into different types of school "correspondent to their ability" was based. However, as analyzed in chapter 2 of this book, in the general circumstances of the post-war period, the ideological emphasis was placed upon equality rather than meritocracy or efficiency. Also, the articles' suggested elements were fundamentally divergent from those supported by the state before the war—allocation of children into different types of secondary schools in terms of their social function for national prosperity. In fact, some individuals like Kido Bantarō and Kawamoto Unosuke, progressive reformers, pointedly insisted that the expression "correspondent to their ability" should be interpreted in the sense of "correspondent to their developmental need." They regarded education as a valuable commodity in itself and recognized that equality demanded effective access to it should not be denied to any child on grounds of lack of academic ability. To put it another way, they demanded a comprehensive secondary schooling for all, regardless of children's differences in academic ability. In order to achieve a shared secondary school experience, which might serve as one step towards greater social homogeneity, they demanded open admission, free tuition, and a universal curriculum. Thus, as explained in the introduction to this study, the initial position of the concept of equality of opportunity in Japan differed significantly from the meritocratic position which Halsey's hypothesis predicted during the period. This interpretation was adopted by the progressives, particularly the Japan Teachers' Union (JTU), as a basic ideology in order to oppose the reverse course whereby the conservatives attempted to roll back the post-war democratic educational reforms in the following thirty years.

The 1950s: Redefining the Concept of Equality of Educational Opportunity

The period of the 1950s could be described as essentially one of consolidation, but also a time when the beginning of important challenges to the implementation of the FLE were developed. Towards the end of the 1950s, criticism about the reality of the new systems began to emerge and the pressure for change towards redefining the concept of equality of opportunity declared in the FLE—which was so important in the early 1960s—began to gather momentum (see chapter 3).

Once the American Occupation of Japan ended in 1952, the Japanese government began to undertake a revision of various legislative legacies of the Occupation, and to modify them according to the domestic conservative ideology of the day. This process became known as the "reverse course." In education, the government, with the Ministry of Education (MOE) and the industrial groups (*Zaikai*), attacked two aspects of the Occupation reforms. First, the conservatives criticized the post-war education system as too foreign and democratic to suit the traditional image of what Japanese education should be. They thought that this resulted in a disharmony between the system and the actuality of the state. They insisted, therefore, that such foreign elements should be re-examined to ensure that the new educational system related more closely to native conditions: There were moves to regain central control by the MOE, attempts to reintroduce ethics courses, and attempts to strengthen central control over teachers and to combat the influence of the JTU. Second, a particularly strong feature of the criticism was a widespread discontent with the inefficiency of the newly established 6-3-3-4 system. The conservatives, especially the Zaikai, were not satisfied with this system and advocated its diversification as essential for industrial and economic reconstruction. Therefore, they suggested the strengthening of vocational education at the lower and upper secondary education level and the establishment of separate vocational colleges.

Behind these criticisms, the philosophical basis of the egalitarian characteristics of the concept of equality of opportunity in the Occupation's educational reform began to be eroded by strong emphasis on efficiency and meritocracy. In fact, during the period, a liberal view of the concept of equality of opportunity was gradually regaining ground within the conservative groups. Concerning the necessity for industrial development proposed by the *Zaikai*, the conservative governments with the Central Council on Education (CCE) began to argue during the period that it would be desirable to diversify the 6-3-3-4 system according to the varying circumstances of (1) the different attainments of children, (2) different localities, and (3) different demands resulting from socio-economic structural changes. Essential to the conservatives' thinking was the belief that the diversification of the 6-3-3-4 single-track system would make it possible to seek out the most able children in the interests of national efficiency and to ensure various educational opportunities according to personal liberty and freedom. These twin themes were a consistent strand in meritocratic strategies designed to provide some new recruits for higher social positions and thus implied equality of opportunity at the *starting* point in the educational competition.

As related directly to equality of opportunity, one notable thing can be said about this diversification reform: Unlike progressive reformers in the Occupation period who conceived of equality mainly as identity or sameness in most cases, the conservatives began to interpret equality in two different ways:

1) equality of educational opportunity began to be defined as the *same* possibility of access for each pupil to *diversified* schools, curriculum, teaching methods, and treatment corresponding to ability;

2) equality of educational opportunity should mean *equal cultivation of different ability* in order to foster a national elite.

Although the idea of providing each child with a suitable education wherever it was found clearly involved some form of equal distribution of educational opportunity and thus appeared to conform to a notion of liberty or freedom of choice, this could have been part of a strategy the primary purpose of which was to serve the industrial and economic development of the state. Certainly in the view of conservatives during the period, industrial development seemed to be more important than individual development. In a series of reports of the CCE and Zaikai, the latter value seemed strongly emphasized: both liberty and efficiency demanded that a national elite should be fostered. These twin themes producing the strategy of meritocracy became central to educational policies in Japan during the 1950s.

The 1960s and the 1970s: The Emergence of a New Concept of Equality of Educational Opportunity

The early 1960s in both Japan and the other industrial countries saw an unprecedented surge in enthusiasm for expansion in education at the secondary and tertiary levels (see chapter 4). The expansion soon gave way to a stress on national efficiency combined with equality of opportunity. The national emphasis on the prevention of the waste of talent accelerated the speed of the educational expansion which covered the whole range from pre-school to higher education. Behind this situation, the new element introduced by the manpower or human capital approach provided a theoretical basis for the expansion and a rationale to justify the change in the education system, lack of educational opportunity being denounced as a waste of valuable human capital. Convinced that an increase in human capital was the most effective investment for the economic prosperity of the nation, successive governments in Japan immediately discussed and grappled with the issues of manpower and educational expansion. The Japanese problem had been to establish diversified educational structures, created for the perpetuation of a governing elite.

After the reverse course of the 1950s, Japanese education entered into a period of expansion of opportunities. This expansion of opportunity was made possible by the recovery and growth of the national economy, which had by the late 1950s already surpassed its pre-war level. During the 1960s, the conservatives produced *The National Income Doubling Plan*, which advanced the trend towards unifying economic development and educational expansion. The series of publications by the CCE and the Economic Deliberation Council (EDC) stressed the link with education through a new concept of equality of educational opportunity—the ability first (*Nōryokushugi*) principle. Under this new ideology, the conservatives' concept of equality of opportunity was to treat all those children of the same measured ability in the same way, irrespective of environmental factors. In contrast to the American and British educational trend during the period, the conservatives in Japan attempted to bring the concept of equality of opportunity back to the liberal concept: This, in essence, was the same concept on which the pre-war Japanese education system and also the tripartite system of secondary education in Britain were based. The conservatives attacked the uniformity of the 6-3-3-4 system and urged very strongly that education should be diversified in accordance with ability. In particular, "the very act of strategically discovering highly talented children at an early age for the purpose of economic growth bespoke a deep desire to control the destiny of Japanese youth."[1] Thus, once again, a very strongly liberal view of equality of educational opportunity was reaffirmed among the conservatives in response to demands for labor and became the conceptualization dominant within government.

However, the conservatives' interpretation of equal opportunity in line with the ideology of ability first faced severe criticism from the progressives, mainly the JTU. The battle over the principle of equal opportunity between the conservatives and the JTU during the 1960s and the 1970s could be seen in the struggle over how to interpret the phrases in Article 26 of the Constitution and Article III of the FLE concerning the people's right to receive an education equally and correspondent to their ability concerning upper secondary education. On the one hand, the Liberal Democratic Party (LDP), the MOE and Zaikai, supporters of the ability first ideology, made a great deal out of the words "according to their ability" as they pressed their arguments for diversification of upper secondary schools in conformity with the reports of the CCE in 1966 and 1971. As logical consequences of such an interpretation, it was argued that at the national level, quality and talent were not fostered for national development and, at the individual level, personal freedom was eroded by an excessive emphasis on equality in terms of the FLE.

On the other hand, progressives, especially the JTU, asserted that all children should be given upper secondary education regardless of their ability and that the principle of ability meant recognition of the principle of individuality. Thus, the JTU established its own concept of equality of opportunity—the *Sabetsu = Senbetsu* (discrimination = selection) principle[2] as a counter-strategy against the conservatives' favored principle—*Nōryokushugi*. Criticizing the so-called "examination hell" in the contemporary Japanese education system, the JTU strongly demanded the establishment of a comprehensive upper secondary school with no selection, based on the 1946 USEM Report. Furthermore, as discussed in chapter 4, this was expressed in a more developed form as the Right to Learning (*Kyōiku-ken*) in a series of reports published by the JTU's Council on Education Reform in the early 1970s. The JTU attempted to promote the development of human character under conditions of equality without the imposition of what they saw as improper forms of nationalism and intensified state control with regard to the opportunity for learning. Thus, under the banner of the *Sabetsu = Senbetsu* principle and the Right to Learning, two major strands can be found in the JTU's principle of equality of educational opportunity:

1) The concept of equality of educational opportunity did not allow discrimination on the basis of academic ability (*Nōryokushugi*).

2) All the nation's children should be given equal access to a comprehensive upper secondary school because they had the same amount of capacity and ability by nature.

Thus, from the 1960s to the end of the 1970s severe disputes frequently unfolded between conservatives and the JTU over the principle of equality of educational opportunity.

In the end, despite the JTU's aspirations for the establishment of a non-selective comprehensive upper secondary school, no basic change occurred in the educational structure. With a few exemptions, students still had to pass an entrance examination to enter upper secondary schools, which were diversified into many different tracks. In this education system, ironically the more emphasis the JTU placed on the egalitarian concept of equal opportunity in education and the more teachers treated children equally in terms of the same curriculum, non-streamed classes, and whole-class teaching methods, the stronger the meritocratic concept became. Because of the stratification of upper secondary schools and then universities, it was difficult if not impossible for lower secondary schools to adapt their teaching to meet the needs of students of different abilities. Teaching had to be designed to prepare students for entrance examinations and to put as many students into prestigious upper secondary schools as possible.Many Japanese scholars described this situation as examination hell, in which the school education system was forced to give top priority to the entrance examination competition. Moreover, degreeocracy, the paramount importance of educational credentials for career success, had given impetus to this situation (see chapter 6). With the emergence of educational credentialism and examination hell, two contradictory principles, egalitarianism and meritocracy, became woven into an allegedly compatible synthesis. In other words, the principle of equality was applied to the lower secondary school in which equal education was given to all students regardless of their academic ability, for the sake of social justice; on the other hand, the principle of meritocracy was applied to the upper secondary school and higher education levels in which students were allocated by strict selection into separate types of school corresponding to their ability for the sake of national efficiency and development.

From the 1980s to the Present Day: From Human Capital to Market Principle Values in Education

The late 1970s and early 1980s saw a sustained, predominantly right-wing critique of education. The conservatives in many advanced industrialized nations began to assert that egalitarianism had brought about a lowering of standards and loss of traditional values in education. Conservative governments in both Japan and other industrialized nations approached these issues in a similar way. For instance, the powerful conservatives Ronald Reagan in the United States, Margaret Thatcher in England, and Nakasone Yasuhiro in Japan adopted a New Right philosophy,[3] encompassing both neo-liberals, who called for decentralization, and neo-conservatives, who called for tough steps towards centralization, in order to bring recovery in the nation's economy. Both strands shared the view that government intervention and investment in education as well as in other public services should be decreased and called for the sliming down of the welfare state and the adoption of the market economy system in all public systems. They attempted to introduce market values in their education system to ensure efficiency and to counter egalitarianism. This heralded the end of the liberal consensus in education. The many elements of this New Right philosophy were reflected in the proposals of the Ad-Hoc Council in Japan,[4] which sought to make a reality of consumer choice and to restore notions of merit (see chapter 5).

Freedom of choice within the Japanese educational system has been one of the most discussed topics in regards to educational reform since the mid 1980s. Particularly in England and the United States, both of which have been very influential as educational models, freedom of choice has been one of the fundamental foundations of the educational system. Other reforms in Japan included the introduction of 6-year secondary schools with a relaxed system of school catchments areas, which would permit more variety as well as allow schools to rest upon the ideology of market-based choice. Critics argued that this would in turn increase the disparity between schools, lowering academic competition to a too-early age and also strengthening the effect of social stratification on educational opportunity. Proponents argued that these education reforms were designed to lower the number of children in tragic situations, so often sensationalized in the media, which were often blamed on the pressures put directly on the children by the educational system. Those who put forward these reforms were the MOE, the CCE, and the LDP-led government. Other aims of reforms included self-realization, self-cultivation, and freedom in learning, which were suggested and driven forward by their proponents.

In 2001, Koizumi Jun'ichirō was elected prime minister, and once again, education was in the spotlight with a suggestion of revising the FLE. His suggested changes tended to follow the market principle, with increased autonomy both for individual schools and for higher education institutions. It is worth noting that many of the reform proposals drew on the English model.[5] Many critics saw the reforms of the Koizumi administration as at least partly responsible for the emergence of the gap society (literally meaning "disparity society" or *kakusa shakai*). Against this backdrop, Labor economists pointed out the importance of the new phenomena of increased casual labor (the so-called *furiitā*) and NEETs. Thus, these tentative education reforms of a neo-liberal type may foreshadow a future shift of the concept of equal opportunity within the context of consumer demand.

Under these circumstances, the meaning of equality of opportunity was variously defined by different types of interpreters, who now cannot be classified into the two rigid political categories—conservatives and progressives—but who certainly have different beliefs, apply different emphases, and make contradictory proposals concerning educational reform. On the one hand, the supporters of neo-conservatism emphasized the establishment of a disciplined society, the restoration of selection in secondary education, and the preservation of traditional values in education. On the other hand, the supporters of neo-liberalism emphasized the establishment of a free market society, the minimization of governmental interference in education, and the maintenance of parental freedom of choice. Thus, in the sphere of recent educational reform in Japan, there was no consensus about what equality of opportunity was or about how it could be achieved.

Table C.1. The Historical Shifts of the Concept of Equality of Educational Opportunity in Post-war Japan and Explanatory Model

	Type of Concept	Practical Outworking
Pre-war period	Liberal-conservative	secondary education for able children vs. secondary education for all
The mid 1940s to 1950	Egalitarian	equal secondary education for all vs. secondary education corresponding to ability
The 1950s	Egalitarian vs. Liberal	6-3-3-4 system vs. diversified system
The 1960s and the 1970s	Liberal-Egalitarian compromise	ability first principle vs. *Sabetsu = Senbetsu* principle
The 1980s to present	Neo-conservatism joined with Neo-liberalism	Patriotism plus market principle

Here, the broad periods which seemed to emerge in the post-war educational development of Japan when the historical transformation of the concepts of equality of educational opportunity is analyzed provide points of illuminating comparison as well as some interesting contrasts. By using the explanatory models (Halsey's thesis) of the concept of equal opportunity explained in the introduction to this book, the periods and the shift of the concepts could be roughly represented in chart form as follows:

Verification: Applicability of the Analyzing Model

The first substantive concern guiding this study was the historical transformation of the concept of equality of educational opportunities in Japan. It has built upon the foundations laid by two scholars of equality of opportunity, Torsten Husén and James Fishkin.

With respect to the evaluation of claims about the processes of the historical shift of equal opportunity, the main theoretical base that has been discussed in this study is the combined Husén-Fishkin Model. This is composed of: three explanatory models of the concept of equality of opportunity devised by Husén: (1) conservative; (2) liberal; and (3) egalitarian, combined with Fishkin's model of the trilemma. The purpose of this section has been to test the applicability of this model in Japanese cultural environments. The combined Husén-Fishkin Model of equal opportunity was described in the introduction. One of the main foundations of this model was noted, i.e., no society can consistently embody all of the three principles of merit, equality of life chances, and family autonomy. If a nation tries to achieve the egalitarian concept, which places special emphasis on the principle of equality of life chances, that society sacrifices either merit or family autonomy. Either the society has to cancel out the advantages that come with a favorable family background, and hence sacrifice family autonomy, or it has to stop awarding desirable positions on the basis of merit alone. Since this study assumes that in real industrial societies family autonomy must be secured as a natural right, it does not deal with the neo-Marxist view.

The second substantive concern governing this study was to identify what peculiarities existed in Japan regarding processes of the historical shift of the concept of equal opportunity. It used Halsey's thesis of equal opportunity to evaluate the way the concept tended to shift. The main prediction of Halsey's thesis dealt with the tendency of the concept to shift historically: The inequalities of social class emerge more clearly as educational opportunities expand quantitatively and, in the long run, the trend of the shift of the concept becomes increasingly similar in different societies as the concept shifts from the liberal (meritocratic) to the egalitarian. Since Japan and other industrialized nations (e.g., England) experienced a great expansion of educational opportunities after World War II, according to this thesis, our comparative analysis should show a global tendency for the concept to shift in a single direction. Thus, with these predictions in mind, this study attempts to bring together the findings of the various chapters and at the same time provide a brief overview of the process of the transformation of equality of educational opportunity.

From the late nineteenth century to the pre-World War II period, both Japan and other industrial nations (like England) were societies sited between conservative and liberal concepts. As chapter 1 argued, equality of opportunity was defined in terms of a liberal variant of the conservative concept. Although the central governments of these countries acknowledged the importance of searching for talent among the masses for the benefit of the nation's development, they did not apply the principle to the secondary education level, not to mention higher education levels. It was assumed that equal educational opportunity existed when the conditions of access to education—for example, rules of admission—were the same for each pupil. Under this notion of equality, only the most wealthy and the most able progressed to secondary education, whilst the bulk of children finished their final years of schooling as senior children in a variety of post-elementary schools. Yet, World War II marked the real turning point as far as secondary education was concerned.

However, at the beginning, Japan and England took utterly different roads to equality of educational opportunity. In England, the initial position of equality of opportunity was the liberal view.[6] The 1944 Education Act had a vision of secondary education for all, and the new organizational framework established by the Act was the tripartite system, namely grammar school as an academic type of school for quite a small number of able children, technical school for fostering technicians, and modern school for the majority. In this new system, children were to be tested through the 11-plus (psychological test), and allocated to one of the three types of secondary schools according to their aptitude and ability. Children were seen to have equality of opportunity to *compete* for a place in grammar school as a result of the removal of external barriers such as class, income, religion, and race. Thus, English society at the time was a society in which the liberal concept held sway. However, by the 1960s, there was growing criticism of the tripartite system. Critics argued that the 11-plus selection reinforced class divisions in society and resulted in a waste of ability. They suggested that early selection reflected social class: Under the tripartite system, children from the wealthier families would have been systematically given developmental opportunities which could reliably be expected to benefit them in the process of meritocratic competition. If every pupil were to be given equal life chances under these circumstances, merit had to be disregarded. Accordingly, the Labor Party, when it came to power again in 1964, pushed for the establishment of comprehensive schools which would remove the differences between various secondary schools. Furthermore, the Plowden Report in 1967 proposed the principle of positive discrimination, which was to enhance the equality of outcome for those from disadvantaged backgrounds.[7] In this situation, the traditional liberal concept was evaluated as weak, and instead equality of opportunity was defined as a reasonably differentiating, or positively discriminating, the treatment of pupils with a matching allocation of educational resources. Thus, Britain in the 1960s was evaluated as a society dominated by the egalitarian concept (although not entirely so, given the continued existence of private education), keeping the autonomy of the family in place but attempting to equalize life chances at the same time, and consequently, it required that meritocracy be sacrificed to some extent, at least in the state education system.

In Japan, by contrast, the initial position of equality of opportunity was the egalitarian view. Chapter 2 showed that the educational provisions of both the New Constitution and the FLE embodied two significant principles: (1) respect for fundamental human rights; and (2) equality of opportunity. These provisions supported the egalitarian view of the concept by emphasizing the sameness of children in terms of their developmental process and their natural right to receive education. In fact, it is noteworthy that the characteristics of positive discrimination, which emerged in England during the 1960s, could be seen in section 2 of Article III of the FLE. On the USEM's advice, Japanese society pursued the establishment of an American-model comprehensive school system without selection, at least within compulsory education (although as in England, this pursuit was not total, since private education continued to exist). Thus, condemning the class distinction in the pre-war education system, Japanese people at the time expected to realize the egalitarian concept which demanded autonomy of the family and equal life chances; that meant limiting or eliminating meritocracy.

However, as observed in chapters 3 and 4, recovery from the war led the Japanese conservatives to re-examine egalitarianism in the new education system and reaffirm many of their traditional values in education. The conservatives began to match their belief in equal opportunity with the necessity for providing various types of schooling according to pupils' ability for further economic development, while assuming a scheme of differentiation of the nation's pupils on grounds of merit. The progressives, especially the JTU, strongly opposed the reforms of the conservatives by working out its own *Sabetsu* = *Senbutsu* principle. Under the 1955 system, the situation became one of unmitigated conflict at the national level. In the end, when it came to educational policies at national level, the conservatives succeeded in replacing the egalitarian concept with the ability first principle without providing proper solutions to reduce social class inequalities in the process of selection. Great emphasis was placed on both *Nōryokushugi* (ability first principle) and parents' freedom of choice in the name of equal opportunity. Under these conditions, the principle of merit—applied to talents as they developed under unequal conditions—became a mechanism for generating unequal life chances.

Having put the above situations together with other elements in the educational policy making process, we are now ready to summarize the main points of the concept of equality of opportunity that have been derived from the findings of this study.

First, despite the obvious political, social and cultural differences, comparable tendencies and characteristics in the process of transformation of the concept have been observed between Japan and other industrial countries. Such characteristics and tendencies are comparable between two different groups (i.e., conservatives and progressives, the LDP and the JTU in Japan, the Conservative Party and the Labor Party in England) which have struggled with each other over the implementation of their policies, employing their commitment to meritocracy and egalitarianism respectively. Since each concept of equality of opportunity had different inherent attractions, its translation into political practices and policies led to major political controversies. As Fishkin argued, the crucial question was whether to define it in terms of liberty or equality. In the case of Japan, this was particularly true in the issue of selection. For example, if defined in terms of the conservatives' espousal of the liberal concept, that is, equal opportunity by merit, it was likely to prove unsatisfactory in relation to equality of life chances. On the other hand, if equality of opportunity were defined in terms of the progressives' espousal of the egalitarian view, there would be problems identifying when the requisite equality had been achieved. In the egalitarian view, equal outcomes did not have to mean identical outcomes, i.e., a situation where all pupils achieved the same cognitive levels. Yet, if we accepted that children would achieve different levels, how would we know that each one received equal opportunities to develop his own potential? Achieving equal opportunity in one area tended to mean sacrificing it in another. Thus, the problems of translating the concepts into practical policies were clearly considerable.

Secondly, the tension between different concepts of equal opportunity increased and was not entirely random or unpredictable. The tension's character could be seen as a product of identifiable features of political, economical, and social life—say, the dominant form of politics being pursued by the central government, the prevailing conditions in the labor market or the individual's demand for social justice. The relationship between these and the particular kind of policy being pursued in and through education was by no means simple or consistent. One could see that the breakdown of the social democratic political consensus between conservatives and progressives had clear consequences for educational policy and reform. For instance, the LDP's educational reform, to align it more closely with the changing needs of a developing capitalist economy, was reflected in a more explicit linking of education to the economy and in certain changes of emphasis within the curriculum. In the egalitarian position supported by the JTU, the idea of social justice was much more important than a consideration of national efficiency or the needs of the economy. It might be said, therefore, that the historical shift of the concept reflected such tensions brought about by competing priorities, limitations of resources, and relative power positions of political groups.

Thirdly, our empirical findings have suggested that the historical transformation of the concept of equality of educational opportunity was more complicated than Halsey's thesis would predict. This is primarily because of the dual role of the concepts of equality of opportunity in the process of industrialization. On the one hand, the concepts serve the meritocratic function to the extent that they affect national development and efficiency. Historically speaking, according to Dore's argument, the late-developing countries ("late starters," like Japan) in modernization tended to place great importance on the selection system. These late starters regarded education's function as being that of a meritocratic mechanism for catching up with developed nations and creating national elites. Dore's thesis of the late development effect offered certain comfort for the Japanese as well as greater understanding of trends in their education system. Dore's late development effect theory stated that (1) academic qualifications were a significant factor in job recruitment; (2) the demand for qualification rose rapidly; and (3) examination-oriented schooling was required for late-starter countries. Perhaps the Confucian ethos, which stresses the encouragement of diligence, might also explain how the meritocratic characteristic of the concept of equal opportunity could prevail without casting doubt on the class inequalities in the process of selection.[8] On the other hand, for instance, in England the concept of equal opportunity had been used in order to reduce class inequalities in education. Historically, in the context of education in England, the concept of equality of opportunity, which had been promoted within the labor movement since the modernization period, tended to move from liberal to egalitarian[9]—contrary to the Japanese case. In the nations where social class issues are remarkable, triggering political, social and cultural disputes, the concept tended to be interpreted in terms of the idea of social justice rather than the idea of fostering talent and the needs of the economy. Egalitarianism treated education as a valuable commodity in itself and argued that equality demanded that effective access to it should not be denied to any citizen. Its main strategies proposed to use a changed educational system as a vehicle for changing the socio-economic structures which they feed. The concept of equality of opportunity was the single most significant way in which debates about redistribution entered educational policy in England. Thus, the transformation of the concept was swayed by the particulars of the modernization process of individual nations.

Fourthly, the shift from a liberal view to an egalitarian one as a measure of equality of opportunity was highly significant, with important implications for policy. As is clear from Halsey's thesis, the introduction of social class issues into the discussion of equal opportunities at the national level shifted the debate firmly in the direction of looking at equality of result. This also tended to move the debate from meritocratic to egalitarian rationales, especially by introducing the concept of positive discrimination in favor of the disadvantaged. In Japan, by contrast, this shift has not yet occurred, because Japanese progressives have not won the argument with conservatives, at least in the eyes of the general public: The two sides are still engaged in an unsolved conflict about the social class issue, with the progressives trying to insist on equality of outcomes. Moreover, the adherence to credentialism among the general public in Japan encouraged a tendency to overlook social class inequalities in the selection process (see chapter 6). It would be this failure to shift which has meant that there are scarcely the rudiments of compensatory education, and that the system of student aid is also very modest. Foreign observers found it hard to understand how it was possible to maintain an ideology of meritocracy when it was clear that wealthier families had better educational chances than less wealthy ones. In this respect, they might conclude that equal opportunity did not seem to have been realized in Japan to the extent that might be supposed in view of the widespread belief in the openness of opportunity.

Finally, relatively little in-depth research has been done in comparing education in different countries from the viewpoint of equality of opportunity. Of the variety of ways of comparing societies, this book might provide a useful explanatory toolkit with which to evaluate the historical shift of the concept of equality of opportunity. The two principles of equal opportunity, egalitarianism and meritocracy, examined in this book might serve as conceptual tools for the formation of a continuum of orientation towards social relations in various societies; one pole of the continuum emphasizes the sameness of children in terms of their developmental process and natural right to access to secondary education, while the other pole marks differences between children in terms of academic ability and expected social function. The trend of the shift of equality of opportunity in Japan has reflected more emphasis on the latter. However, in this conceptual analogy, one faces the ultimate paradox of one's belief in equality of opportunity. On the one side, meritocracy, favored by conservatives, has the potential, by diversifying the intake to higher education, to increase social mobility to the extent that it affects socio-economic achievement independently of social background. Yet, on the other side, the progressives' acceptance of egalitarianism, highlighted in the policy of positive discrimination and the establishment of comprehensive secondary schooling in the English case and in the principle of *Gakushūken* (right to learning) in the Japanese case, embodies a potentiality to sanction wider access to a higher level of education. In this respect, it is not too much to conclude that the conceptual transformation of equality of opportunity has been, and probably will continue to be, dependant upon its position on the continuum between the ideas of egalitarianism and liberty or, in other words, between the emphasis upon equal life chances and merit.

Future Prospects

In conclusion, the present writer would like to point out some possible directions in which this study could be extended. The first is to enlarge the scope of cross-national comparison. The present writer became aware of the limitations of a study that simply compares Japan (implicitly or explicitly) with England and Halsey's model. In order to fully examine the concept of equality of opportunity and the similarities or differences in the way the concept has shifted, further industrial nations should be added to the analysis.

The other direction that could be taken to expand the perspective of this study involves gender, ethnicity, and the disabled. One of the limitations of this study stems from its exclusion of these issues. Exclusion of such issues was not intentional, but rather was an inevitable consequence of the limitation of space available for the analysis. In particular, the exclusion of the gender issue from analysis may have serious consequences for the discussion of equality of opportunity because despite post-war educational expansion, gender inequalities still remain in most societies including Japan. Reflecting this situation, there is widespread interest in the study of gender in more recent American, British and Japanese research on equality of educational opportunity.[10] Therefore, in the not too distant future, we can expect the development of research on equal opportunity that incorporates the gender issue and to that compares the process of the shift in the concept of equality of opportunity among women with that among men.

Routes to Greater Social Inequalities by Private Schools in England

Since this study concentrates on the concept of equal opportunity and educational policies relating to state secondary schools, a field in which major changes, events, and decisions have taken place since the end of World War II, little attention has been given to the other parts of the education system, in particular, private schools (independent schools). In selecting historical documents, this study focuses upon public statements relating to the terms equality, and equal opportunity that were made mainly by central administrative bodies, rather than private ones.

As argued in this final part, the historical shift of the concept of equality of educational opportunity, particularly from the 1940s to the 1960s in Japan and England, seemingly moved in opposite directions in Japan and England, at least on the theoretical level. However, if we take account of the issues of private schools in both countries, it might be said that the shift of the concept of equal opportunity was not as straightforward as Halsey's thesis predicted.

Seen from the perspective of evaluating the effectiveness of national educational reform in establishing a more equal society, the educational policies formulated by the Labor Party to promote equality of opportunity were conspicuously lacking any synoptic view over the entirety of secondary education. Indeed, the majority of the Labor Party, excepting extreme left-wingers, focused on social and educational reform within the existing institutional framework rather than outside it. In other words, the Labor Party could not abolish the private school (independent schools), many of which are elite institutions educating children from the more wealthy and privileged classes.

According to Kang, the general silence of political parties concerning the private schools, and the Labor Party's ambivalent attitude towards them, was explicit evidence of the unclear differences between the Conservative and the Labor Party in England:

> Behind Labor's hesitation to raise this issue as a major political dispute there was not only Labor's unwillingness to deny the value of freedom in education, but also the difficulty in finding finance to abolish the public schools or absorb them into the State system. Such a stance illustrated the way in which equality of opportunity had been defined as including the concept of "separation" in education.[11]

Kang explains that both the Conservative Party and the Labor Party had conceived equality of opportunity as being compatible with the significant principle of freedom in their practical applications to educational issues. From the mid 1960s the existence of such ambiguous stances between political parties in England began to be clear. The existence of the private schools, which were attended 2006 by about 7.0 percent of children, but whose leavers took about 40 percent of places at Oxford University and 38 percent at Cambridge University, became one of the major political issues militating against equality of opportunity. Nevertheless, as Kang points out, "There still remains the theoretical difficulty in supporting the predominance of the value of equality of opportunity over that of freedom, as well as the financial one."[12] This was where the concept of equality of educational opportunity stood in England.

Thus, even though there were some structural differences in the secondary school system between Japan and England, the Labor Party's acceptance of private schools and a small number of grammar schools clearly demonstrated the extent to which most politicians in England accepted a compromise between the liberal and egalitarian concepts (partly for motives of political practicality). In this context, as mentioned before, the meaning of equal opportunity was ambivalent and defined poorly. Depending on the interpreter and the state secondary school system, equal opportunity was defined differently.

Recent Signs of a Growing Sense of Unfairness in Japan

It seems reasonable to suppose that the dramatic nature of post-war political, social, and economic changes partly contributed toward establishing a society of degreeocracy dominated by the lack of attention given to the issue of social class in the debate on equality of educational opportunity in Japan. Despite this popular image of degreeocracy, cross-national comparisons by sociologists show no evidence that educational opportunities were more open in Japan than in England and the United States.[13] Certainly, after World War II, Japan experienced an expansion of its education systems. However, expansion of the system did not weaken the effect of social origin on educational attainment. The results of various studies suggested that educational opportunities were limited by the various resources with which an individual grew up; educational attainment was largely determined by the amount of the family's economic and cultural capital, not only in the other industrialized countries, but also in Japan. The characteristics of degreeocracy do not seem to receive much support from our empirical analysis. These findings lead to the conclusion that the unique sense of Japanese egalitarianism may not reflect the reality of material and cultural inequality.

In recent years, however, reliable nationwide surveys have indicated that a significant proportion of Japanese people regard inequality as the attribute that best characterized contemporary Japanese society,[14] though the upsurge of national debate over equal opportunity in education has not come yet.

Japanese people have become aware that opportunities for educational advancement are not open to all individuals and that various social background characteristics influence the attainment of education. Consideration turned to the inequality of educational opportunity at an individual level. People were not entirely satisfied with their education system, where degreeocracy was imposed *a priori* upon them and the intense competition was the consequence of again

Table C.2. The Sense of "Unfairness" among Japanese People[15]

(a) Overall unfairness

fair	2.8
mostly fair	28.3
not so fair	45.7
not fair at all	18.8
DK/NA	4.4
Total	100 (N=2704)

(b) Unfairness because of	SA	ASE	DA	DK/NA
(1) sex	30.4	53.1	14.2	2.3
(2) age	23.0	52.1	21.4	3.5
(3) school education	48.6	39.6	9.7	2.2
(4) occupation	33.8	48.2	14.6	3.4
(5) wealth	39.0	45.0	12.5	3.4
(6) family stock	36.6	41.7	16.5	5.1
(7) lineage	24.2	44.6	26.6	4.6
(8) nationality	37.8	38.7	17.8	5.7

Source: *The National Survey of Social Stratification and Social Mobility* (SSM) 1995.

giving advantages to those who were privileged to start with them. In fact, social scientists have discovered signs of growing educational inequality in recent years. Some research findings show an increasingly large proportion of entrants to Japan's most prestigious universities coming from private school backgrounds (see chapter 6). In particular, they emphasize the growing number of privileged students who have attended private 6-year secondary school as opposed to three years of lower secondary school followed by three years of upper secondary school. These private schools, similar to the Public Schools in England, which charged considerable fees and catered to the upper-middle class, not only offered a heightened possibility of educational success, but also passed on what Bourdieu calls the cultural capital of the elite to their students. Parents who could afford to send their children to more expensive institutions greatly improved those children's educational chances. This tendency (since the 1990s) has been increasing in an age when the birth rate is in decline.

Having made the above observations, can it be said that Japanese people are able to learn how to tackle social class issues in education from the experiences in other western countries? As to the social class issue, this study has used the

English case of equality of opportunity as the main focus, where possible drawing comparisons with Japan. The results of this study suggest that Japanese people need to reconsider, and explore more deeply, the various possible meanings of terms such as equality of opportunity, equality, ability, social class, and meritocracy and see how these have been treated and debated over in different periods in other industrialized countries. As has been examined in this book, the issue of social class inequalities has disappeared from the official educational debate in Japan since the mid 1960s. It has not yet reappeared and/or been reconsidered under recent conditions, yet it has always held first place in England. It might be said that Japanese people can gain many insights that could help to solve contemporary class issues from cases in other industrial nations. The findings of this study might give them useful information to answer significant questions such as: How has the issue of social class inequalities been treated and discussed in the debate on equality of educational opportunity? How different are Western nations' advocacies of egalitarianism from Japan's? On what basis do reformers in other industrial nations assess equal opportunity? Why has the policy of compensatory education or positive discrimination needed to be implemented? Why is there so much awareness of the degree to which equality of opportunity in the sense of equality of results has been realized in the other industrialized societies? Thus, much of what other societies experienced after World War II seems to be still relevant to the contemporary situation in Japan.

Notes

1. Horio, *Educational Thought and Ideology in Modern Japan*, 219.
2. This term was coined by Kariya, *Taishū Kyōiku Shakai no Yukue*.
3. For further details of a New Right philosophy, see Friedman, *Capitalism and Freedom*; Hayek, *The Constitution of Liberty*; Levitas, *The Ideology of New Right*; and Gamble, *The Free Economy and the Strong State*.
4. Uchida, *Rinkyōshin no Kiseki*; Fukayama, *Rinkyōshin de Kyōiku ha Dō Kawaruka*; and Aspinall, *Unions and the Politics of Education in Japan*, 145–72.
5. On this subject, see Eades, Goodman, and Hada, *The "Big Bang" in Japanese Higher Education*.
6. See Kang, *Educational Policy and the Concept of Equal Opportunity in England*, 142–88.
7. Department of Education and Science, *Children and Their Primary Schools* (the Plowden Report).
8. For instance, see Fosco, *Japan: Patterns of Continuity*; and Sugimoto and Arnason, *Japanese Encounters with Postmodernity*.
9. See Kang, *Educational Policy and the Concept of Equal Opportunity in England*.
10. Roos, *Gender and Work: A Comparative Analysis of Industrial Societies*; and Goldthorpe and Clive, "On the Class Mobility of Women: Results from Different Approaches to the Analysis of Recent British Data" *Sociology*, no. 20 (1986): 531–55; Okamoto and Naoi, *Josei to Shakai Idō*; and Hashimoto, *Danjo Kyōgaku no Shiteki Kenkyu*.
11. Kang, *Educational Policy and the Concept of Equal Opportunity in England*, 252.
12. Ibid.
13. For example, see Ishida, *Social Mobility in Contemporary Japan*.

14. In recent analysis, see Miyano, Fukōheikan to shakai kaisō.
15. *Note:* Question (a) read: Generally speaking, do you think that society is fair? Question (b) read: Apart from an overall evaluation of fairness, do you think that fairness exists in the following aspects of contemporary Japanese society? SA= Strongly Agree, ASE= Agree to Some Extent, DA=Disagree

Appendix 1

The Japanese School System in 1937

Pre-war education in Japan involved a diverse and hierarchical system of post-elementary education. The system classified students early (at the start and finish of middle school) and then concentrated on providing an education closely related to the resultant future career path chosen for each child. Academic education required for university was only provided for a select few who made it to the higher schools—almost all of whom went to university. Teachers of such students were trained at normal schools designed exclusively for that purpose. Colleges and higher technical schools provided further professional training for those middle-school graduates who failed to pass the higher-school examination. For those who failed to enter the 5-year middle schools which served as the gateway to all of the above courses, there were a variety of opportunities for those whose education terminated: girls' high school for girls, and vocational, technical, and further elementary schools for boys.

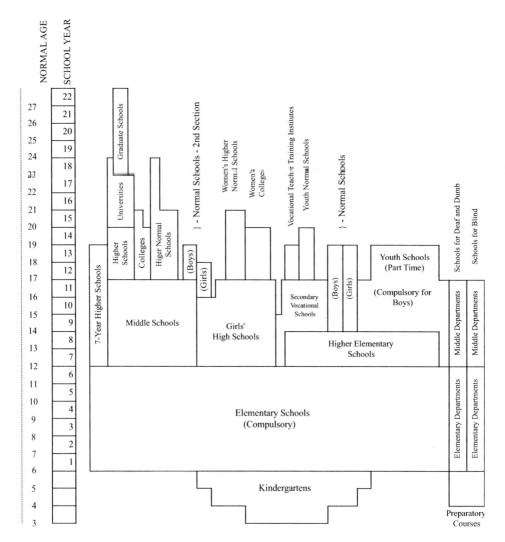

Source: Kansai Society for Educational Administration, 197.

APPENDIX 2

THE JAPANESE SCHOOL SYSTEM IN THE 1980S

The post-war education system aimed to end the undemocratic elitism of the multi-track pre-war system. This was called a unified, single-track "6-3-3-4 system" and was based on a simplified U.S. model. However, the old compulsory 6-year elementary schools would remain. Secondary education, which had formerly taken place in selective 5-year middle schools, would be divided so all children would attend compulsory 3-year lower secondary schools (*chūgakkō*), while further secondary education was to be provided in 3-year, American-style comprehensive upper secondary schools (*kōtōgakkō*). All higher education, including that which had formerly taken place in normal schools and lower-status technical colleges, was henceforth to be provided in undifferentiated 4-year universities. The old elite higher schools would be phased out—transformed into low-status local universities—and all institutions were to be co-educational. Five-year colleges of technology were also established in 1961.

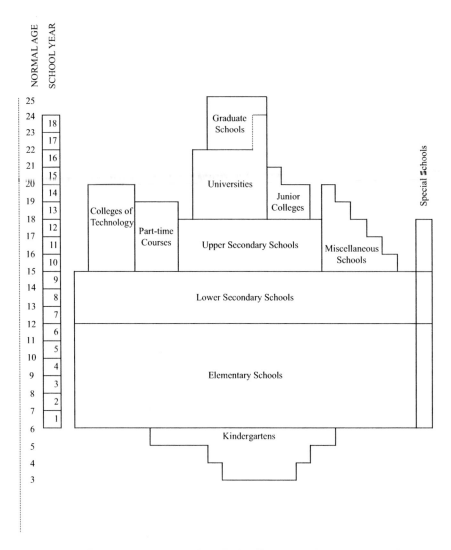

Source: http://www.mext.go.jp/b_menu/hakusho/html/hpae196301/hpae196301_2_010.html.
Ministry of Education, Culture, Sports, Science and Technology, 18 September 2010.

Appendix 3

The Japanese School System in 2008

In 1992, aiming at a diversification of the post-war state secondary education system, the LDP government established a new 6-year state secondary system in a small number of experimental schools. This system diversified the existing state secondary education system on two different tiers: on the one hand, there was the present 3-3-year lower and upper secondary schools, with entrance examinations to upper secondary schools; and on the other hand were the new 6-year schools which would conduct an entrance examination at age 12, with each school recruiting pupils from a wide range of school districts.

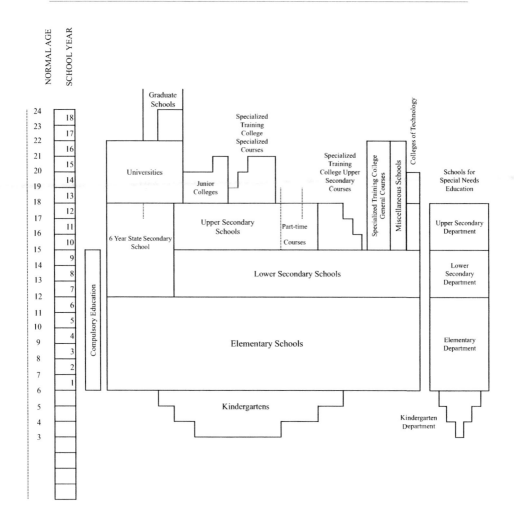

Source: http://www.mext.go.jp/english/org/struct/010.htm.

BIBLIOGRAPHY

Abe, A. *Kodomo no Hinkon.* Tokyo: Iwanami Shoten, 2008.

Abe, Y. *Kyōikugaku jiten,* vol. I. Tokyo: Iwanami Shoten, 1936.

Amano, I. *Education and Examination in Modern Japan.* Tokyo: University of Tokyo Press, 1990.

———. "Education in a Modern Affluent Japan." *Assessment in Education* 4, no. 1 (1997).

Amano, I., and M. Aso. *Education and Japan's Modernization.* Tokyo: Ministry of Foreign Affairs, Japan, 1972.

Arikura, R., and I. Amagi. *Kyōiku kankei hō II.* Tokyo: Nihon Shinpyōronsha, 1958.

Asahi Shinbun. "Educational Opportunity Depends on Parents' Income," 21 May 2006.

Asahi Shinbun weekly AERA. "A 6-year State Secondary Education System," 3 February 1997.

Aspinall, R. *Unions and the Politics of Education in Japan.* New York: State University of New York Press, 2001.

Aspinall, R., and P. Cave. "Lowering the Flag: Democracy, Authority and Rights at Tokorozawa High School." *Social Science Japan Journal* 4, no. 1 (2001): 77–91.

Beauchamp, E. R., and J. M. Vardaman, Jr., eds. *Japanese Education since 1945: A Documentary Study.* Armonk, New York: M. E. Sharpe, 1994.

Bernstein, B. *Class Codes and Control,* 2nd ed., vol. 3. London: Routledge & Kegan Paul, 1977.

Bourdieu, P., and J. C. Passeron. *Reproduction in Education, Society and Culture.* London: Sage, 1977.

Bowles, S., and H. Gintis. *Schooling in Capitalist America: Educational Reform and the Contradictions of Economic Life.* New York: Basic Books, 1976.

Cabinet Office (Sōrifu). *The Mass Survey of Opinion of Citizen's Life.* Tokyo, 1987.

Cave, P. "Educational Reform in Japan in the 1990s: 'Individuality' and Other Uncertainties." *Comparative Education* 37, no. 2 (2001): 173–191.

———. "Japanese Educational Reform: Development and Prospects at Primary and Secondary Level." In *Can the Japanese Change Their Education System?,* ed. R. Goodman and D. Phillips. Oxford: Symposium Books, 2003.

Chūō Kyōiku Shingikai (Central Council on Education). *Kyōiku no Chūritsu no Iji ni Tsuite.* Tokyo: Monbushō, 1954.

———. *Kyōiku no Seijiteki Chūritsusei Iji ni Kansuru Tōshin.* Tokyo: Monbushō, 1954.

———. *Shōchūga'kkō Gakushū Shido Yōryō Kaichō an.* Tokyo: Monbushō, 1958.

———. *Kōki Chūtō Kyōiku no Kakujū Seibi ni Tsuite no Tōshin.* Tokyo: Monbushō, 1966.

———. *Kitaisareru Ningenzō.* Tokyo: Monbushō, 1966.

————. *Kongo ni Okeru Gakkō Kyōiku no Sōgōteki na Kakujū Seibi no Tame no Kihonteki Shisaku ni Tsuite*. Tokyo: Monbushō, 1971.

————. *Reform of Various Education Systems to Make Them Relevant to a New Age*, Report of the 14th session of the CCE. Tokyo: Monbushō, 1991.

————. "Chūō Kyōiku Shingikai Dainiji Tōshin," *Monbushō*, no. 1451. Tokyo: Monbushō, 1997.

————. *21 Seiki o Tenbō Shita Waga Kuni no Kyōiku no Arikata ni Tsuite*. Tokyo: Monbushō, 1997.

————. *Shōshika to Kyōiku*. Tokyo: Monbushō, 2000.

Coleman, J. S. et al. *Equality of Educational Opportunity*. Cambridge, Mass: Harvard University Press, 1969.

Collins, R. *The Credential Society: An Historical Sociology of Education and Stratification*. New York: Oxford University Press, 1979.

Cummings, W. K. *Education and Equality in Japan*. Princeton: Princeton University Press, 1980.

Department of Education and Science (England). *Children and Their Primary Schools* (Plowden Report). London: HMSO, 1967.

Dore, R. P. *Education in Tokugawa Japan*. Berkeley: University of California Press, 1965.

————. *The Diploma Disease*. London: George Allen & Unwin, 1976.

Duke, B. *Japan's Militant Teachers*. Honolulu: University of Hawaii Press, 1973.

Eades, J., R. Goodman, and Y. Hada, eds. *The 'Big Bang' in Japanese Higher Education*. Melbourne: Trans Pacific Press, 2004.

Ehara, T. *Gendai Kōtō Kyōiku no Kōzō*. Tokyo: Tokyo Daigaku Shuppankai, 1984.

Fishkin, J. S. "Liberty versus Equal Opportunity." In *Equal Opportunity*, E.F. Paul, F.D. Miller and J.Paul (eds). Oxford: Basil Blackwell, 1987.

Floud, J. et al. *Social Class and Educational Opportunity*. London: William Heinemann, 1956.

Forster and d'Ercole, Income Distribution and Poverty in OECD Countries in the Second Half of the 1990s,2005.

Fosco, M. *Japan: Patterns of Continuity*. Tokyo: Kōdansha, 1971.

Friedman, M. *Capitalism and Freedom*. Chicago: University of Chicago Press, 1962.

Fujita, H. "Social and Economic Benefits of Educational Credentials: A Cross-societal Comparison." *Kyōiku Shakaigaku Kenkyu*, no. 38 (1983).

————. *Kyōiku Kaikaku*. Tokyo: Iwanami Shoten, 1997.

Fujita, H. et al. *Kyōiku to Shijyō* (Kyōikugaku nenpō). Seori shobō, 1996.

Fukayama, M., ed. *Rinkyōshin de Kyōiku ha Dō Kawaruka*. Tokyo: Rōdōjunpōsha, 1986.

Galutung, J. "Social Structure, Education Structure and Life-long Education." *Reviews of National Policies for Education, Japan*. Paris: OECD, 1971.

Gamble, A. *The Free Economy and the Strong State*. London: Macmillan Education, 1988.

Genda, Y. "The 'NEET' Problem in Japan." *Social Science Japan*, no. 32. Tokyo: University of Tokyo, 2005.

Genda, Y., and E. Kyokunuma. *NEET*. Tokyo: Gentousha, 2004.

Goldthorpe, J. H., and P. Clive. "On the Class Mobility of Women: Results from Different Approaches to the Analysis of Recent British Data," *Sociology*, no. 20 (1986).

Goodman, R. *Who's Looking at Whom?: Japanese, South Korean and English Educational Reform in A Comparative Perspective*. Oxford: Nissan Institute of Japanese Studies, Occasional Paper, 1989.

Hall, I. P. *Mori Arinori*, Cambridge: Harvard University Press, 1973.

Hall, R. K. *Education for a New Japan*. New Heaven, CT: Yale University Press, 1949.

Halsey, A. H. *Educational Priority* (The Halsey Report). London: HMSO, 1972.

Halsey, A. H., J. Floud, and C. A. Anderson. *Education, Economy and Society*. New York: The Free Press, 1961.

Halsey, A. H. et al. *Origins and Destinations*. Oxford: Clarendon Press, 1980.

Hashimoto, N. *Danjo Kyōgaku no Shiteki Kenkyu*. Tokyo: Ōtsuki Shoten, 1992.

Hashizume, S. *Gakureki Henjyū to Sono Kōzō*. Tokyo: Dai'Ichihōki, 1976.

Hayami, T., and T. Hasegawa. "Gakugyō Seiseki no In'Gakichaku," *Japanese Journal of Educational Psychology*, no. 27 (1979).

Hayao, K. *The Japanese Prime Minister and Public Policy*. Pittsburgh: University of Pittsburgh Press, 1993.

Hayek, F. A. *The Constitution of Liberty*. London: Routledge & Kegan Paul, 1960.

Hirahara, H. *Gimu Kyōiku/Danjo Kyōgaku*. Tokyo: Gakuyō Shobō, 1978.

———. *Kyōiku to Kyōiku Kihonhō*. Tokyo: Keisō Shobō, 1996.

Hisaki, Y., E. Suzuki, E. and H. Imano, eds. *Sengo Kyōiku Ronsou Shiroku*. Tokyo: Dai'Ichi Hōki, 1980.

Holloway, S. D. et al. "Causal Attributions by Japanese and American Mothers and Children about Performance in Mathematics," *International Journal of Psychology*, no. 21 (1986).

Hood, C. *Japanese Education Reform: Nakasone's Legacy*. New York: Routledge, 2001.

Horio, H., and M. Yamazumi. *Kyōiku Rinen*. Tokyo: Tokyo Daigaku Shuppankai, 1976.

Horio, T. *Gendai Kyōiku no Shisou to Kōzō*. Tokyo: Iwanami, 1971.

———. "Chūkyōshin Kaikaku Kōsō to Kokumin no Gakushū Kyōiku Ken." In *Kyōiku*. Tokyo: Kokudosha, 1971.

———. *Gendai Nihon no Kyōiku Shisou*. Tokyo: Aoki Shoten, 1979.

———. *Educational Thought and Ideology in Modern Japan*. Tokyo: University of Tokyo Press, 1988.

———. *Gendai Shakai to Kyōiku*. Tokyo: Iwanami Shinsho, 1997.

Hunter, J. *The Emergence of Modern Japan*. London: Longman, 1989.

Husén, T. *Social Background and Educational Career: Research Perspectives on Equality of Educational Opportunity*. Paris: Centre for Educational Research and Innovation, OECD, 1972.

Ichikawa, S. *Kyōiku Gyōsei no Riron to Kōzō*. Tokyo: Gyōsei, 1975.

Iizaki, A. *Kokumin no Kyōikuken*. Tokyo: Aoki Shoten, 1972.

———. *Kyōiku no Kikaikintou, Kyōikukihonhō Bunken Senshu*, vol. 3. Tokyo: Gakuyō Shobō, 1978.

Imada, T. *Shakai Kaisō to Seiji* Tokyo: Tokyo Daigaku Shuppankai, 1991.

Inui, A. *Nihon no Kyōiku to Kigyō Shakai*. Tokyo: Ōtsuki Shoten, 1990.

Ishida, H. *Social Mobility in Contemporary Japan*. London: Macmillan, 1993.

Ishikawa, S. *Nihon Kyōikushi*. Tokyo: Tamagawa Daigaku Shuppanbu, 1987.

Jackson, B., and D. Marsden. *Education and the Working Class*. London: Routledge & Kegan Paul, 1966.

Jencks, C. et al. *Inequality: A Reassessment of the Effect of Family and Schooling in America*. New York: Basic Books, 1972.

Jiyūminshutō (Liberal Democratic Party). *Ge'kkan Jiyūminshutō*, 21 December 1997.

Kaigo, T. *Japanese Education: Its Past and Present*. Tokyo: Kokusai Bunka Shinkōkai, 1968.

Kamei, H., et al. *Chūkyōshin Tōshin Kara Yomu 21 Seiki no Kyōiku*. Tokyo: Gyōsei, 1996.

Kaneko, M. *Kyōiku Hōgaku to Kyōiku Saiban*. Tokyo: Keisō Shobō, 1969.

———. *Kokumin no Kyōikuken*. Tokyo: Iwanami, 1971.

———. *Kyōiku-hō*. Tokyo: Yūhikaku, 1978.

Kang, Hee-Chun. *Educational Policy and the Concept of Equal Opportunity in England*. Seoul: Sekyugsa, 1986.

Kariya, T. *Taishū Kyōiku Shakai no Yukue*. Tokyo: Chūkō Shinsho, 1995.

———. *Kaisōka Nihon to Kyōiku Kiki*. Tokyo: Yūshindō, 2001.

Kawai, A., and T. Muroi, eds. *Kyōiku Kihonhō Rekishi to Kenkyu*. Tokyo: Shin Nihon Shuppan, 1998.

Keizai Shingikai (Economic Deliberation Council). *Kokumin Shotoku Baizō Keikaku*, 27 December 1960. Tokyo: Keizai Shingikai.

———. *Shotoku Baizō Keikaku ni Tomonau Chōki Kyōiku Keikaku Hōkoku*. Tokyo: Keizai Shingikai, 1960.

———. *Jinteki Nōryoku Seisaku ni Kansuru Tōshin* (Task and Countermeasure for Development of Human Abilities and in Pursuits of Economic Expansion). Tokyo: Keizai Shingikai, 1963.

Kersten, R. "Liberal School of History." *Japan Forum* 11, no. 2 (1999): 191–203.

Kida, H. *Kyōiku Gyōseigaku*. Tokyo:Yūshindo Kobunsha, 1982.

Kikkawa, T. "Effect of Educational Expansion on Educational Inequality in Post-industrialized Societies: A Cross-cultural Comparison of Japan and the United States of America," *International Journal of Japanese Sociology* 13, no. 1 (November 2004): 100–19.

Kikuchi, J., ed. *Kyōiku to Shakai Idō, Gendai Nihon no Kaisō Kōzō*, vol. 3. Tokyo: Tokyo Daigaku Shuppankai, 1993.

Kitaoka, S. *Jimintō*. Tokyo: Yomiuri Shinbunsha, 1995.

Kobayashi, N., and M. Kaneko. "Kyōku Hanrei 100 Sen," *Jurist*, no. 41 (1973).

Kobayshi, T. *Society, Schools and Progress in Japan*. Oxford: Pergamon Press, 1976.

———. "From Education Borrowing to Educational Sharing: the Japanese Experience." In *Cultural Identity and Educational Policy*, ed. Colin Brock. London: Croom Helm, 1985.

Kokumin Kyōiku Kenkyusho, ed. *Minshuteki Kōkō Kyōiku no Sōzō, Kokumin Kyōiku*. Tokyo: Kokumin Kyōiku Kenkyusho, 1967.

Kokuritsu Kyōiku Kenkyūsho. *Nihon Kindai Kyōiku 100-Nen Shi*, vol. I. Tokyo: Kokuritsu Kyōiku Kenkyūsho, 1974.

Komori, K., ed. *Kōkō Seido Kaikaku no Sōgōteki Kenkyu*. Tokyo: Taga Shuppan, 1986.

Kosaka, K. *Social Stratification in contemporary Japan*. London: Kegan Paul International, 1994.

Kubo, Y. *Tai'nichi Senryō Seisaku to Sengo Kyōiku Kaikaku*. Tokyo: Sanseido, 1984.

Kudomi, T. *Kyōsō no Kyōiku*. Tokyo: Rōdō Junpōsha, 1993.

Kurasawa, T. *Gakkō Rei no Kenkyū*. Tokyo: Kōdansha, 1978.

Kuroha, R. *Gakkō to Shakai no Shōwashi*. Tokyo: Dai'Ichi Houki, 1994.

Kurosaki, I. *Kōkyōikuhi no Kenkyu*. Tokyo: Aokishoten, 1980.

Kurosaki, I. et al. *Kyōiku Shi-zō no Saikouchiku*. Tokyo: Seori Shobō, 1997.

Kyōiku. Tokyo: Kokudosha.

Kyōiku no Sengoshi Henshū Iinkai (KSHI). *Kyōiku no Sengoshi*, 4 vols. Tokyo: San'chi Shobō, 1986.

Lebra, T. S. *Japanese Patterns of Behavior*. Honolulu: University of Hawaii Press, 1976.

Levitas, R., ed. *The Ideology of New Right*, London: Polity Press, 1986.

Lincicome, M. *Principles, Praxis, and the Politics of Educational Reform in Meiji Japan*. Honolulu: Hawaii University Press, 1993.

Maki, M. *Kyōikuken*. Tokyo: Shin Nihon Shuppan-Sha, 1971.

Marshall, Byron K. *Learning to be Modern: Japanese Political Discourse on Education*. Colorado: Westview Press, 1994.

Marutani, Y. *Fukuzawa Yukichi Kenkyu*. Tokyo: Souei, 2002.

Ministry of Education, Culture, Sports, Science &Technology. *Survey times of Household Expenditure per Student*. Tokyo, 2004.

Ministries of Education, Health and Welfare, Labor, and Construction. *Kongo no Kosodate Shien Notameno Sisaku no Kihonteki Houkou ni Tsuite* (Basic Orientations to Assist Child-Raising) (Angel Plan), Tokyo, 1995.

———. *Jyūtenteki ni Suisinsubeki Shōshika Taisaku no Guteiteki Jissikeikaku ni Tsuite* (About the Implementation of Concrete Plans for Importantly Recommended Counter Policy against Low Fertility) (New Angel Plan). Tokyo, 1999.

———. *Heisei 18 Nendo Ban Rōdō Keizai no Bunseki* (*Rōdō Hakusho*) (Heisei 18 Analysis of Labor Economics). Tokyo, 2005.

Miura, A. *Karyū-Shakai*. Tokyo: Koubunsha, 2005.

Miyajima, T., and H. Fujita. "Bunka no Kōzō to Saiseisan ni Kansuru Ji'ssyōteki Kenkyu," *Tokyo Daigaku Kyōiku Gakubu Kiyou* 32 (1992).

Miyano, M. *Fukōheikan to shakai kaisō*, National Survey of Social Stratification and Social Mobility (SSM), series no. 8. Tokyo, 1995.

Monbujihō. Tokyo: Monbushō, various years.

Monbushō (Ministry of Education). *Nihon Kensetsu no Kyōiku Houshin* (The Educational Policy for Construction of a New Japan Shin). Tokyo: Monbushō, 1945.

———. *Shin Kyōiku Shishin* (A Guide for the New Education). Tokyo: Monbushō, 1946.

———.*Shinsei Chugakkō Shinsei Kōtōgakkō Nozomashi I Un'Eino Shisin* (A Desirable Guideline for Administration of the New Lower and Upper Secondary Schools). Tokyo: Monbushō, 1949.

———. *Rokusansei o Sonzoku Seshimurubeki Riyu* (The Reasons for Preserving the 6–3-3–4 System). Tokyo: Monbushō, 1951.

———. *Kōyku Sa'sshin Shingikai Yōran* (A Handbook of the Educational Reform Council). Tokyo: Monbushō, 1952.

———. *A Plan for Developing Human Capital and Reform of the Examination System in Monbujihō*. Tokyo: Monbushō, 1960.

———. *Kokuritsu Kōgyō Kyōin Yōsei no Se'chi Touni Kansuru Ringi Sochi Hōan* (An Emergency Bill Concerning Teacher Training in National Technical Schools). Tokyo: Monbushō, 1961.

———. *Kyōiku Hakusho* (White Paper on Education): *Nihon no Seichō to Kyōiku* (Japan's Development and Education). Tokyo: Monbushō, 1962.

———. *Shōwa 36 Nendo Zenkoku Chūgakkō I'ssei Gakuryoku Chousa Ji'sshi Yōkō* (Outline for Simultaneously Implementation of Nationwide Scholastic Achievement Test for Secondary School on Shōwa 36). Tokyo: Monbushō, 1962.

———. *Kōtōtgakkō Seito Kyūzō Taisaku to "Kōkō Zen-Nyū Undō" no Kahi* (A Measure for Suddenly Increasing the Number of Upper secondary School Students and Advisability of Upper Secondary School for All Movement). Tokyo: Monbushō, 1962.

———. *Kōkō Nyūshi Seido Kaisei Shōrei* (A Ministerial Ordinance to Reform the Entrance Examination of Upper Secondary School). Tokyo: Monbushō, 1963.

———. *Chuga'kkō Sotsugyōsha no Shinro Jyōkyō*. Tokyo: Monbushō, 1968.

———. *Gakusei 100 Nenshi*, vol. 2. Tokyo: Monbushō, 1972.

———. *Outline of Education in Japan*. Tokyo: Monbushō, 1985.

———. *Chūō Kyōiku Shingikai Dai'Niji Tōshin*,in *Monbushō*, no. 1451. Tokyo: Monbushō, 1997.

———. *The Education Reform Plan for the 21ˢᵗ Century, the Rainbow Plan, the Seven Priorities Strategies*. Tokyo: Monbushō, 2001.

Monbushō Hourei Kenkyukai, ed. *Kyōiku Kihonhō no Kaisetsu*. Tokyo: Monbushō, 1974.

Moriguchi, K. "Shin'Gaku no Kitei Sho'inshi ni Kansuru Ichikenkyu." In *kyotodaigaku Kyōiku Gakubu Kiyou*, no 6.

Motoyama, Y. *Meiji Zenki Gakkō Seiritsushi*. Tokyo: Miraisha, 1965.

Munakata, S. *Kyōiku Kihonhō*. Tokyo: Shinpyōsha, 1966.

Murata, A. "Sengo no Nōryokubetsu Ga'kkyū no Hensen," *Hanazono Daigaku Kenkyu Kiyou*, no. 14. Hanazono Daigaku, 1983.

Musgrove, F. *School and the Social Order*. Chichester: John Wiley and Sons, 1976.

Nagai, K. *Kenpō to Kyōiku Kihonken*. Tokyo: Keisō Shobō, 1970.

———. *Kokumin no Kyōkuken*. Tokyo: Hōritsu Bunkasha, 1973.

Nakano, Y. "Kaisō to Gengo," *Kyōiku Shakaigaku Kenkyu*, no. 29 (1974).

Namimoto, K. *Kyōiku Seisaku to Kyōiku no Jiyū*. Tokyo: Seibundō, 1971.

———. *Gendai Kyōiku Seisaku no Tennkai to Doukou*. Tokyo: Gakuyō Shobō, 1987.

Namimoto, K., and A. Mikami. *"Kaisei" Kyōiku Kihonhō o Kangaeru*. Tokyo: Kitaki Shuppan, 2008.

Nihon Kyōiku Ga'kkai. *Kakutō no Bunkyō Seisaku*. Tokyo: Nihon Kyōiku Ga'kkai, 1955.

Nihon Kyōiku Shinbun, "A 6-year State Secondary Education System," 22 February 1997.

Nikkeiren. *Shin Kyōiku Seido Saikentōni Kansuru Yōbō* (Recommendation for Reconstruction of the New Education System). Tokyo: Nikkeiren, 1952.

———. *Tōmen Kyōiku Seido Kaizen ni Kansuru Yōbō* (Recommendation for the Improvement of the Current Education System). Tokyo: Nikkeiren, 1954.

————. *Kagaku Gijutsu Kyōiku Kōshin ni Kansuru Iken* (Our View Concerning the Improvement of Science and Technical Education). Tokyo: Nikkeiren, 1957.

Nikkyōso (Japan Teachers' Union). *Kyōiku Hakusho* (White Paper on Education). Tokyo: Nikkyōso, 1950.

————. *Kyōshi no rinri kōryō* (A Code of Ethics for Teachers): *Kyōiku hakusho* (White Paper on Education), 1 May 1950.

————. *Kōkō Nyūshi Haishi, Zen'in Nyūgaku Undō no Hōshin* (Abolition of Entrance Examination in Upper Secondary School, A Policy of Upper Secondary School for All Movement). JTU 21ˢᵗ Conference, Tokyo, 1959.

————. *Gakute Ji'sshi ni Kansuru Monbudaijin Eno Shitsumonsho* (Questions towards Minister of Education on Implementation of the Scholastic Achievement Test). Tokyo: Nikkyōso, 1961.

————. *Watashitachi no U'ttae* (Our Complaint). Tokyo: Nikkyōso, 1961.

————. *How to Reform Japan's Education: A Report of Nikkyōso—Council on Education Reform.* Tokyo: Nikkyōso, 1975.

————. *Nihon no Kyōiku* (Japanese Education). Tokyo: Nikkyōso, various years.

Nishi, T. *Unconditional Democracy, Education and Politics in Occupied Japan 1945–52.* Stanford: Hoover Institution Press, 1982.

Okada, A. "Equality of Opportunity in Post-war England and Japan: A Comparative Study of Educational Policy, 1944–1970," unpublished Ph.D. thesis, Oxford University, 1998.

————. "Secondary Education Reform and the Concept of Equality of Opportunity in Japan." *Compare* 29, no. 2 (1999): 171–89.

————. "Japan as a Prototype of the 'Degreeocracy' Society?" *Educational Review* 23, no. 3 (2001).

————. "Education of whom, for whom, by whom? Revision of the Fundamental Law of Education in Japan." *Japan Forum* 14, no. 3 (2002).

Okamoto, H., and M. Naoi, eds. *Josei to Shakai Idō.* Tokyo: Tokyo Daigaku Shuppankai, 1990.

Okano, K., and M. Tsuchiya. *Education in Contemporary Japan.* United Kingdom: Cambridge University Press, 1999.

Ota, T. *Sengo Nihon Kyōikushi.* Tokyo: Iwanami Shobō, 1978.

Park, Y. H. *Bureaucrats and Minister in Contemporary Japanese Government.* Berkeley: University of California Press, 1986.

Passin, H. *Society and Education in Japan.* New York : Teachers College Press, 1965.

Rinji Kyōiku Shingikai (Ad-Hoc Council on Education). "Kyōiku Kaikaku ni Kansuru Daiichiji Tōshin." *Rinkyōshin Dayori,* special ed. 2–3, 26 June 1985,

————. "Kyōiku Kaikaku ni Kansuru Dainiji Tōshin," *Rinkyōshin Dayori,* special ed. 5, 23 April 1986.

Phillips, D., and R. Goodman, eds. *Can the Japanese Change Their Education System?* Oxford: Oxford Studies in Comparative Education, 2003.

Prime Minister Office. *Heisei 15 Nendo Kokumin Seikatsu Hakusho* (Heisei 15 White Paper of Nations Lives). Tokyo: Sorifu, 2003.

Roesgaard, M. *Moving Mountains: Japanese Education Reform.* Aarhus: Aarhus University Press, 1998.

Rohlen, T. "Is Japanese Education Becoming Less Egalitarian? Notes on High School Stratification and Reform." *Journal of Japanese Studies* 3 (1977).

————. *Japan's High Schools.* Berkeley, University of California Press, 1983.

————. "Conflict in Intuitional Environments: Politics in Education." In *Conflict in Japan,* ed. Ellis S. Krauss et al. University of Hawaii Press, Honolulu, 1984.

Ronza. "Dai Ronshō." Tokyo: Asashishinbunsha (January 2001).

Roos, P. *Gender and Work: A Comparative Analysis of Industrial Societies.* New York: State University of New York Press, 1985.

Sasaki, Y. *"Kaisei" Kyōiku Kihonhō.* Tokyo: Nihon Bunkyō Shuppan, 2009.

Sato, H. *Beikoku Tai'Nichi Kyōiku Shisetsudan ni Kansuru Sōgtōteki Kenkyu.* Tokyo: Kokuritsu Kyōiku Kenkyusho, 1991.

Sato, T. *Fubyōdō Shakai Nihon*. Tokyo: Chūōshinsho, 2000.

Schoppa, L. J. *Education Reform in Japan: A Case of Immobilist Politics*. London: Routledge, 1991.

Seirei Shimon Iinkai (Advisory Committee for Ordinance Revision). *Kyōiku Seido no Kaikaku ni Kansuru Tōshin* (Recommendations for Educational Reform). Tokyo, Monbushō, 1951.

Sengo Nihon Kyōiku Shiryō Shūsei Henshū Iinkai (SNKSHI). *Sengo Nihon Kyōiku Shiryō Shūsei*, 12 vols. Tokyo: San'ichi Shobō, 1982.

Shimahara, N. *Adaptation and Education in Japan*. New York: Praeger, 1976.

Shimizu, S. *Tuijō Nihonkoku Kenpō Shingiroku*. Tokyo: Yūhikaku, 1962.

Shimizu, Y. *20 Nen Go no Kyōiku to Keizai*. Tokyo: Tōyōkan Shuppansha, 1961.

Shimonaka, Y. *Ban'nin no Kyōiku: Shimonaka Yasaburō Kyōikuronshū*. Tokyo: Heibonsha, 1974.

Shinbori, M. *Gakureki–Jitsuryoku Shugi o Kobamu Mono*. Tokyo: Diamond, 1966.

———. *Gakubatsu*. Tokyo: Fukumura Shuppan, 1969.

Shirahase, S.,. *Henkasuru Shakai no Fubyōdō*. Tokyo: Tokyo Daigaku Shuppannkai, 2006.

Smethurst, R. J. *The Origins and Policies of the Japan Teachers' Union 1945–56*. Ann Arbor: University of Michigan Press, 1967.

Sugihara, S. *Kyōiku Kihonhō*. Tokyo: Kyōdō, 1974.

Sugimoto, Y., and J. P. Arnason. *Japanese Encounters with Postmodernity*. London: Kegan Paul International, 1995.

Suzuki, E. *Kyōiku Gyōsei*. Tokyo: Tokyodaigaku Shuppankai, 1970.

———. *Nihon Senryō to Kyōiku Kaikaku*. Tokyo: Keisō, 1983.

Tachibanaki, T. *Nihon no Keizai Kakusa*. Tokyo: Iwanamishoten, 1998.

Takahashi, H. *Sengo Kyōiku Kaikaku to Shidō Shuji Seido*. Tokyo: Kazama Shobō, 1995.

Takakura, S. *Kyōiku ni Okeru Kousei to Fukousei*. Tokyo: Kyōiku Kaihatsu Kenkyusho, 1996.

Takeuchi, H., and M. Aso, eds. *Nihon no Gakurekishakai ha Kawaru*. Tokyo: Yūhikaku, 1981.

Takeuchi, Y. *Kyōsō to Kyōiku*. Tokyo: Sekaishisōsha, 1981.

Tanaka, H. *Sengo Nihon Seijishi*. Tokyo: Kōdansha Gakujutsu Bunko, 1996.

Tanaka, K. *Kyōiku Kihonhō no Riron*. Tokyo: Yūhikaku, 1961.

Taniguchi, T. *Nihon Chūtō Kyōiku Kaikakushi Kenkyu*. Tokyo: Dai'Ichihōki, 1988.

Thurston, D. R. *Teachers and Politics in Japan*. Princeton, NJ: Princeton University Press, 1973.

Tokyo Daigaku Kōhō Iinkai. *Gakunai Kōhō*, no. 906–02, 25 November 1991.

Tokyo Daigaku Kyōikugakubu Kyōjudan. *Iwayuru Seirei Shimon Iinkai no 'Kyōikuseido Kaikaku ni Kansuru Tōshin ni Taisuru Iken*. Tokyo: Tokyo Daigaku, 1951.

Traphagan, J., and J. Knight, eds. *Demographic Change and the Family in Japan's Aging Society*. New York: State University of New York Press, 2003.

Tsuchimochi, Gary H. *Education Reform in Post-War Japan: The 1946 U.S. Education Mission*. Tokyo: University of Tokyo Press, 1993.

Tsukasaki, M., and M. Tsukasaki. *Kyōiku no Kikai Kintou Towa*. Tokyo: San'chi Shobō, 1976.

Uchida, K. *Rinkyōshin no Kiseki*. Tokyo: Dai'Ichi Hōki, 1990.

Uehara, S. *Kyōiku Gyōseigaku*. Tokyo: Fukumura Shuppan, 1991.

Umene, S. *Nihon no Kyōiku Dōarubekika*. Tokyo: Keisō Shobō, 1972.

———. *Nihon no Kyōiku*. Tokyo: Gyōsei, 1975.

United States Education Mission (USEM). *Report of the United States Education Mission to Japan*, submitted to the Supreme Commander for the Allied Powers, Tokyo, 30 March 1946, Westport, CT.

Ushiogi, M. "Shinro Ke'ttei Katei no Pasu Kaiseki," *Kyōiku Shakaigaku Kenkyu*, no. 30 (1975).

———. *Gakureki Shakai no Tenkan*. Tokyo: Tokyo Daigaku Shuppankai, 1978.

———. "Yureru Gakureki Shakai," *Gendai no Exprit*, no. 152 (1980).

Ushiogi, M., and T. Sato. "Shakaikaisō to Gakugyō Seiseki ni Kansuru Ji'ssyōkenkyu," *Nagoya Daigaku Kyōikugakubu Kiyō* 26 (1979).

Watanabe, A. *Sengo Nihon no Saishōtachi*. Tokyo: Chūōkōronsha, 1995.

Yamada, M. *Parasito Shinguru no Jidai.* Tokyo: Chikumashobō, 1999.

———. *Kibō Kakusa Shakai.* Tokyo: Chikumashobō, 2005.

Yamazaki, M. *Jimintō to Kyōiku Seisaku.* Tokyo: Iwanami Shinsho, 1986.

Yamazumi, M. *Nihon Kyōiku Shōshi.* Tokyo: Iwanami Shoten, 1987.

Yashiro, N. *Gendai Nihon no Byouri Kaimei.* Tokyo: Tōyō Keizai Shinpōsha, 1980.

Yokohama Kokuritsu Daigaku Gendai Kyōiku Kenkyusho, eds. *Chûkyōshin to Kyōiku Kaikaku.* Tokyo: San'ichi Shobō, 1973.

Yomiuri Shinbun Sengoshi Han, ed. *Kyōiku no Ayumi.* Tokyo: Yomiuri Shinbunsha, various years.

Yoneda, T. *Kindai Nihon Chūgakkōseido no Kakuritsu.* Tokyo: Tokyo Daigaku Shuppankai, 1992.

Yoneyama, S. "Japanese 'Education Reform': The Plan for the 20th Century." In *Japan: Change and Continuity,* ed. M. Javed, J. Graham, and H. Miyajima. London: Routledge, 2002.

Zen-nyu Zenkyo, ed. *Kōkō Zen'in Nyūgaku Mondai Zenkoku Kyōgikai Seimei.* Tokyo: Zen-nyū Zenkyo, 1962.

INDEX

ability 4, 9, 16, 19, 28, 32, 34–37, 41–46, 48, 50–51, 59–60, 62–64, 68–70, 73, 75, 82, 84–87, 89–90, 95–102, 104, 108, 115, 120, 122, 125,130, 135, 142–145, 147, 149–150, 152, 162, 164–167, 169, 171–172, 175, 179
 first (as adjective) 47, 81–82, 84, 85–87, 92, 97, 102–104, 143, 165, 171–172
academic attainment 72, 101
achievement 7, 9, 13–14, 21, 72–73, 85, 116, 125, 138n47, 144, 149, 151, 157
ACOR 56–57, 59–62, 76n9, 77n14, 77n17
Ad Hoc Council on Education see AHCE
Advisory Committee for Ordinance Revision (*Seire Shimon Iinkai*) see ACOR
AHCE 109, 111, 113, 116, 120, 126, 133
Amano, I. 76n10, 142–143
American Occupation 1, 3, 17n4, 30–31, 33, 44, 55–56, 67, 126, 162–163
assessment 87, 89, 122, 130, 144

birth rate 17, 117, 145, 153, 178,
Bourdieu, P. 10, 178
Bowles, S., and H. Gintis 10, 13
Britain 153, 165, 171
bullying (ijime) 113, 118, 120, 126, 128, 134, 144, 149
bunkyōzoku see education zoku
bureaucrats 6, 75, 121
business
 representatives (*zaikai*) 143
 sector 81, 83, 85, 87, 94, 96, 126
 world 24, 121

CCE 4–5, 7, 16, 64–66, 68, 72, 77n32, 82, 85, 94, 96–100, 103–104, 108–111, 115–120, 121–124, 126, 137n26, 135, 139, 157, 164–166, 168
childhood 63, 148
child-rearing 154, 156, 158

children 3–9, 11–14, 20–25, 27–29, 30, 34–37, 39–43, 44–51, 57, 59–65, 68–69, 70–76, 80, 82–89, 90–92, 94–96, 99–104, 108, 110, 115, 117–119, 121–126, 130, 134–135, 139, 140–142, 144–149, 151, 154–157, 161–162, 164–168, 170–172, 174–176, 178
choice 5, 10, 14–16, 34, 101, 110–116, 120–125, 130, 135, 148, 164, 168, 172
Chūkyōshin see CCE
Chūō Kyōiku Shingikai (Central Council on Education) see CCE
CI&E (*Minkan Jōhō Kyōiku Kyoku*) 32–33, 54n32
Civil Information and Education Section see CI&E
class
 bias 34, 59, 72–73, 75
 issue 7
clubs 121
community 14, 21, 85, 102. 109–110, 116, 134
competition 90, 94, 110–112, 118, 120–122, 124, 130, 134, 142–148, 164, 167–168, 171, 177
comprehensive secondary school 43, 59, 162, 175
consensus 45, 50, 134, 167–168, 173
conservative 3–6, 11–12, 16, 37–38, 41, 43, 46–48, 50–51, 52n25, 56–57, 59, 65–66, 68–69, 74–76, 83–87, 91, 99–101, 103–104, 108, 120, 127–128, 135–136, 163–170, 172–175
Constitution 1, 3, 16, 31, 38–40, 42–45, 47–51, 52n18, 53n30, 56, 59, 68, 86, 90, 116, 126, 133–134, 136, 162, 165, 171
Course of Study 87–88, 94, 148
creativity 15–16, 113, 115, 117, 144
criteria 2, 35, 51, 82, 87, 118, 144, 150
curriculum 4, 24–25, 39, 56, 63, 67, 78n41, 86, 88–89, 94, 97–98, 108, 115, 117, 121–122, 128–129, 135, 163–164, 167, 173

decision-makers 2
democracy 32–33, 38, 76n3, 129
deregulation 112, 117, 152
discipline 10, 64, 70, 72, 132, 143, 168
discrimination 28–29, 35, 43, 46, 48, 70, 76, 91, 99, 101, 104, 149, 162, 166
disparity society 139, 157, 168
distinctive elements 149
Dore, R. P. 141–143, 173
doryoku (efforts of studying) 149
draft (of New Constitution) 38–39, 41–42, 44–48

economy 4, 9, 31, 62, 64, 80–81, 83, 85, 87, 88, 92–93, 103, 111, 113, 115, 127, 152, 154, 156–157, 165, 167, 173–174
EDC (Economic Deliberation Council: Keizai Shingikai) 16, 64, 81, 83–86, 96–97, 99, 104, 165
ERNC (Education Reform National Conference: Kyōiku Kaikaku Kokumin Kaigi) 117, 126–133, 135–136
education policy 66–67, 80, 121
educational
    reform 3–4, 7, 16–17, 23, 30–33, 41, 44–45, 49, 52n7, 55, 74–75, 92, 97, 102, 105n11, 109, 112, 116
    sociologist 7, 69, 143–144, 148–149, 157
education system 3, 7, 9–10, 15, 19–24, 26, 29, 31–34, 36–37, 39, 41–43, 45–51, 54–57, 59–66, 68, 70–72, 74–76, 83, 85–87, 90, 92, 96, 101–103, 108–111, 113–115, 117–121, 123, 125–128, 130–131, 133–135, 141, 143–145, 160–167, 171–173, 176–177, 183, 185
egalitarianism 6, 8, 10, 16, 49, 57, 60, 62, 68, 75, 85–86, 91, 102, 104, 150, 160, 167, 172, 174–175, 177, 179
elite education, 104, 115
England 8–9, 13–15, 26, 34, 50, 167–168, 170–179
Entrance examination 73, 94, 96, 100–101, 110, 118–119, 121, 123, 125, 141, 143–144, 150, 166–167, 185
ERC (Educational Reform Counciil: Kyōiku Sa'ssin Iinkai) 44–45, 47–50, 60
examination hell (shiken-jigoku) 118, 120–123, 130, 143–145, 149, 166–167
extra tuition 145

family 6–7, 10–12, 17, 21, 24, 28–29, 49, 73, 99, 101–102, 116, 125–126, 139–140, 146–147, 149, 153, 157, 162, 169–171, 177
fertility 145

Fishkin, J. S. 10–12, 169, 172
FLE (Fundamental Law of Education: Kyōiku Kihonhō) 1–4, 16, 31, 38, 42, 44–45, 48–51, 56, 59, 61, 67, 85–86, 89–90, 96, 99, 104, 111, 116, 126–135, 162–163, 165–166, 168, 171
Floud, J. 13
forward-thinking 113
Fujita, H. 60, 121
furiitā 152–153, 157, 168

Galtung, J. 141, 144
gakubatsu (school cliques) 144–145, 150
gakureki-shakai (degreeocracy) 141
gakurekishugi (degreeocracy) 157
GDCE (Group for Discussion of Culture and Education: Bunka to Kyōiku ni Kansuru Kondankai) 110–111
Genda, Y. 152–153
GHQ (General Headquarters) 32, 54
Gini co-efficient 147
graduation 94, 115, 144

Halsey, A. H. 163, 169–176
Hatoyama, I 32
Hatoyama, Y 132, 154–157
hensachi 118, 144
higher education 3–4, 7, 15, 22, 25, 32, 36, 44, 50, 82, 92, 98, 114, 124–125, 130, 143–145, 149, 154, 161, 165, 167–16, 170, 175, 183
high school 34, 92, 99, 103, 108, 118–119, 127–128, 145, 147–148, 154–158, 181
Horio, T. 88
human rights 27, 44, 47–48, 60, 102, 171
Husén, T. 8–9, 11–12, 169

identity 128, 164
ikiru chikara 117–118, 137n26
individualism 61, 68, 85
inequality 7, 10, 17, 30, 40–41, 51, 70, 73, 86, 101, 104, 115, 119, 124, 141, 147–152, 158, 177–178

JDP (Japan Democratic Party) 66, 73, 132
JCP (Japan Communist Party) 35–37, 74
Jencks, C. 13
Jobless youth 152–153
JSP (Japan Socialist Party) 35–37, 45, 55, 66, 68, 74, 90–91, 112
JTU (Japan Teachers' Union: Nikkyoso) 4, 6, 55–57, 61–61, 66–76, 76n3, 77n32, 78n40, 78n59, 83, 88–96, 99–104, 112–113, 128, 149, 163, 165–167, 172–173
juku (cram school) 119, 139

kakusa shakai (gap society) 7, 139, 150–152, 157, 168
Kang, Hee-Chun 8–9
Kariya,T. 8, 69–71, 100–101, 149–150
Koizumi, J 131–134, 136, 152, 168
kōnai bōryoku see school violence
kosei (individuality) 113
Kyōiku Kihonhō see FLE
Kyoto University 119

LDP (Liberal Democratic Party) 6, 64, 66–68, 72, 75, 78n40, 80–81, 83, 85, 87, 104, 105n20, 112, 117, 121, 126, 128–129, 131–132, 135, 143, 148–149, 154, 166, 168, 172–173, 185
life-long learning 109, 132
life-time employers 143

mass education 21, 150
Meiji period 21–23, 28, 39
Meiji Restoration 20, 22
Ministry of Internal Affairs (*Sōmushō*) 145, 151
Monbushō (Ministry of Education) *see* MOE
Monbukagakushō see MOE
MOE (Ministry of Education/Ministry of Education, Culture, Sports, Science & Technology) 3, 16, 32–33, 36–38, 49–51, 53n32, 55, 61–67, 75, 77n28, 78n40, 82–83, 85, 87–96, 99–100, 103–104, 105n9, 106n46, 109–113, 116, 118, 126, 130, 148, 163, 166, 168

Nakasone, Y 16, 105n11, 108–114, 116, 133, 135, 136n1, 167
national elite 2–5, 26, 43, 75, 109, 121–122, 141, 150, 164, 173
national identity 55, 130
nationalism 24, 67, 103, 133, 166
NEETs 152–154, 157, 168
Nihon Kyōsantō see JCP
Nihon Shakaitō see JSP
Nikkeiren (Federation of Employers' Associations) 62–64
Nikkyōso see JTU

OECD 141, 147

positive discrimination 14, 171, 174–175, 179
post-war
   Constitution 3
   education system 3, 31, 33, 55, 57, 62, 70, 128, 131, 133–134, 163, 183
   Japan 4, 54, 112, 157, 169
   Occupation 3
   period 2–3, 5, 8, 15, 36, 73, 120, 128, 162

Rinji Kyōiku Shingikai (Ad Hoc Council on Education) see AHCE
Rinkyōshin see AHCE

SAT (Scholastic Achievement Test) 87–91, school
   district system 23, 92
   violence 113, 120, 128
Seirei Shimon Iinkai see ACOR
selection process 145, 149–150, 174
self-esteem 149
Schoppa, L. J. 62
six-year secondary schools 114
social class 69, 72–74, 103–104, 124–126, 141, 145, 148–150, 170–172, 174, 177–179
standard curricula 150
streaming 69–72, 75, 98, 100, 109
subject 25, 34, 86–87, 89–90, 98, 103, 115, 129

Tachibanaki, T. 151
Teachers 163, 167, 181
Tokyo University 59–60, 119

ultra-nationalist 25, 32
United States 54, 66, 92, 133, 149, 167–168, 177
USEM (United States Education Mission) 33–34, 36–37, 43, 50, 77n16, 162, 166, 171

vocational education 57, 60–62, 65, 70–71, 90, 163

well-being 84

Yamada, M. 152
yutori kyōiku 7, 139, 148

zaikai (business representatives) 57, 62, 64–66, 69, 72, 75, 77n27, 143, 163–164